ART DECO LONDON

FRANCO PFALLER

AMBERLEY

ABOUT THE PHOTOGRAPHER

Franco is a Swiss photographer who has been living in London since 1994. This is his second book for Amberley Publishing after *London's Riverside in Photographs*. He also has a trilingual photo book published in Switzerland called *Mein Wallis – Mon Valais – My Valais* and a photo book in French called *La Tzoumaz – Au fil des saisons*. His website is www.yourpanorama.ch and you can find him on most social media platforms under @yourpanorama.

First published 2025

Amberley Publishing
The Hill, Stroud
Gloucestershire, GL5 4EP

www.amberley-books.com

ISBN 978 1 3981 2187 4 (print)
ISBN 978 1 3981 2188 1 (ebook)

British Library Cataloguing in Publication Data.
A catalogue record for this book is available from the British Library.

Typesetting by SJmagic DESIGN SERVICES, India.
Printed in the UK.

Appointed GPSR EU Representative:
Easy Access System Europe Oü, 16879218
Address: Mustamäe tee 50, 10621, Tallinn, Estonia
Contact Details: gpsr.requests@easproject.com, +358 40 500 3575

INTRODUCTION

The Art Deco movement, short for Arts Décoratifs, was named after the 'Exposition Internationale des Arts Décoratifs et Industriels Moderne' that was held in Paris in 1925. The exhibition had 16 million visitors and 15,000 exhibitors. From Europe, Art Deco spread to the US and Britain where it became a favourite for buildings that were associated with the modern age – cinemas, swimming pools, office buildings, department stores, garages and power stations to name a few. In the US, some of the most famous skyscrapers (e.g. the Chrysler Building or the Empire State Building) were built in the Art Deco style. Known for its bold shapes, geometric patterns, clean lines, and bright colours, Art Deco emphasises elegance, functionality and modernity. This movement became a defining style of the early twentieth century, leaving a lasting impact on design principles and aesthetics that continue to influence contemporary architecture.

The following photos are mainly external shots, as Art Deco interiors would be a project for another book. Having said that, I wanted to include a few interior images and the choice was made easy for me after having visited the Buzz Bingo Hall in Tooting. The building is magnificent, and it would have been a shame not to share some of those impressions. I also wanted to show that Art Deco lives on, and the proof for this is in the beautiful five-star Beaumont Hotel which only opened its doors in 2014 on a site that was originally a garage. I am grateful to have been allowed to take a few photos of the stunning interiors.

I hope to have included the most well-known buildings in London such as the Battersea Power Station, the Hoover Building and the Dorchester, as well as some surprise entries. There are also quite a few London Underground stations in the book, but far from all that serial Tube station architect Charles Holden designed. Each photograph is accompanied by a brief description, noting the architect, the listing status and the completion date. While these details provide valuable context, they are not intended to be comprehensive.

When I talked about this book to friends, most said I have to include the Michelin House in Chelsea. So I did... even though it is not strictly speaking Art Deco but British Art Nouveau. Let's consider it a pioneer in Art Deco, however, as it is built very much in that style.

All these buildings are now around 100 years old and some have only survived thanks to being listed. Many are currently undergoing major refurbishments and my patience was often tested when I travelled through London only to find out that another of my subjects was hidden behind scaffolding. Most trips were made either on foot or by public transport (my 60+ card came in handy), the exception being one very early morning journey across town to take photos of the Charlton Lido before it opened to the public (and thanks are owed for allowing me to come in) and another one to Richmond as the station during the day is very busy. Some of the unlisted buildings have undergone substantial extensions over time, but these have been executed with such taste that only the most knowledgeable observer would notice.

There are many ways I could have structured the book and I decided to do it in roughly alphabetical order of the postcode (I have a feeling this might be a first). It should make it easier to go and visit if you so desire. Many of the buildings have changed names countless times since being built or even since being listed (depending on the function or the current sponsor/owner). Therefore, some buildings you might know under a different name.

Franco

Troxy

The Grade II listed Troxy, designed by George Coles, opened as a cinema in 1933. After ceasing operations as a cinema in 1960, it served as a venue for the Royal Opera and later as a bingo hall. Today, it stands as one of London's coolest live venues. E1 OHX

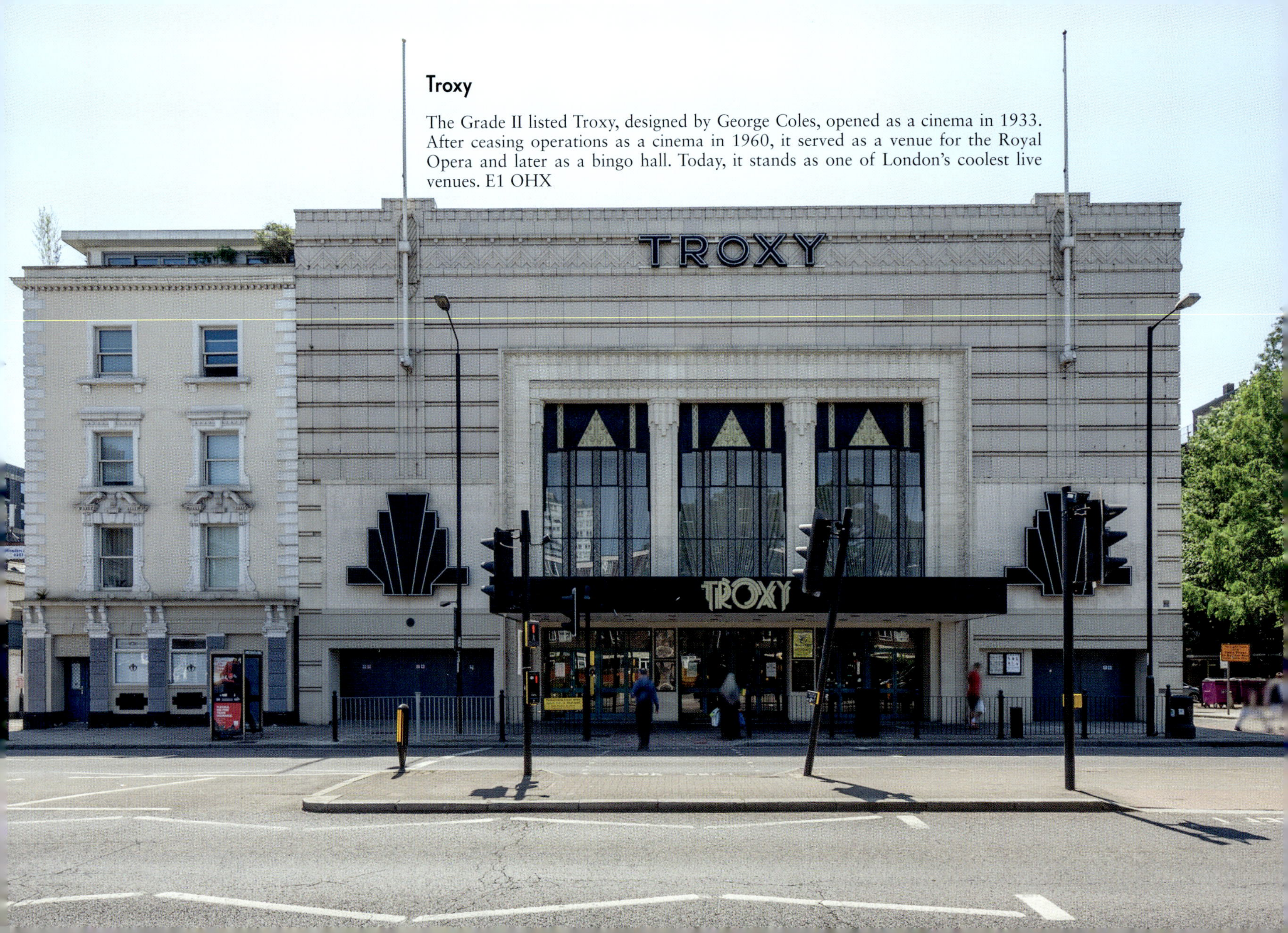

People's Palace

The 'new' People's Palace opened in 1937, replacing the Queen's Hall, which was destroyed by fire. The Queen's Hall, originally the concert hall for the first People's Palace, remains in situ and is now called the Queen's Building. Both buildings are currently part of Queen Mary University. The exterior of the new People's Palace was designed by Campbell Jones and Smithers, with reliefs by Eric Gill, while the interior was designed by George Coles. It is a Grade II listed building. E1 4NS

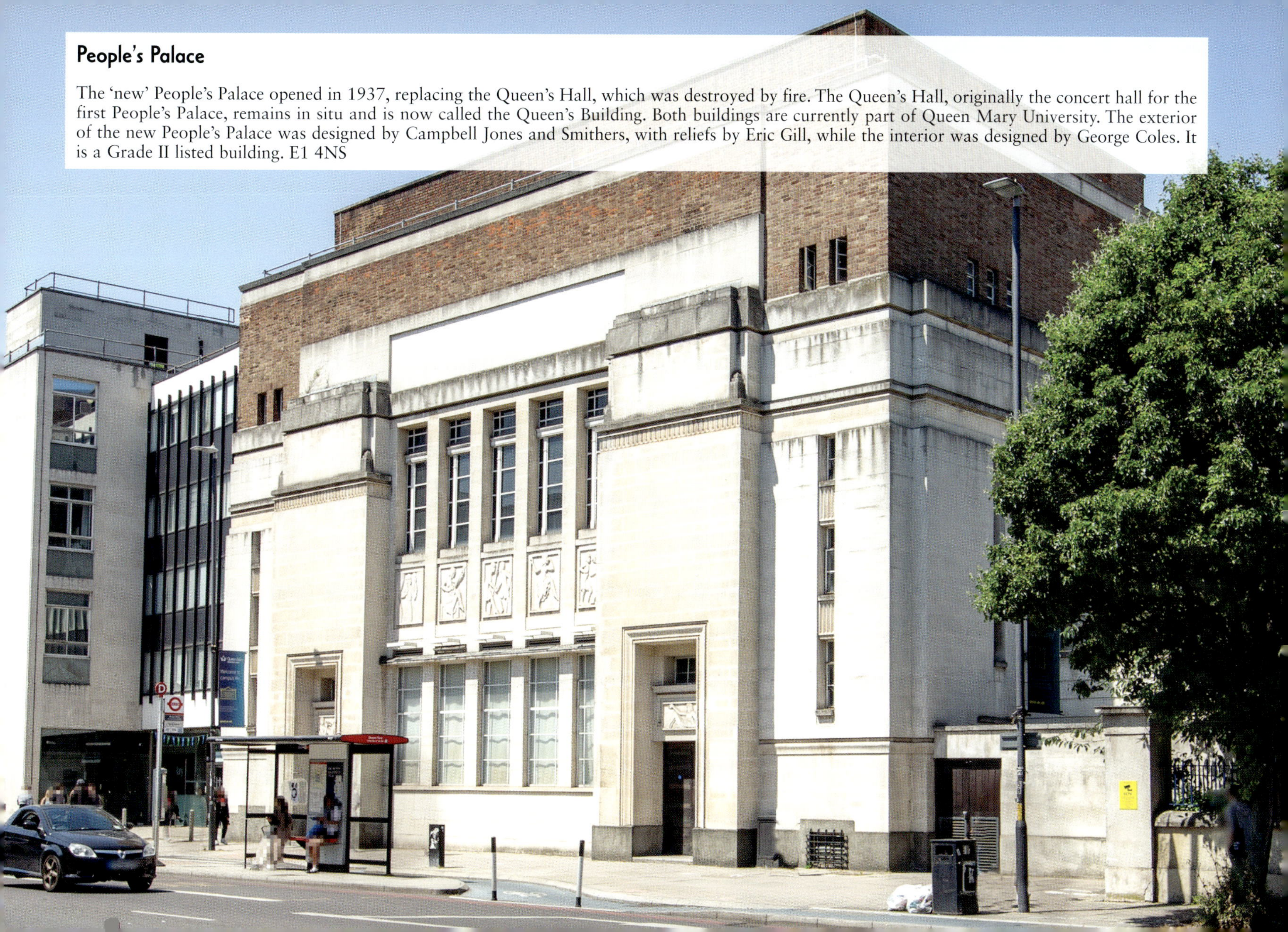

Walthamstow Stadium

The Grade II listed entrance to the once mighty Walthamstow Stadium, designed by Thomas & Edge Ltd, was built in 1932. The stadium was one of London's premier dog-racing tracks and also hosted speedway and stock car races over the years. It is now a complex of flats. E4 8SJ

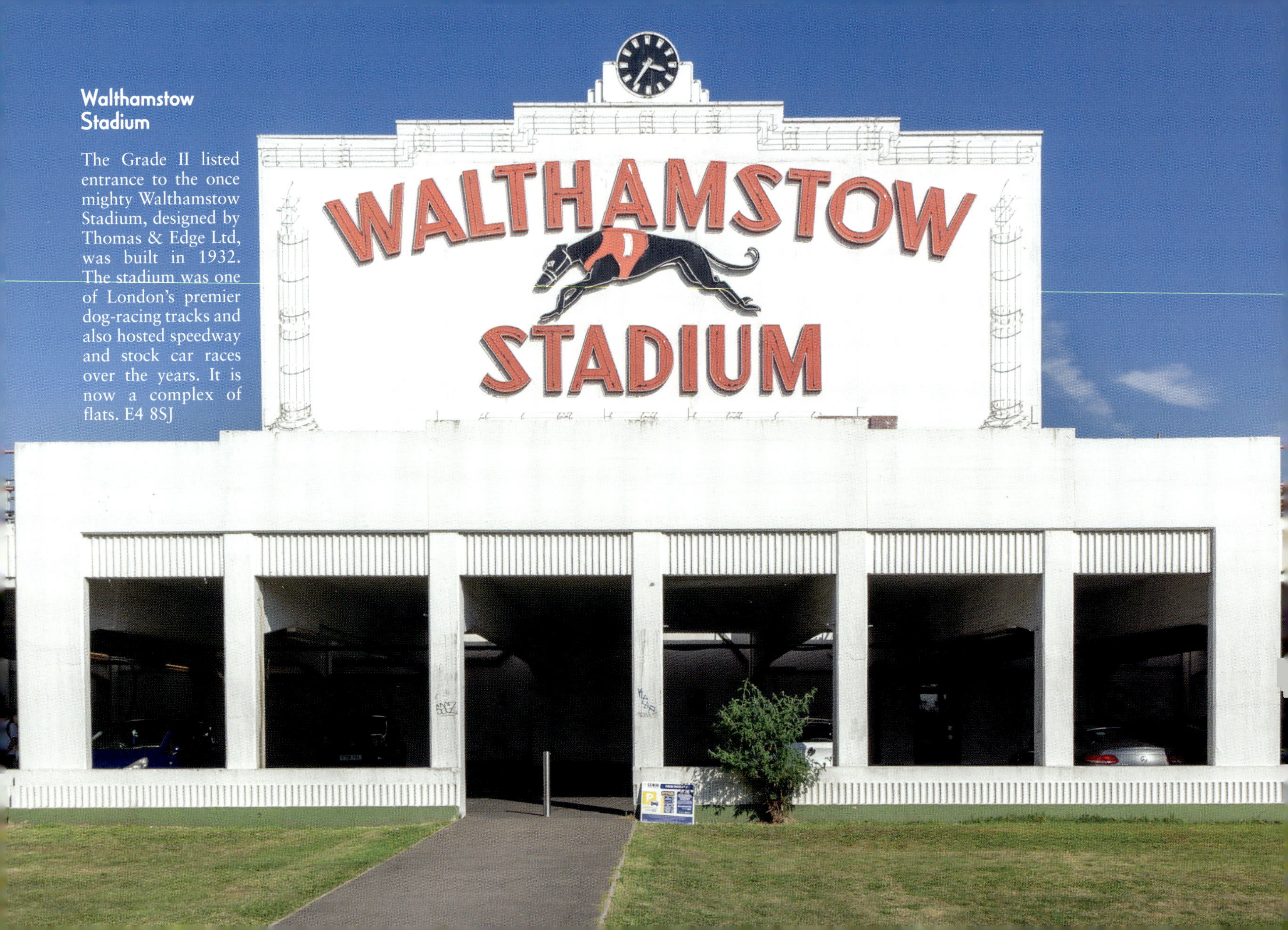

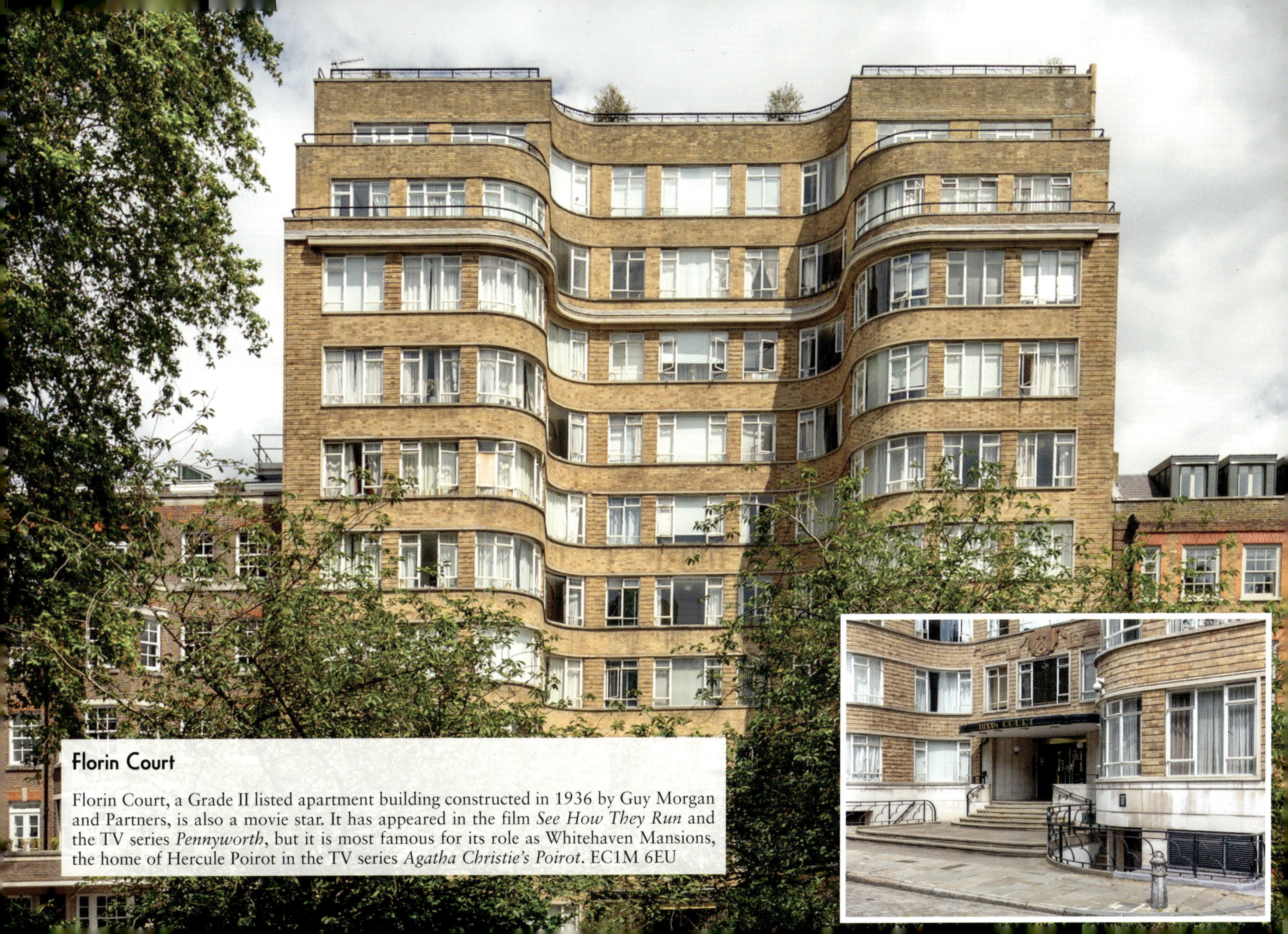

Florin Court

Florin Court, a Grade II listed apartment building constructed in 1936 by Guy Morgan and Partners, is also a movie star. It has appeared in the film *See How They Run* and the TV series *Pennyworth*, but it is most famous for its role as Whitehaven Mansions, the home of Hercule Poirot in the TV series *Agatha Christie's Poirot*. EC1M 6EU

The Lab

The Lab Building, now a residential complex, was formerly known as the Metropolitan Water Board Laboratory. Serving as the laboratory, research, and office building for the Metropolitan Water Board (later Thames Water), it was designed by Stanley Hall and Easton and Robertson and built in 1937. It is a Grade II listed building. EC1R 4TW

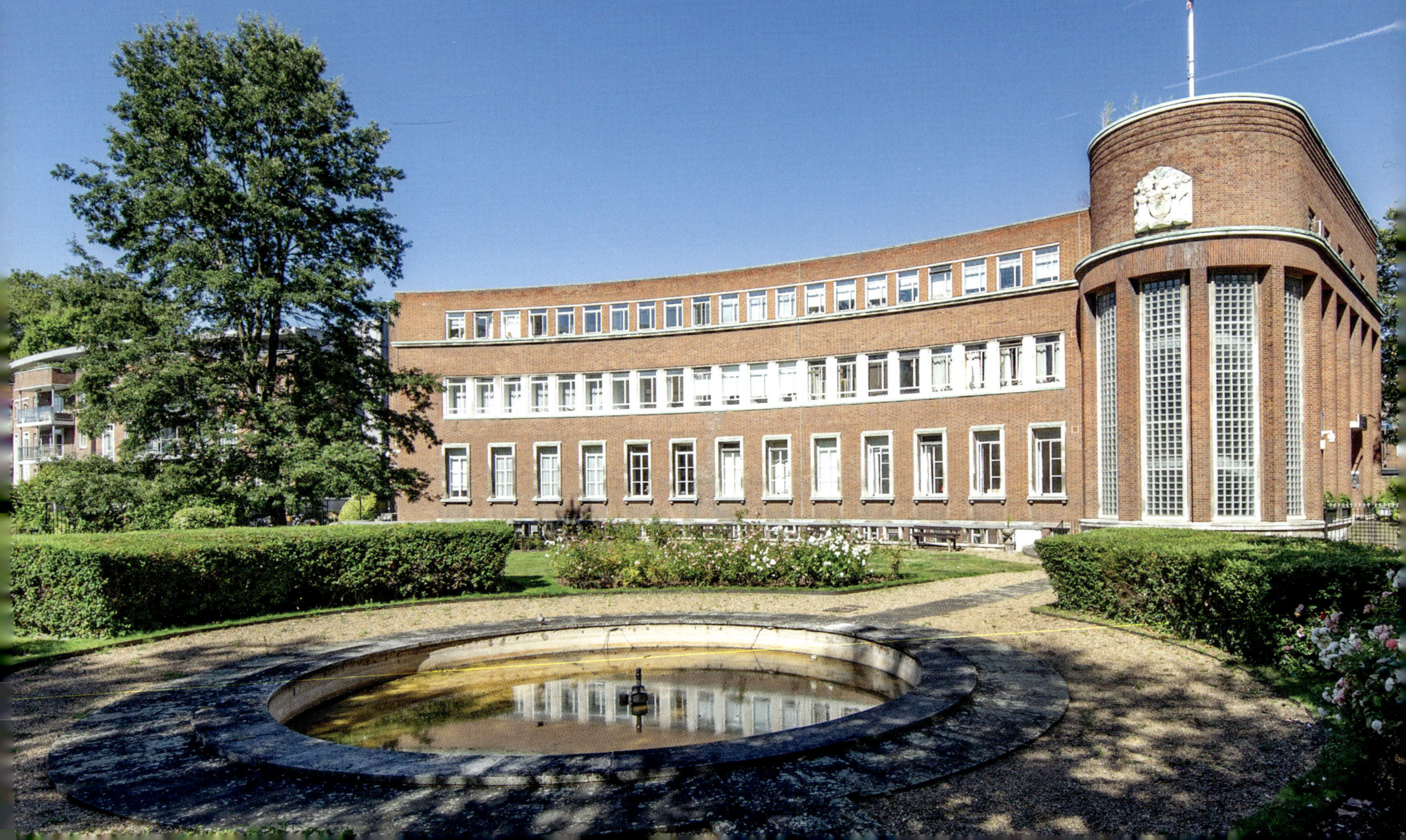

Ibex House

Completed in 1937, this Grade II listed office building was designed by Fuller, Hall and Foulsham. It is an excellent example of a 'modernistic' office block. EC3N 1DY

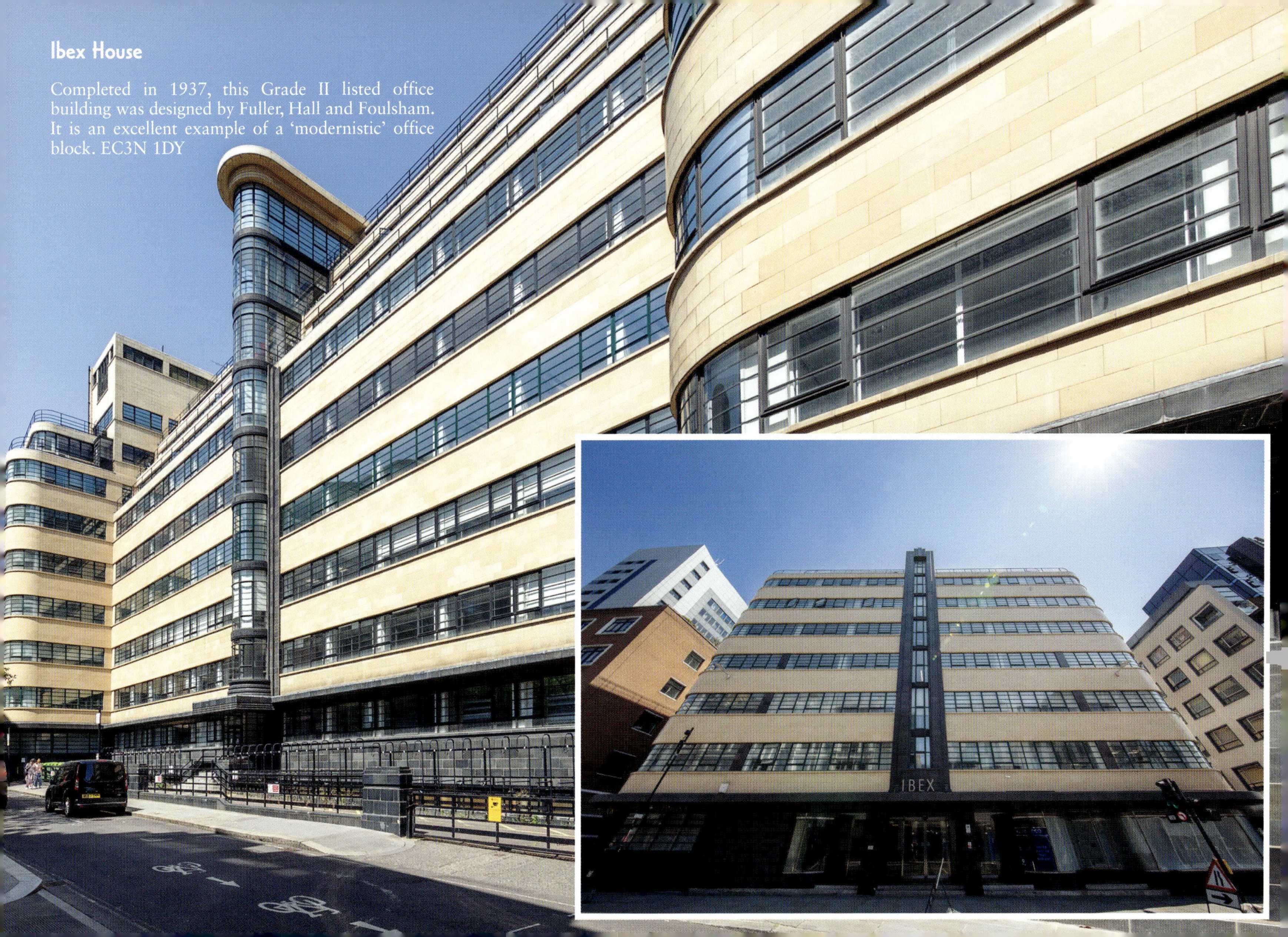

Adelaide House

Adelaide House, a Grade II listed building next to London Bridge, was constructed in 1925 and was the tallest office block in the City at the time. Designed by Sir John Burnet and Thomas S. Tait, it features a facade of Portland stone and white granite with a marked vertical emphasis, characteristic of Art Deco design. EC3R 8AJ

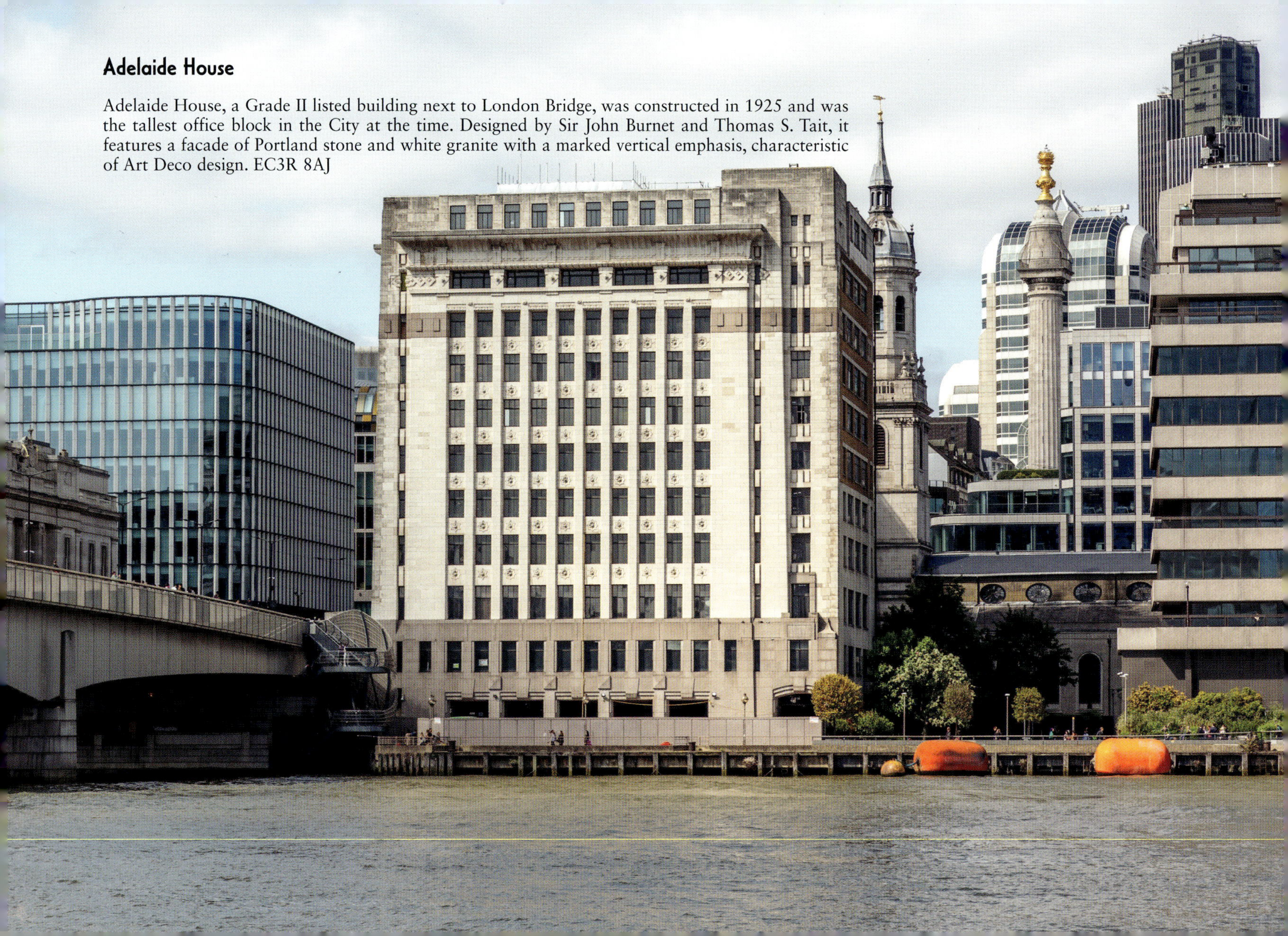

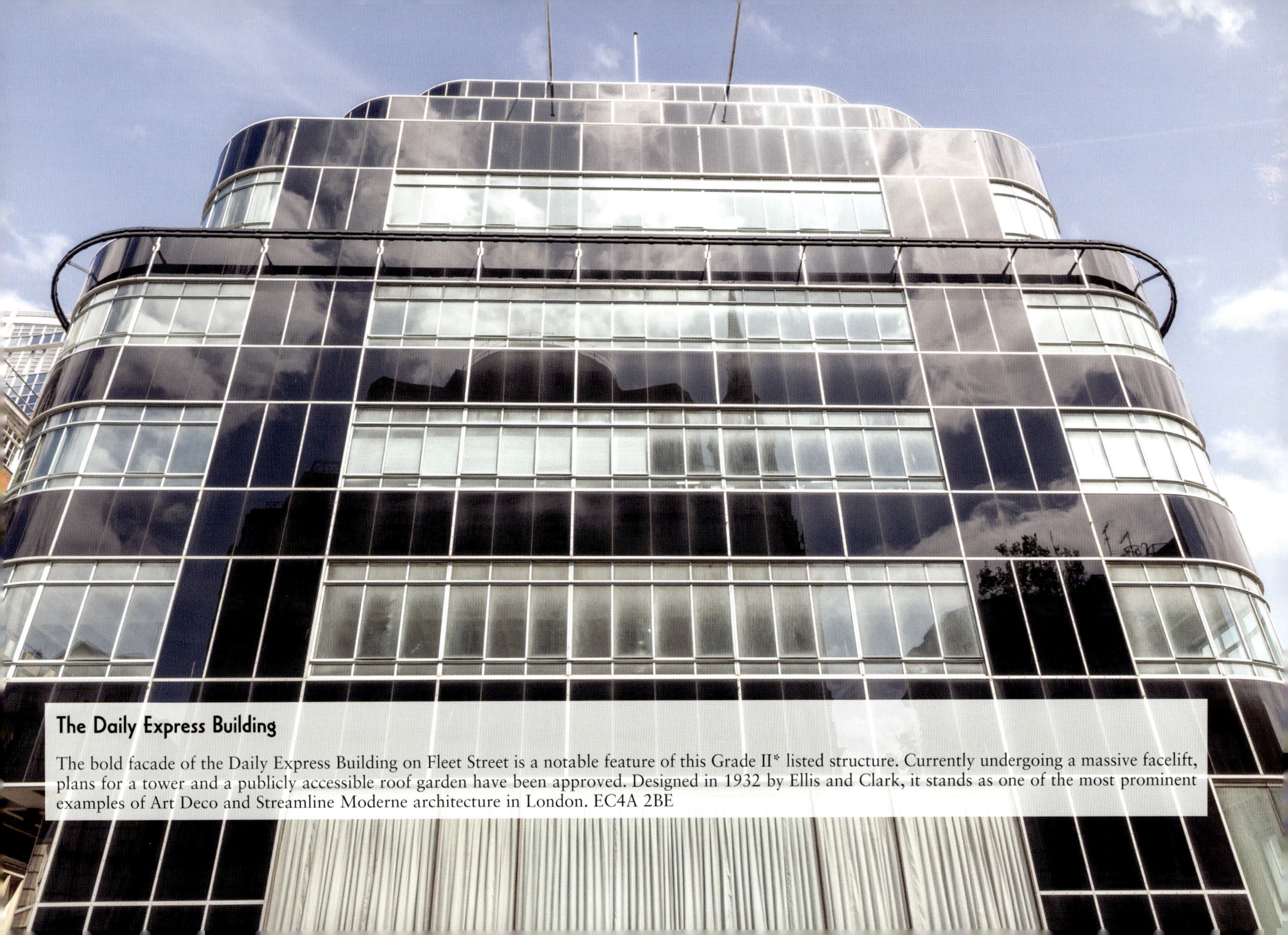

The Daily Express Building

The bold facade of the Daily Express Building on Fleet Street is a notable feature of this Grade II* listed structure. Currently undergoing a massive facelift, plans for a tower and a publicly accessible roof garden have been approved. Designed in 1932 by Ellis and Clark, it stands as one of the most prominent examples of Art Deco and Streamline Moderne architecture in London. EC4A 2BE

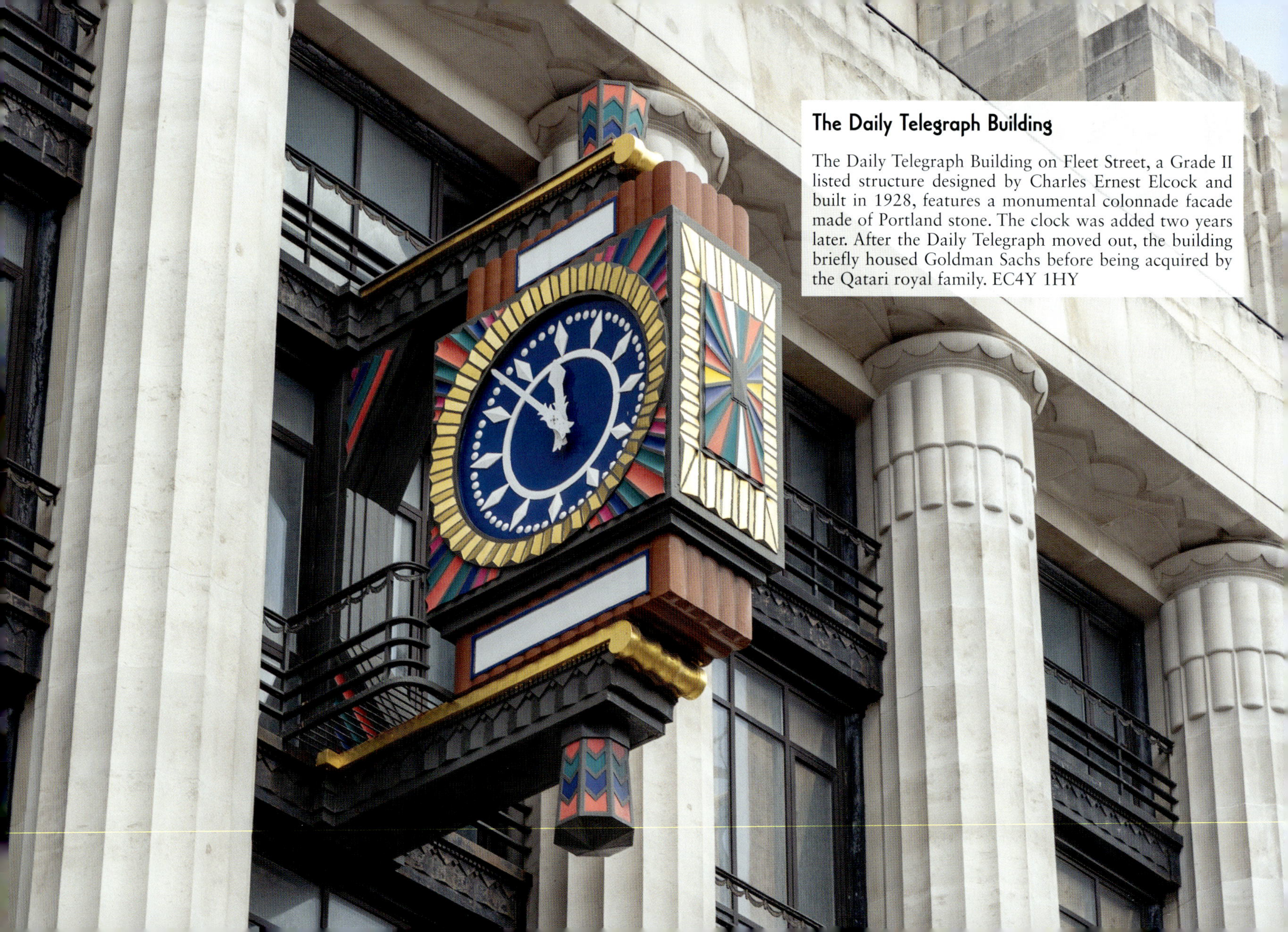

The Daily Telegraph Building

The Daily Telegraph Building on Fleet Street, a Grade II listed structure designed by Charles Ernest Elcock and built in 1928, features a monumental colonnade facade made of Portland stone. The clock was added two years later. After the Daily Telegraph moved out, the building briefly housed Goldman Sachs before being acquired by the Qatari royal family. EC4Y 1HY

Unilever House

The Unilever Building, a collaboration between James Lomax Simpson and Burnet, Tait & Partners, was constructed between 1930 and 1932 in a neoclassical Art Deco style. This Grade II listed building features a facade of Portland stone and is distinguished by its Ionic columns spanning the fourth to the sixth floors. EC4Y 0JP

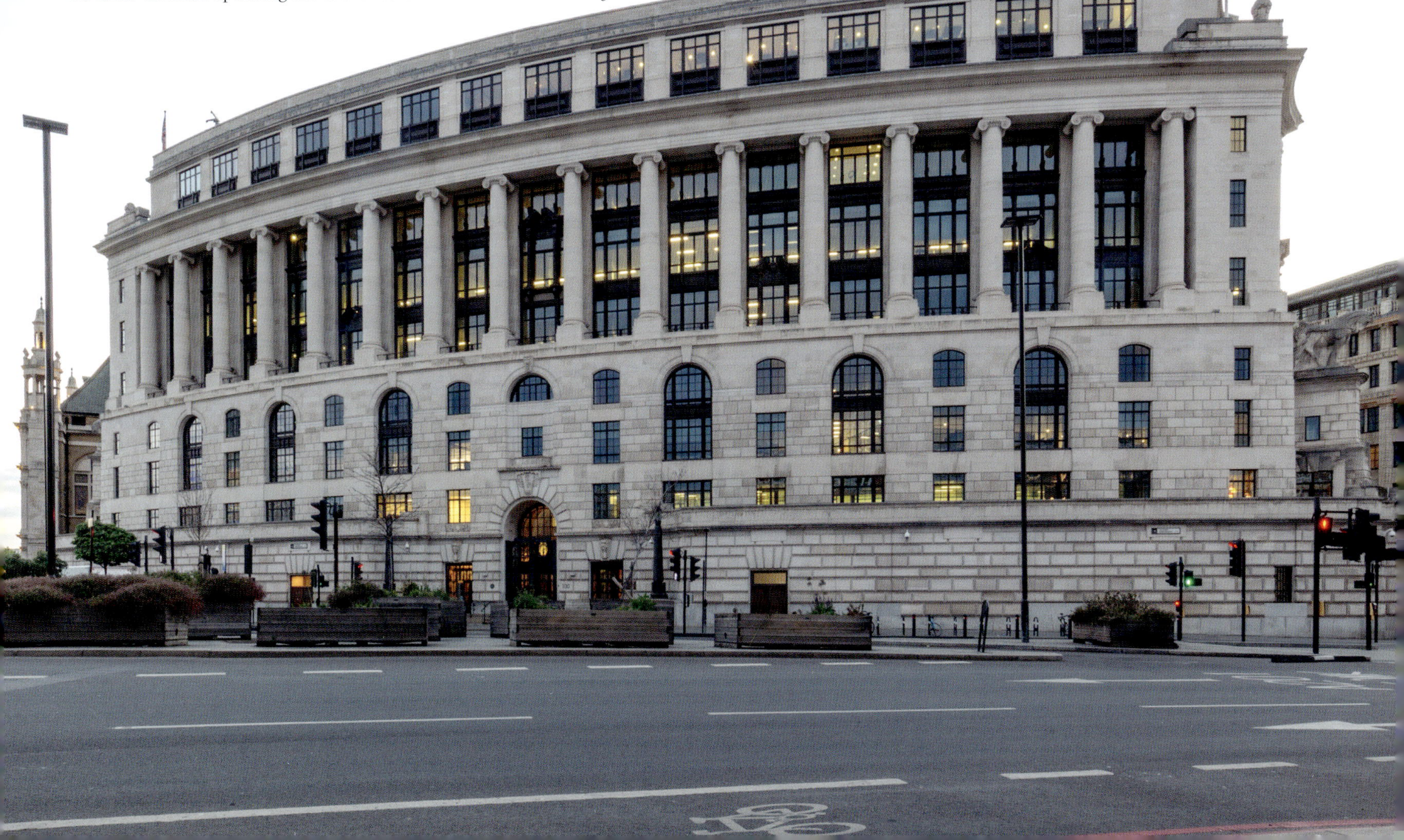

Sudbury Town Station

Sudbury Town Station, built in 1931 and listed as Grade II*, served as the prototype for Charles Holden's groundbreaking modernist 'box' style design for the Piccadilly line extension. (More about Holden later.) HA0 2LA

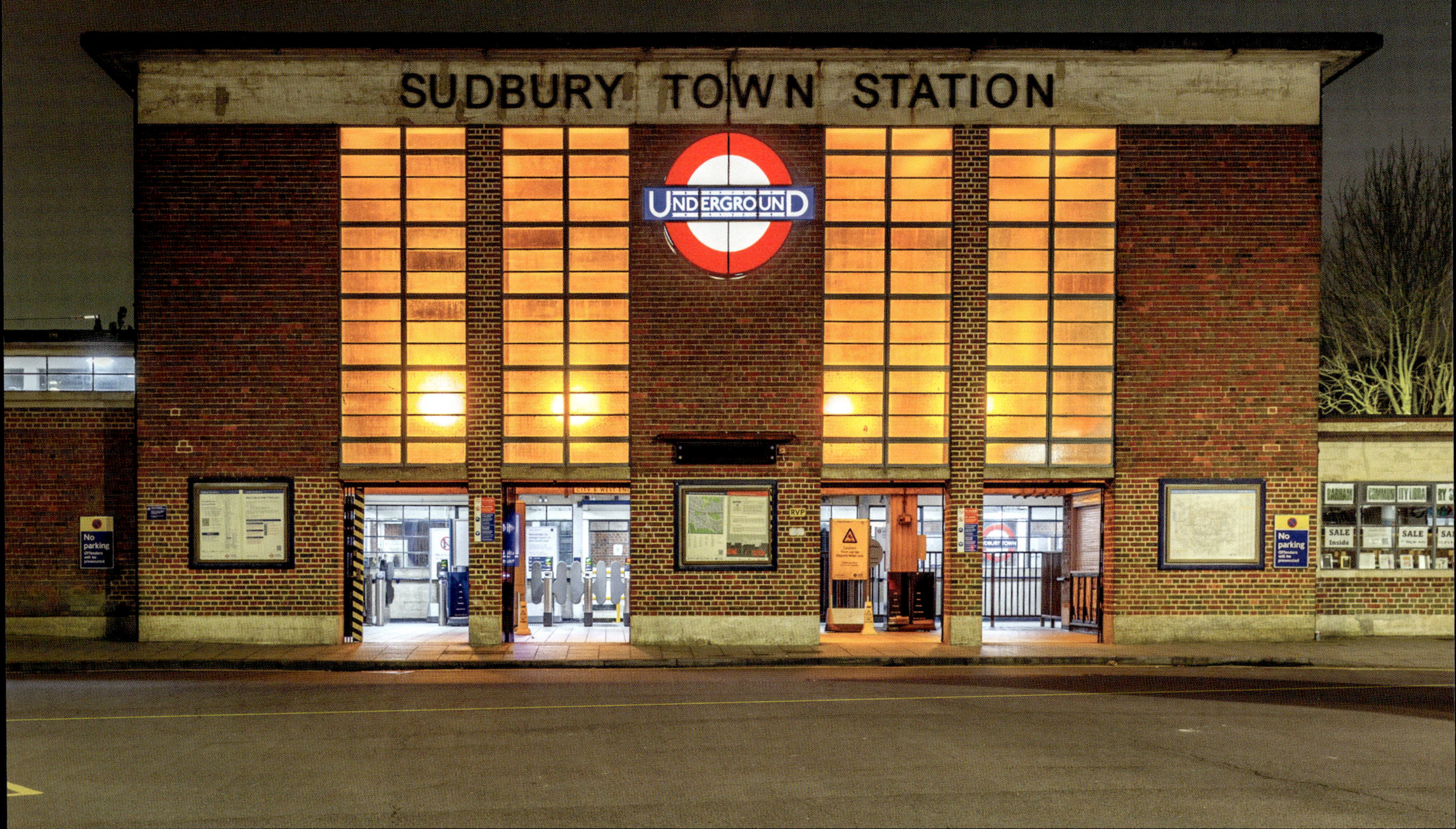

Zoroastrian Centre

Designed by F. E. Bromige, this Grade II* listed building was constructed in 1936 as a cinema. Over the years, it underwent several name changes, including Odeon, Gaumont, and ACE Cinema, and also served as a nightclub and a wine bar. Today, it is known as the Zoroastrian Centre, serving as the secretariat and principal venue for Zoroastrianism in Europe, the world's oldest monotheistic faith. HA2 9TL

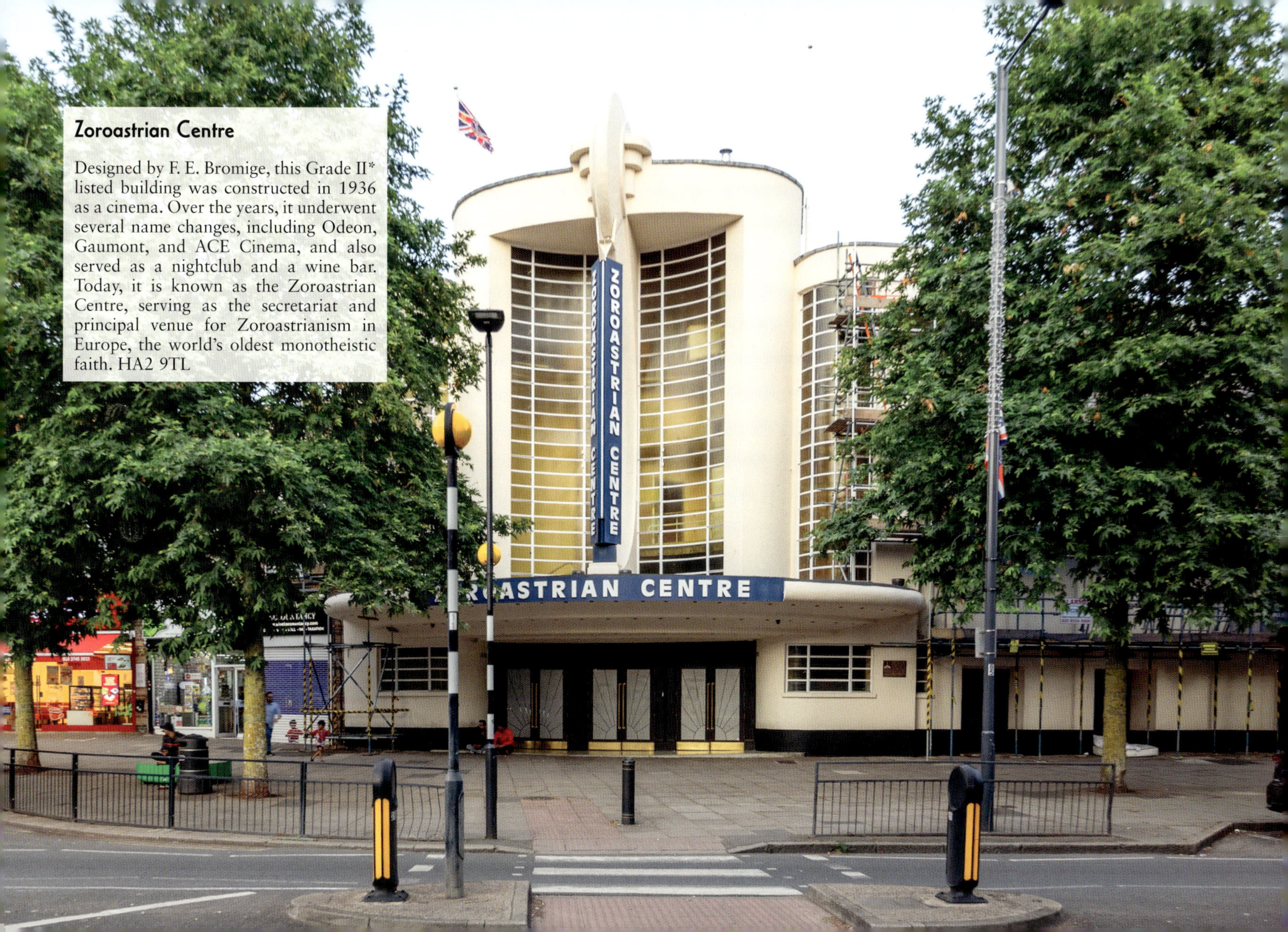

Rayners Lane Station

Rayners Lane Station, opened in 1938, was designed by New Zealand architect Reginald Uren and Charles Holden. This Grade II listed building on the Piccadilly line showcases the 'Sudbury Box' style, which Holden first introduced at Sudbury Town Station. HA5 5EG

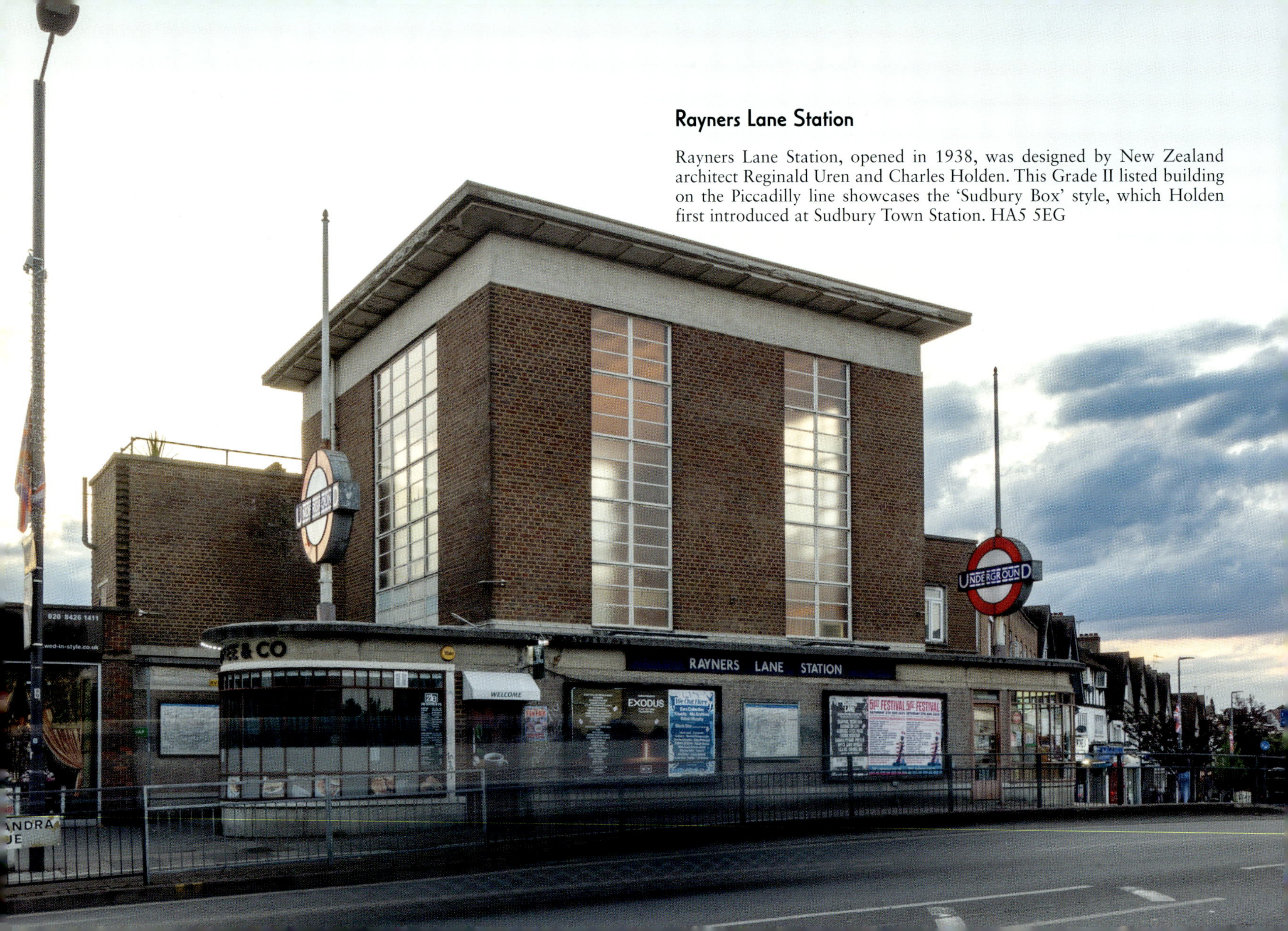

John Keble Church

Built in 1936, the John Keble Church is the only church dedicated to, you guessed it, John Keble. He was one of the leaders of the Oxford Movement, a group of high churchmen in the Church of England, many of whom switched eventually to Catholicism. The church was designed by D. F. Martin-Smith and is Grade II listed. HA8 9NT

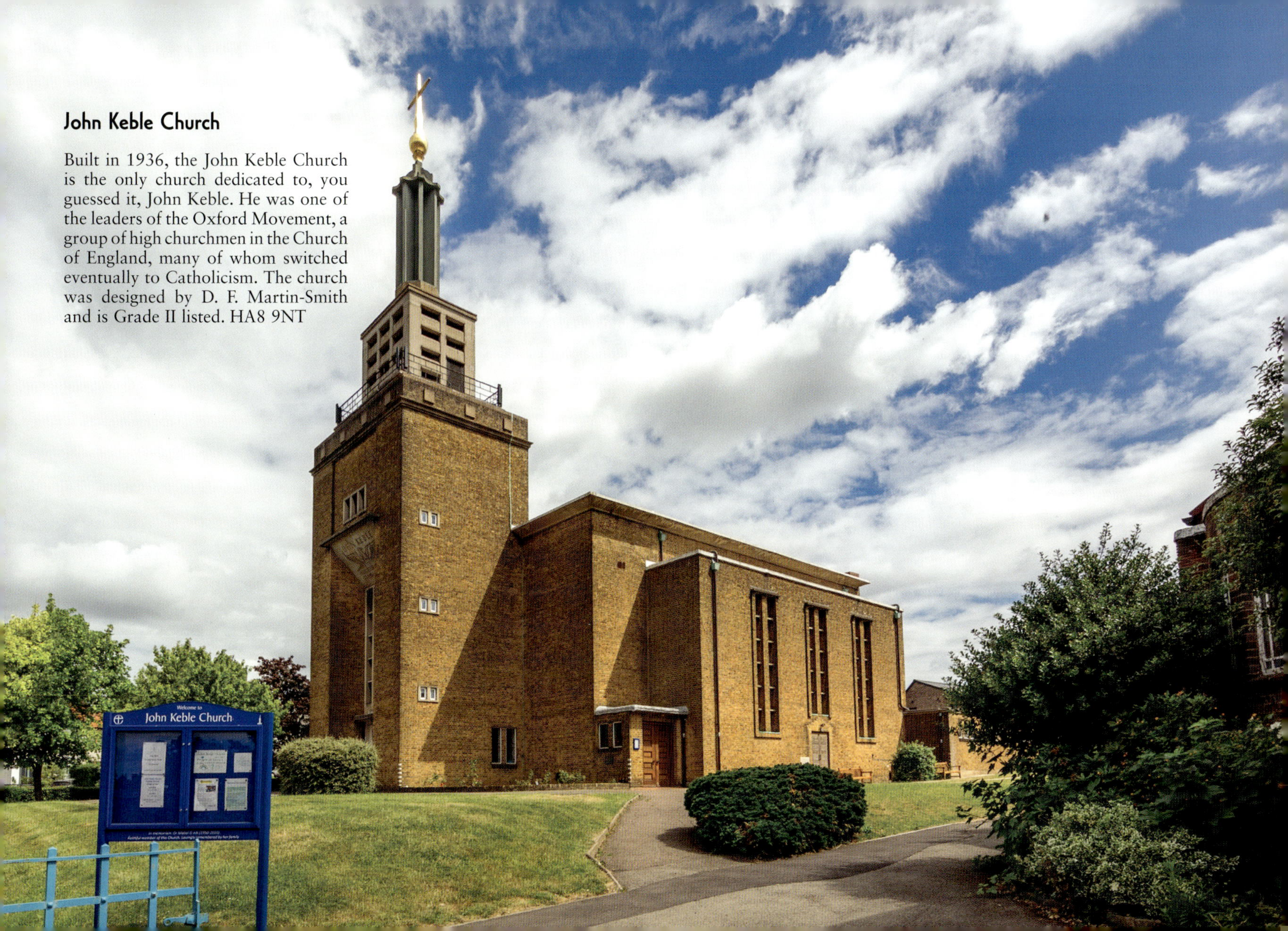

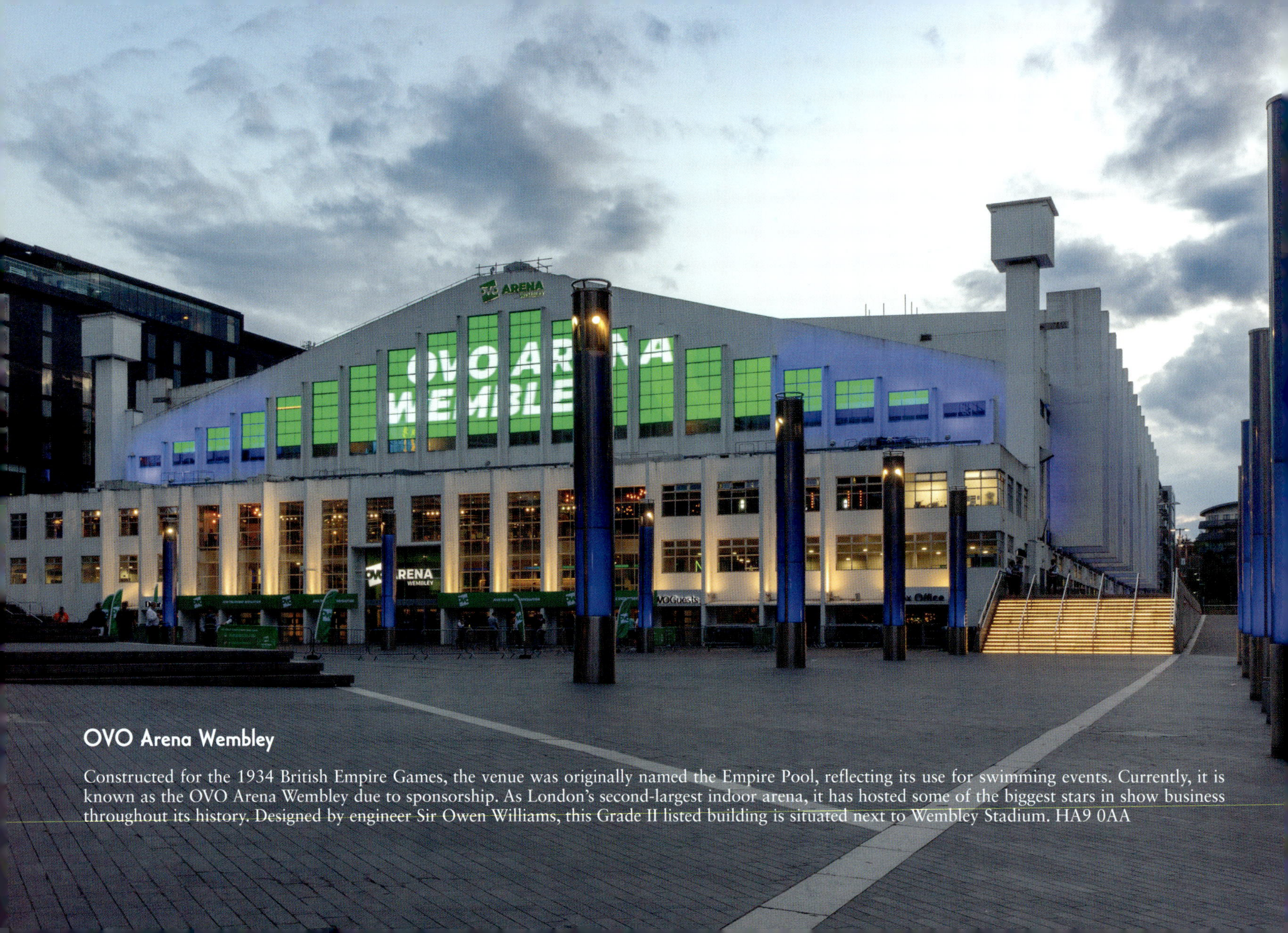

OVO Arena Wembley

Constructed for the 1934 British Empire Games, the venue was originally named the Empire Pool, reflecting its use for swimming events. Currently, it is known as the OVO Arena Wembley due to sponsorship. As London's second-largest indoor arena, it has hosted some of the biggest stars in show business throughout its history. Designed by engineer Sir Owen Williams, this Grade II listed building is situated next to Wembley Stadium. HA9 0AA

Sunspan House – New Malden

This dwelling is among the ten remaining Sunspan Houses, a collaborative design effort by Wells Coates and D. Pleydell-Bouverie. These houses were prefabricated, characterised by a square plan with one curved side strategically positioned to optimise sunlight exposure throughout the day. KT3 3UH

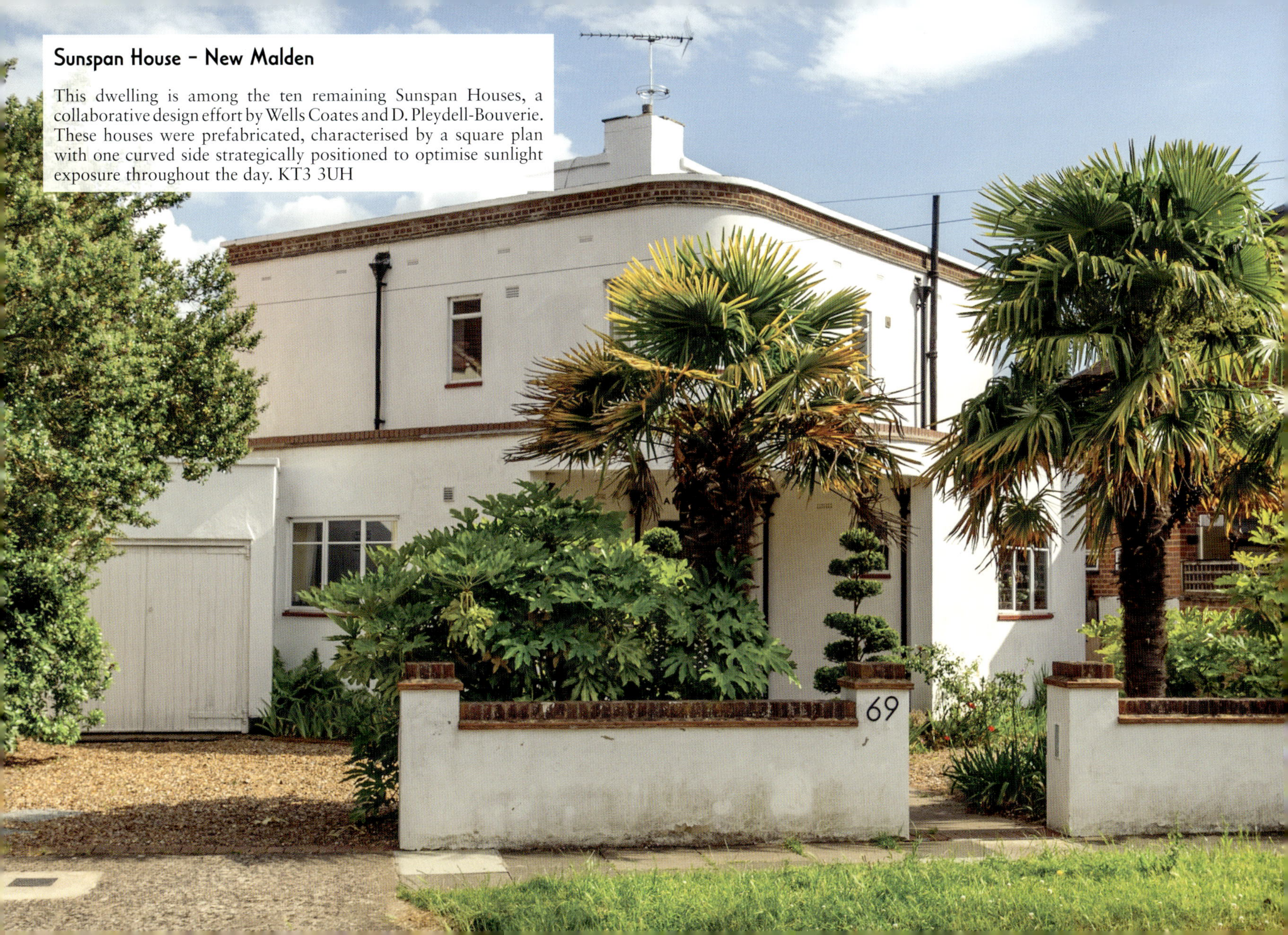

Surbiton Station

Surbiton Station, crafted by James Robb Scott and completed in 1937, stands as one of Britain's most exemplary modernist train stations. This stunning Grade II listed edifice has graced the silver screen, notably appearing in films and TV series, most prominently in *Harry Potter and the Half-Blood Prince*. KT6 4PE

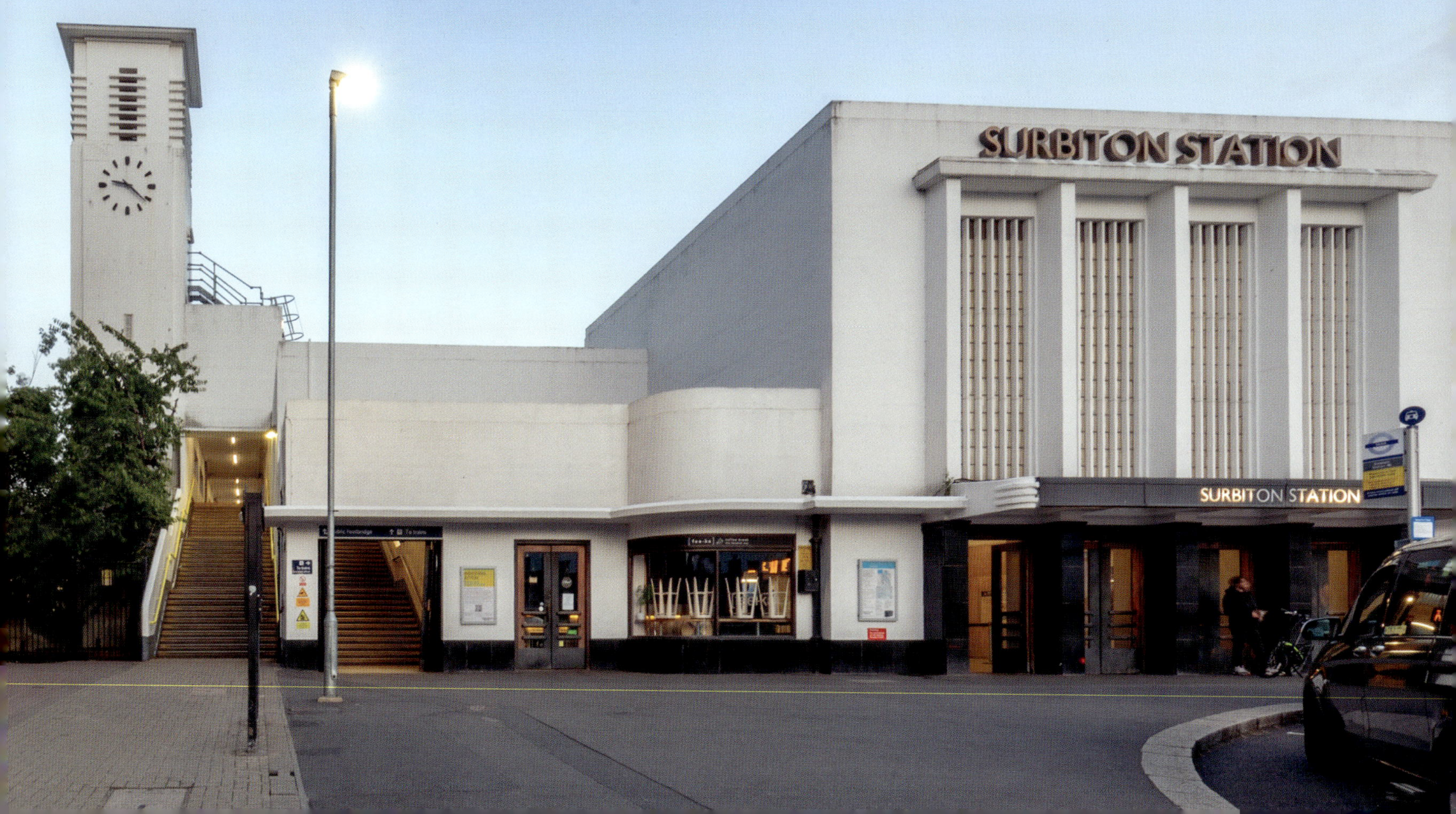

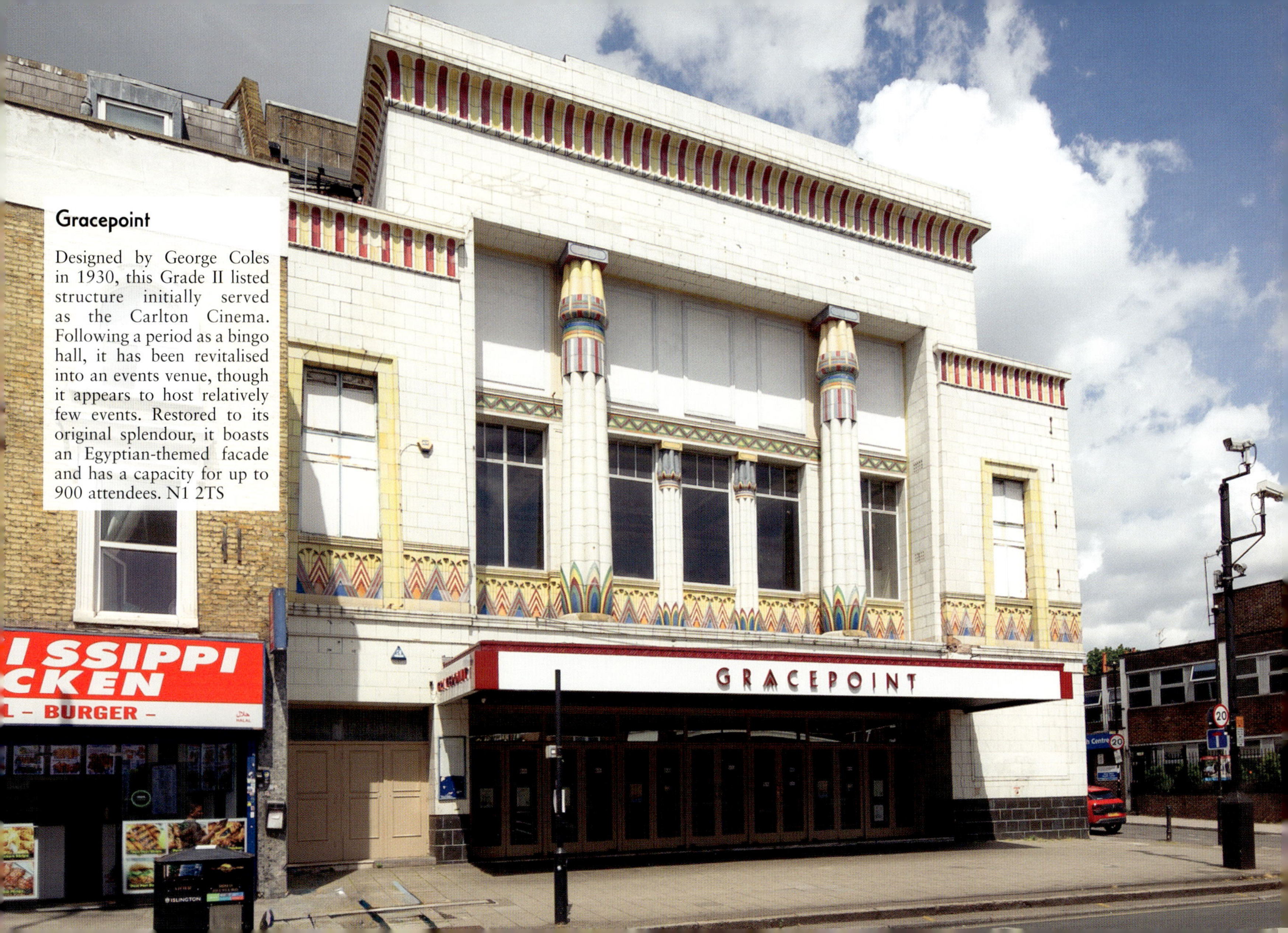

Gracepoint

Designed by George Coles in 1930, this Grade II listed structure initially served as the Carlton Cinema. Following a period as a bingo hall, it has been revitalised into an events venue, though it appears to host relatively few events. Restored to its original splendour, it boasts an Egyptian-themed facade and has a capacity for up to 900 attendees. N1 2TS

Islington Town/Assembly Hall

The Grade II listed Islington Town Hall, designed by E. C. P. Monson, was built in three stages over the period from 1922 to 1930 (when the Assembly Hall was opened). N1 2UD

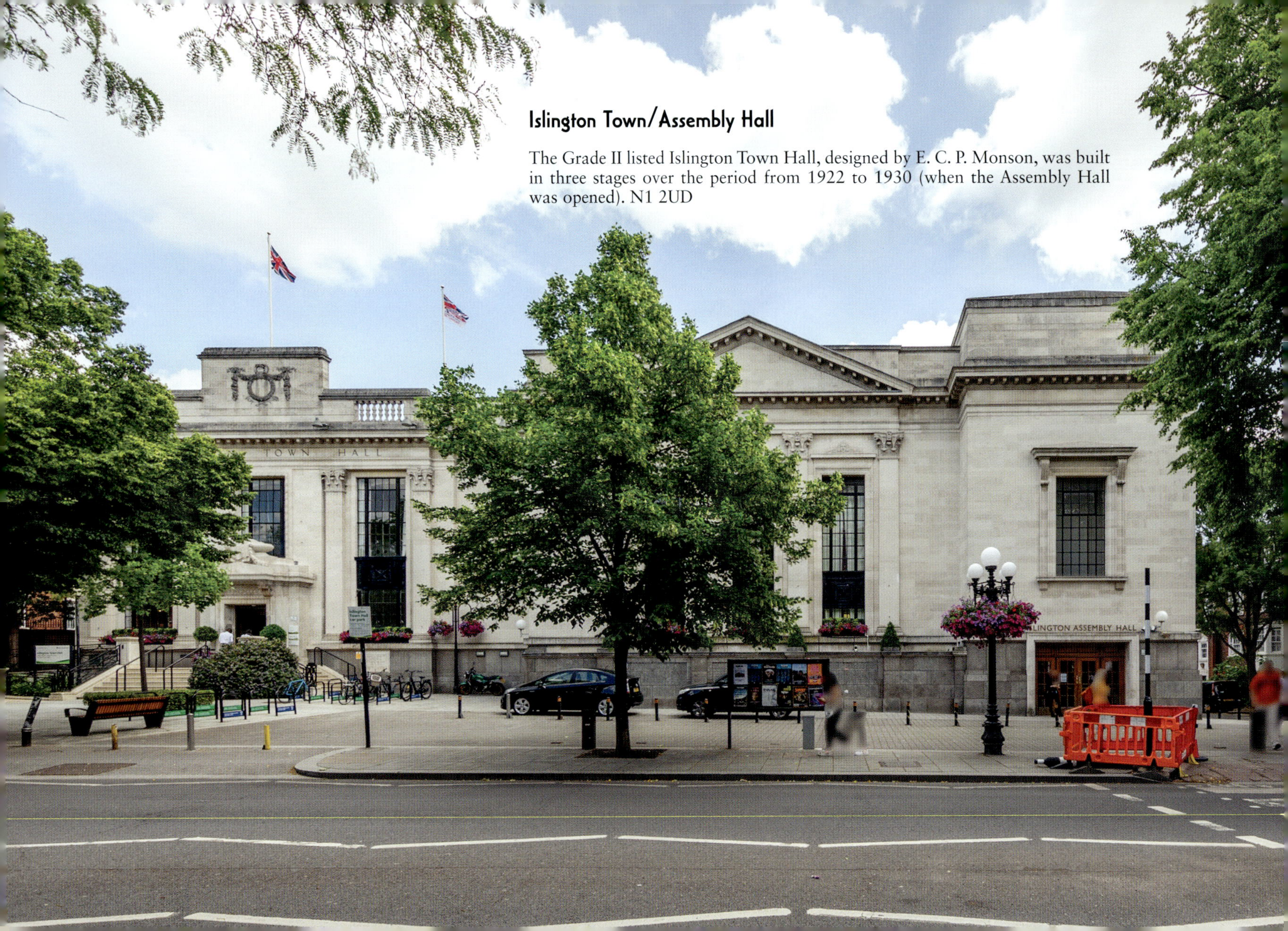

Phoenix Cinema

Originally constructed in 1910 as the East Finchley Picturedrome (later known as the Coliseum and the Rex), the Phoenix Cinema underwent a significant Art Deco renovation in 1938. The front was designed by Howes and Jackman, while the auditorium received a makeover by renowned cinema interior designers Mollo and Egan. It is now a Grade II listed building. N2 9PJ

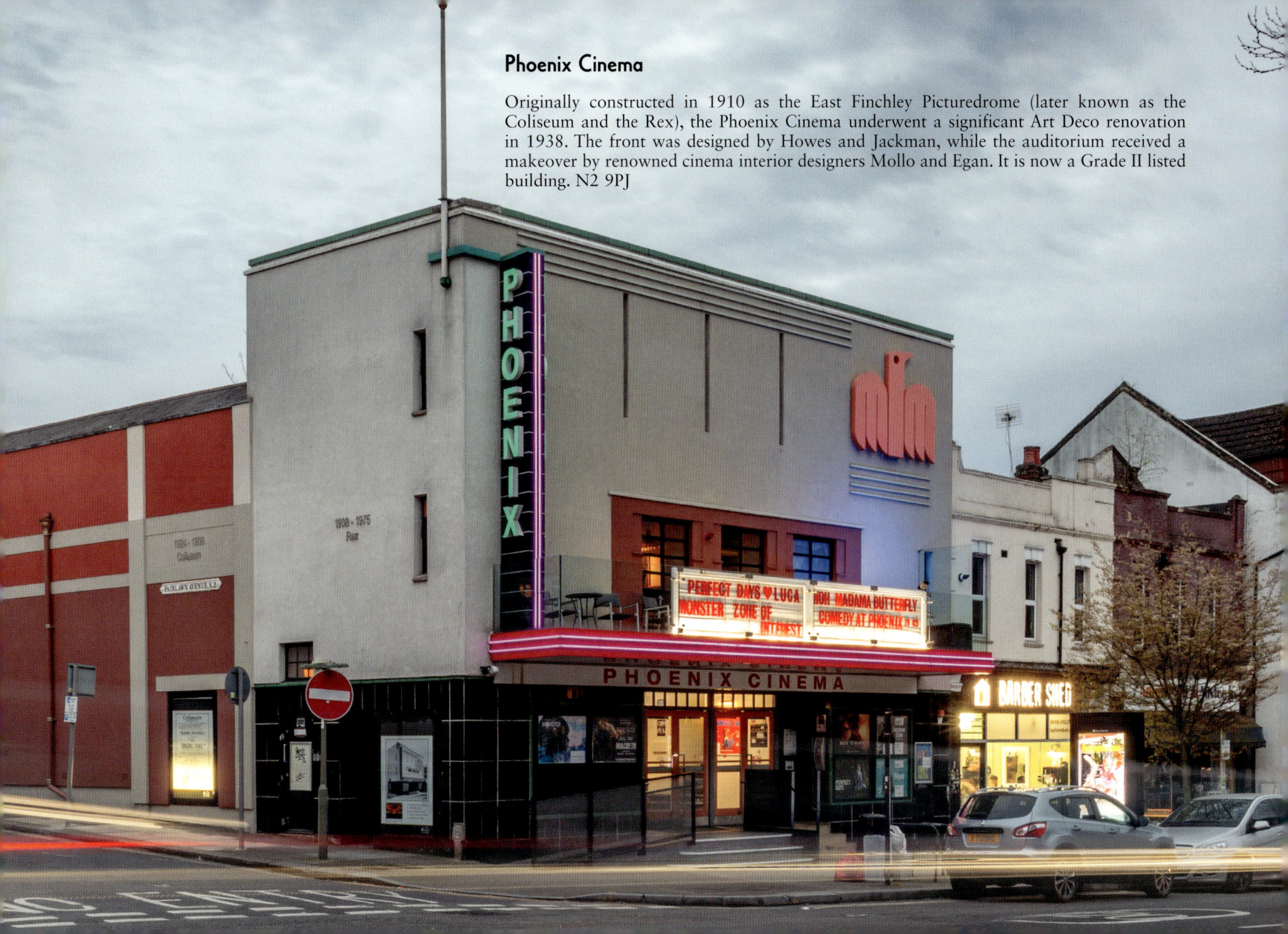

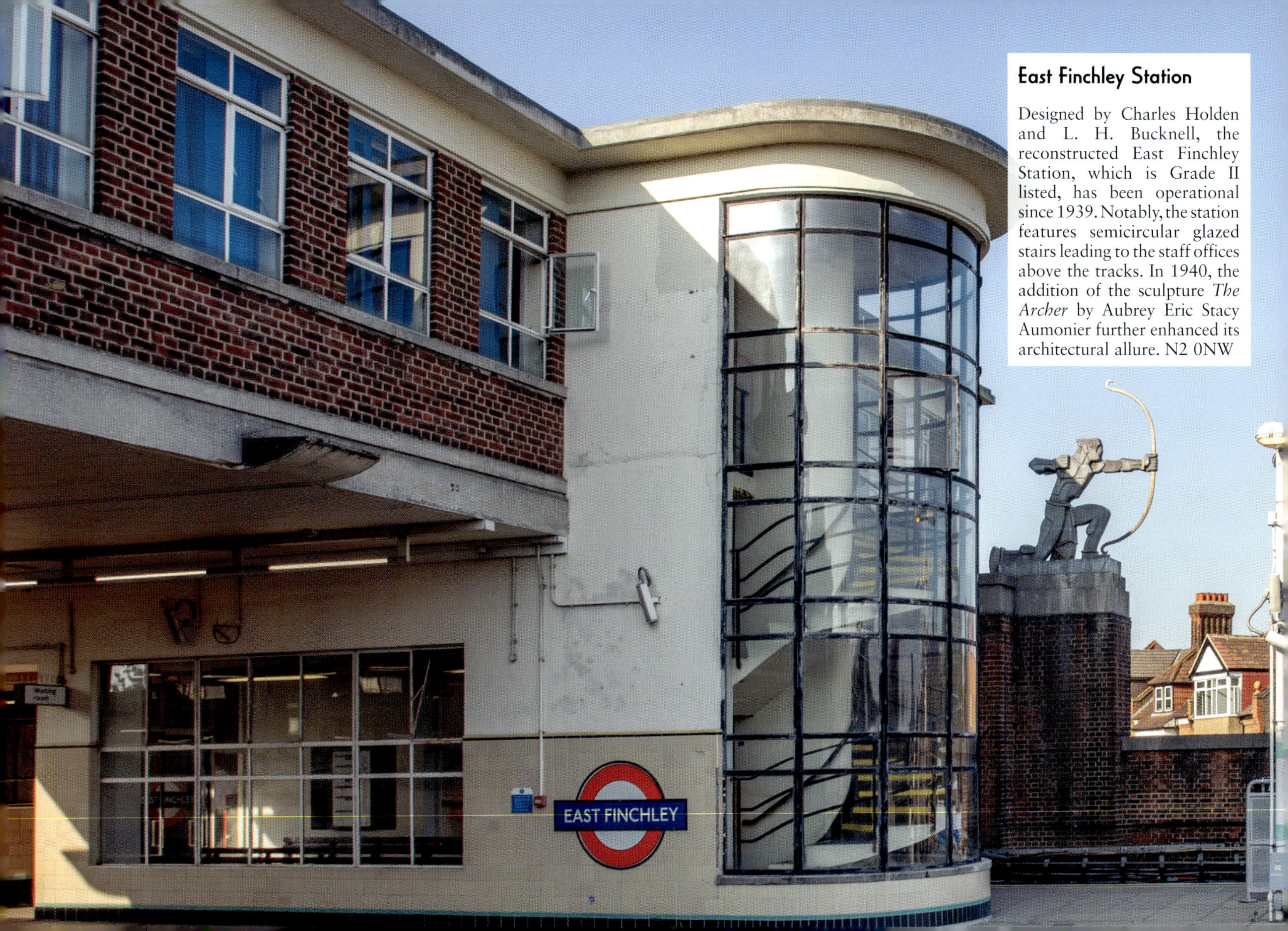

East Finchley Station

Designed by Charles Holden and L. H. Bucknell, the reconstructed East Finchley Station, which is Grade II listed, has been operational since 1939. Notably, the station features semicircular glazed stairs leading to the staff offices above the tracks. In 1940, the addition of the sculpture *The Archer* by Aubrey Eric Stacy Aumonier further enhanced its architectural allure. N2 0NW

Rainbow Theatre (ex)

Opened in 1930 as the Finsbury Park Astoria, designed by Edward A. Stone, it was hailed as one of the largest cinemas in the world. Over the years, its focus shifted from cinema to music, evolving through various names until it became the renowned Rainbow Theatre in 1971, earning itself a Grade II* listing. The roster of bands and musicians gracing its stage reads like a who's who in rock and roll. Following its final concert in 1981, the venue fell silent, occasionally hosting unlicensed boxing matches. Presently, it is under the ownership of the Universal Church of the Kingdom of God, a Brazilian Pentecostal church. N4 3NX

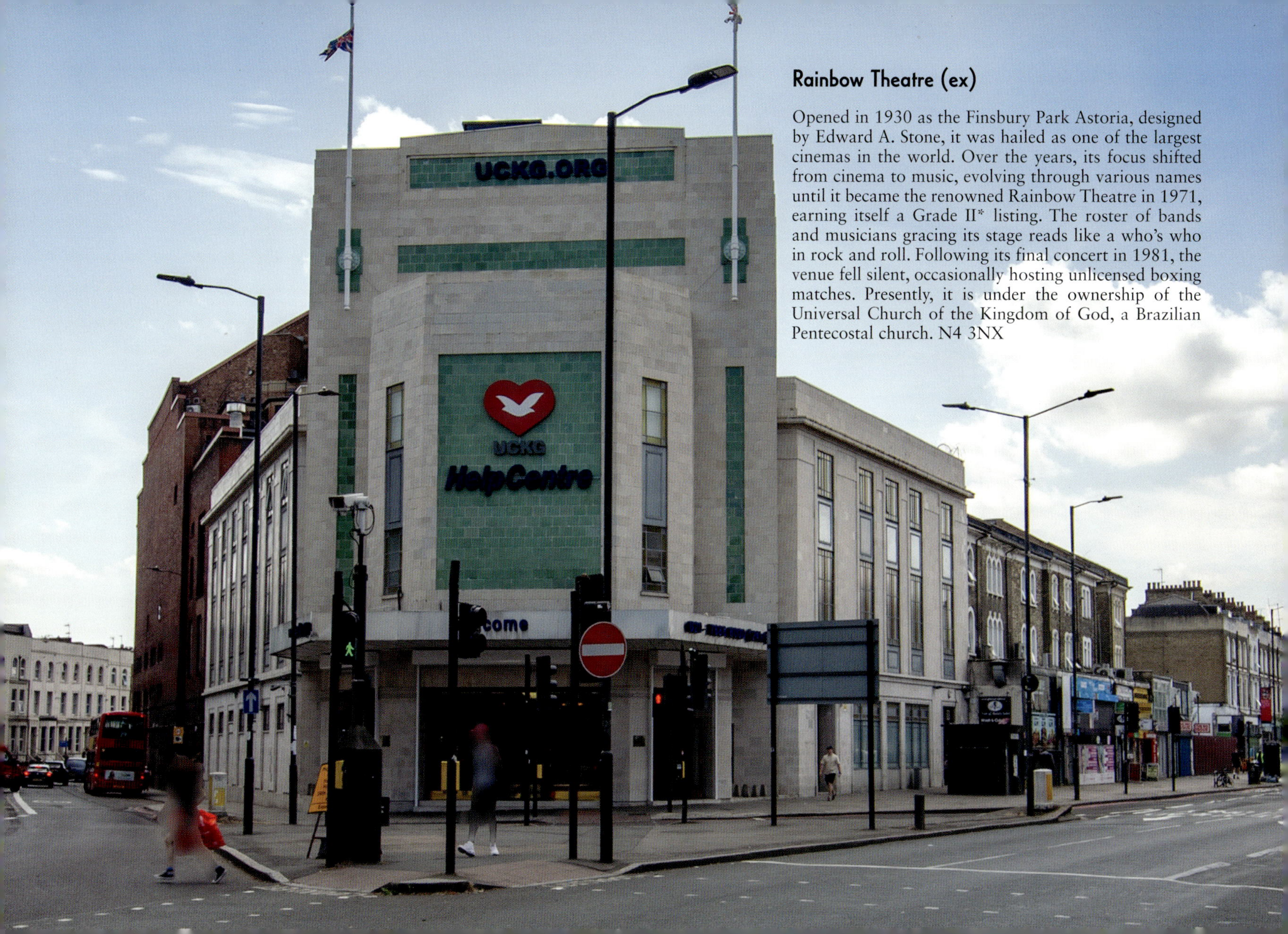

Arsenal Stadium (ex)

The Art Deco East Stand, designed by William Binnie, was added to the old Arsenal Stadium in 1936. When the football club moved to the new Emirates Stadium in 2006, the old stadium was redeveloped into Highbury Square, a complex with over 700 properties. The Grade II listed East Stand was thoughtfully incorporated into this project. N5 1FJ

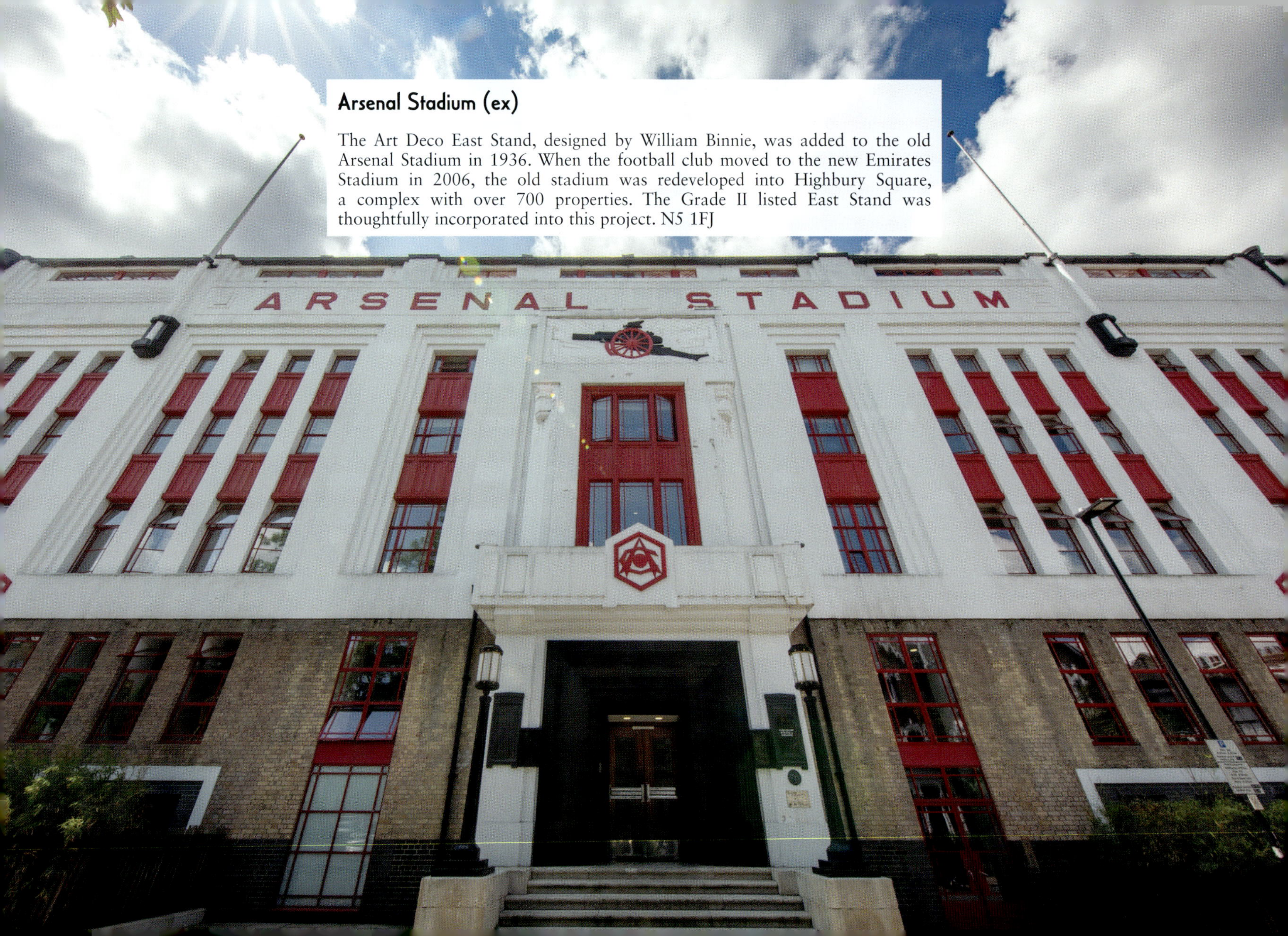

92 Frobisher Road

In 1938, cinema architect Ernest Bromige built a new Art Deco facade to the existing Premier Cinema. Following this transformation, it was renamed the Regal Cinema. Over the years, the building has undergone numerous changes, serving as a bingo hall, laser game centre, church, cinema once more and back to a church. However it looks like Jesus has left the building – when I took the photo, they were looking for a new tenant. N8 0QX

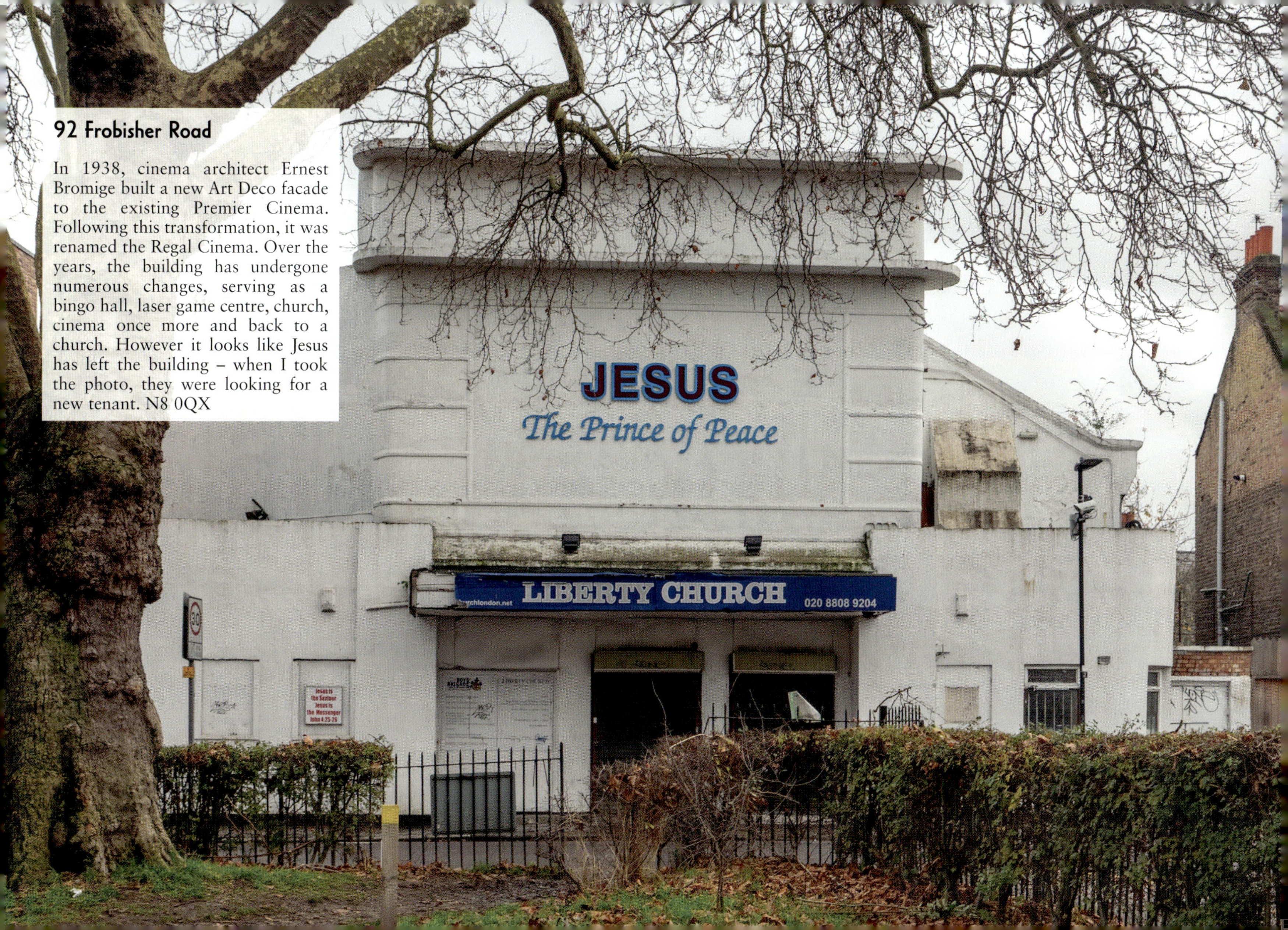

Arnos Grove Station

Constructed in 1932, the Grade II* listed Arnos Grove Station is a prime example of Charles Holden's modernist architecture for the Piccadilly line extension. Renowned architectural critic Jonathan Glancey praised it as one of the world's foremost modern buildings, calling it 'This king, queen, and all princes of a metro station.' In his review, Glancey also honoured the station with title of *Gesamtkunstwerk* – a complete and unified work of art. N11 1AN

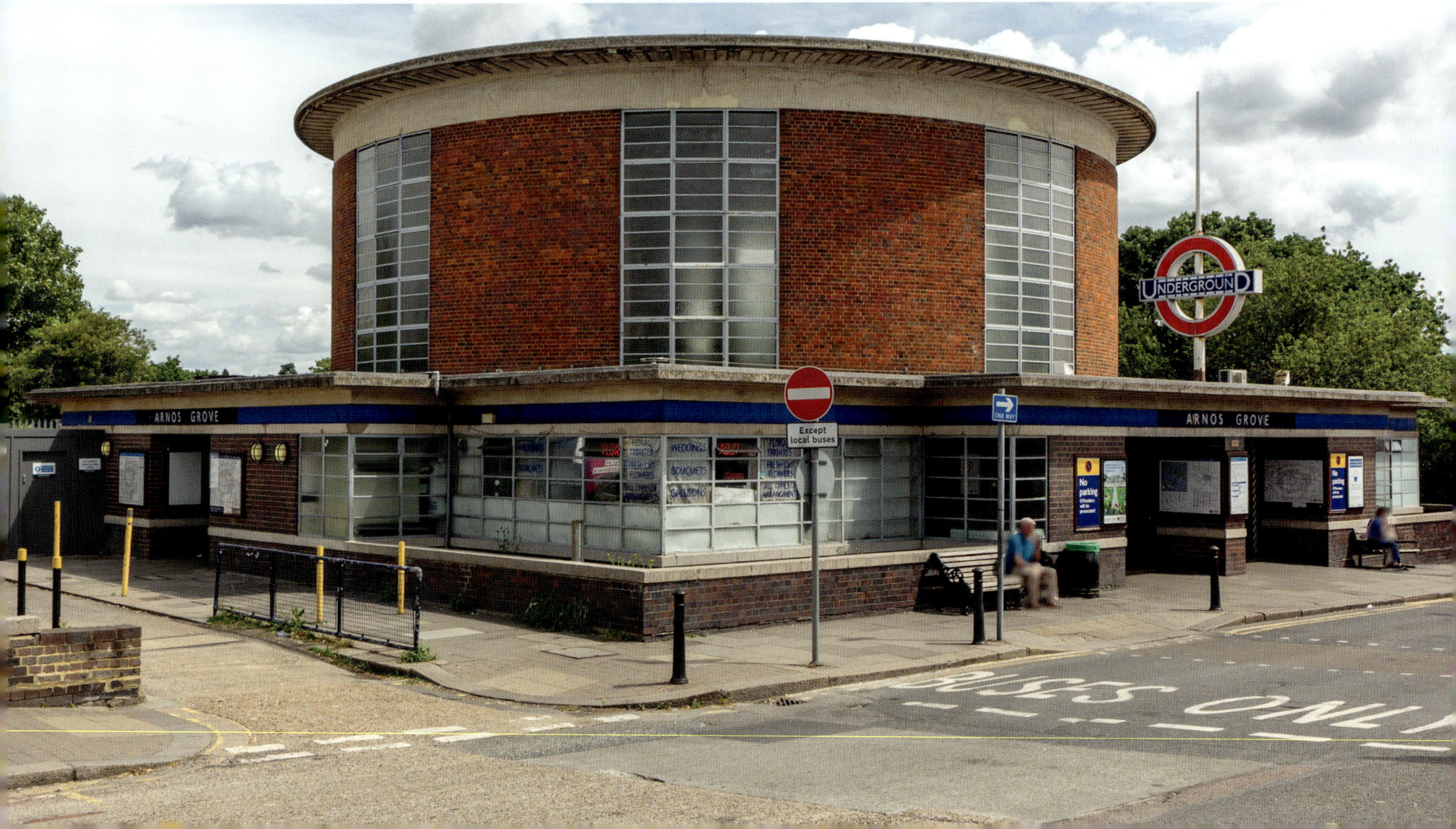

Southgate Station

The 'flying saucer' among Underground stations stands as one of Charles Holden's most iconic creations. This Grade II* listed station opened its doors in 1933. Holden's name is prominently featured in this book, reflecting his extensive portfolio, which includes, among other projects, the design of over forty Underground stations. N14 5BJ

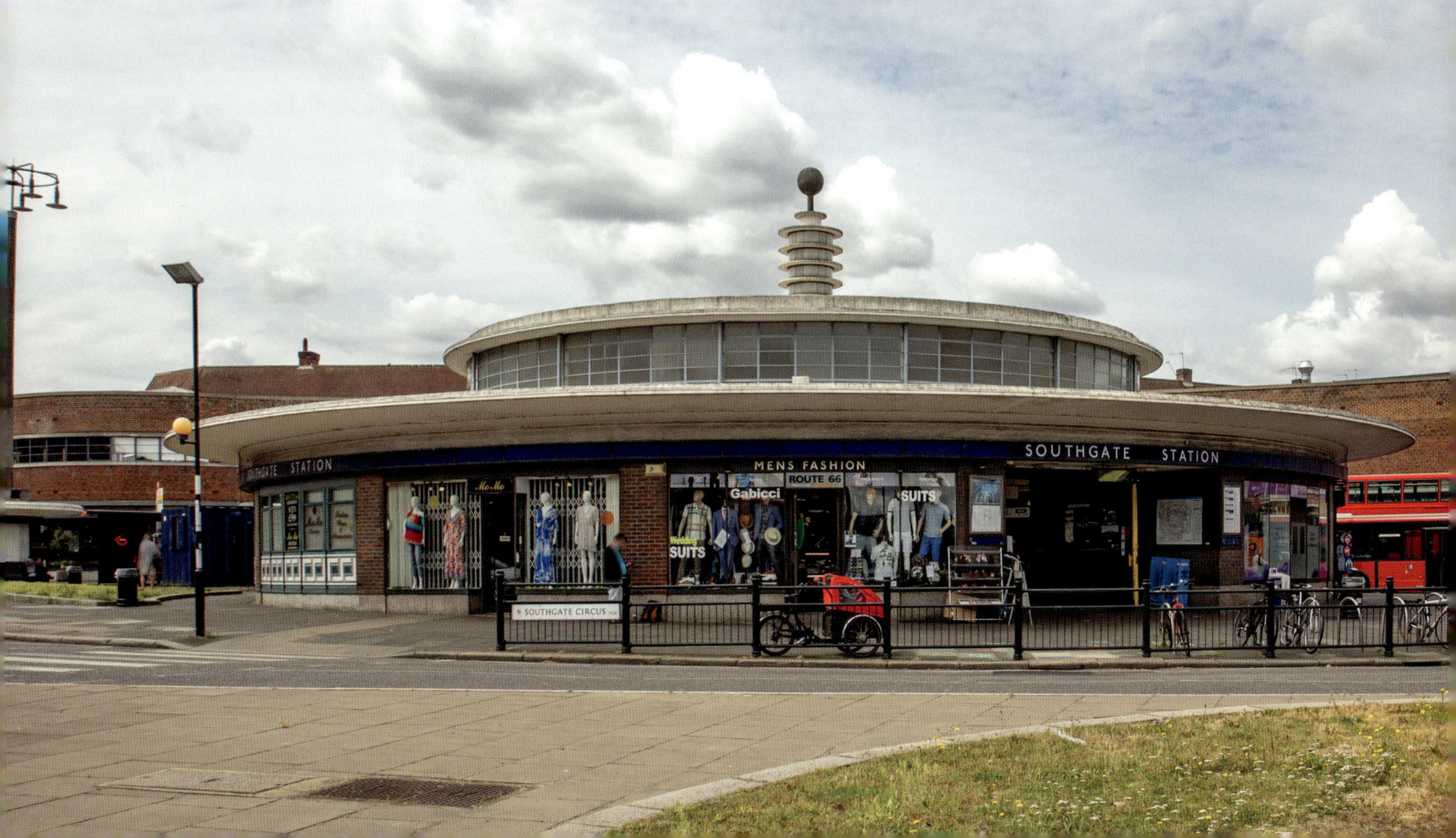

Grange Park Methodist Church

The Grange Park Methodist Church was designed by Charles H. Brightiff. It opened in 1938 and is also known as 'the Church in the Orchard'. N21 2EU

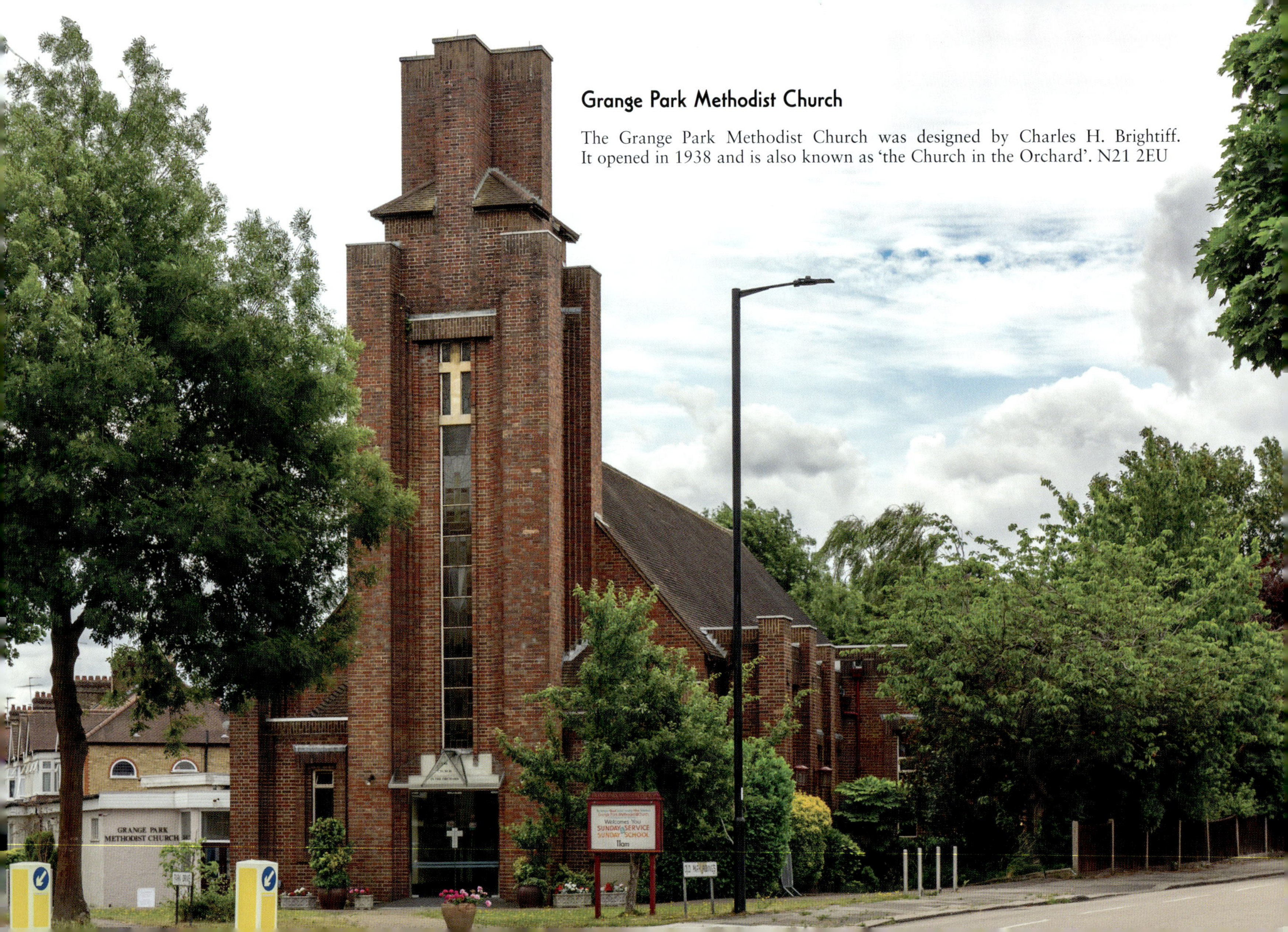

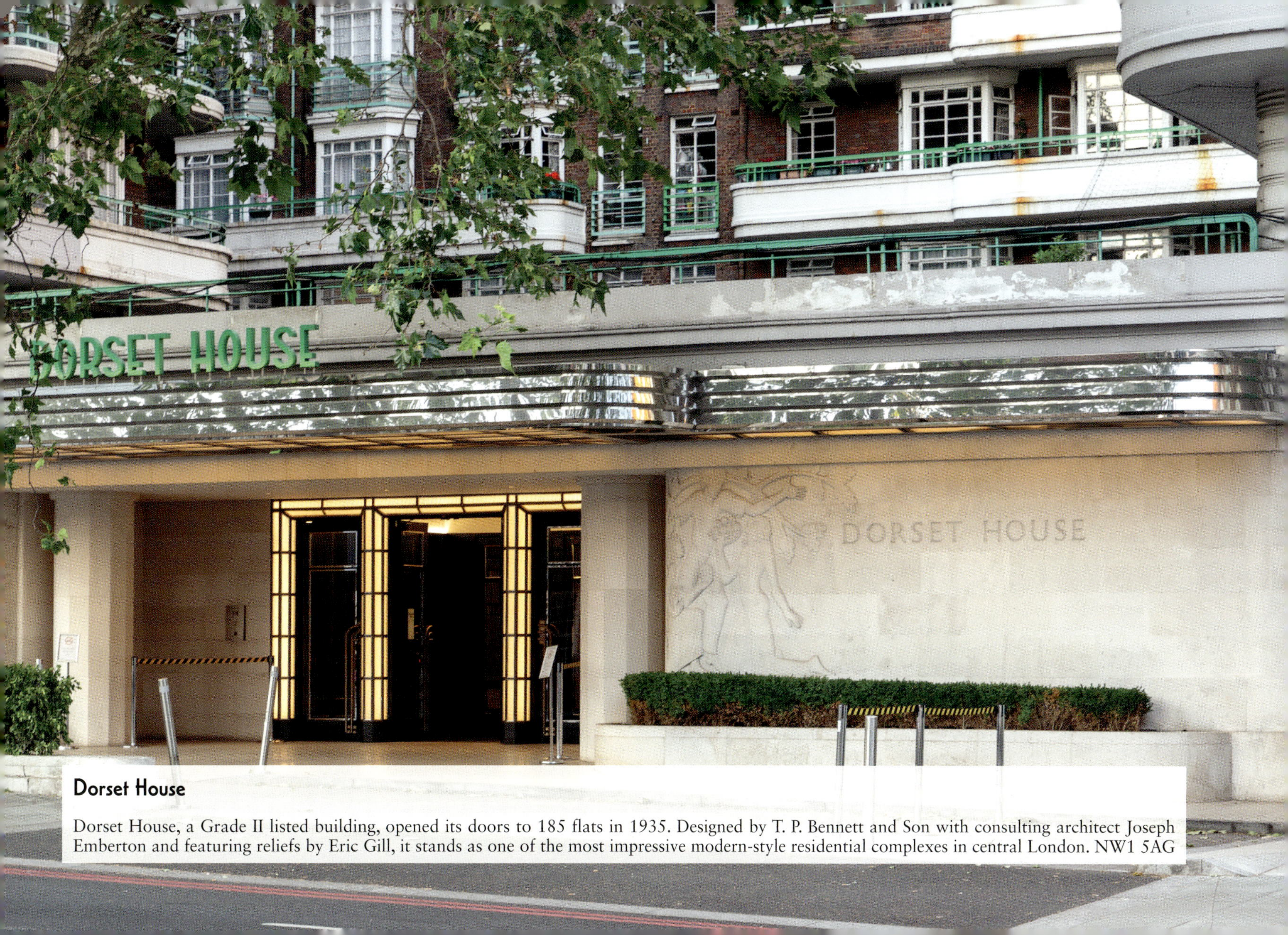

Dorset House

Dorset House, a Grade II listed building, opened its doors to 185 flats in 1935. Designed by T. P. Bennett and Son with consulting architect Joseph Emberton and featuring reliefs by Eric Gill, it stands as one of the most impressive modern-style residential complexes in central London. NW1 5AG

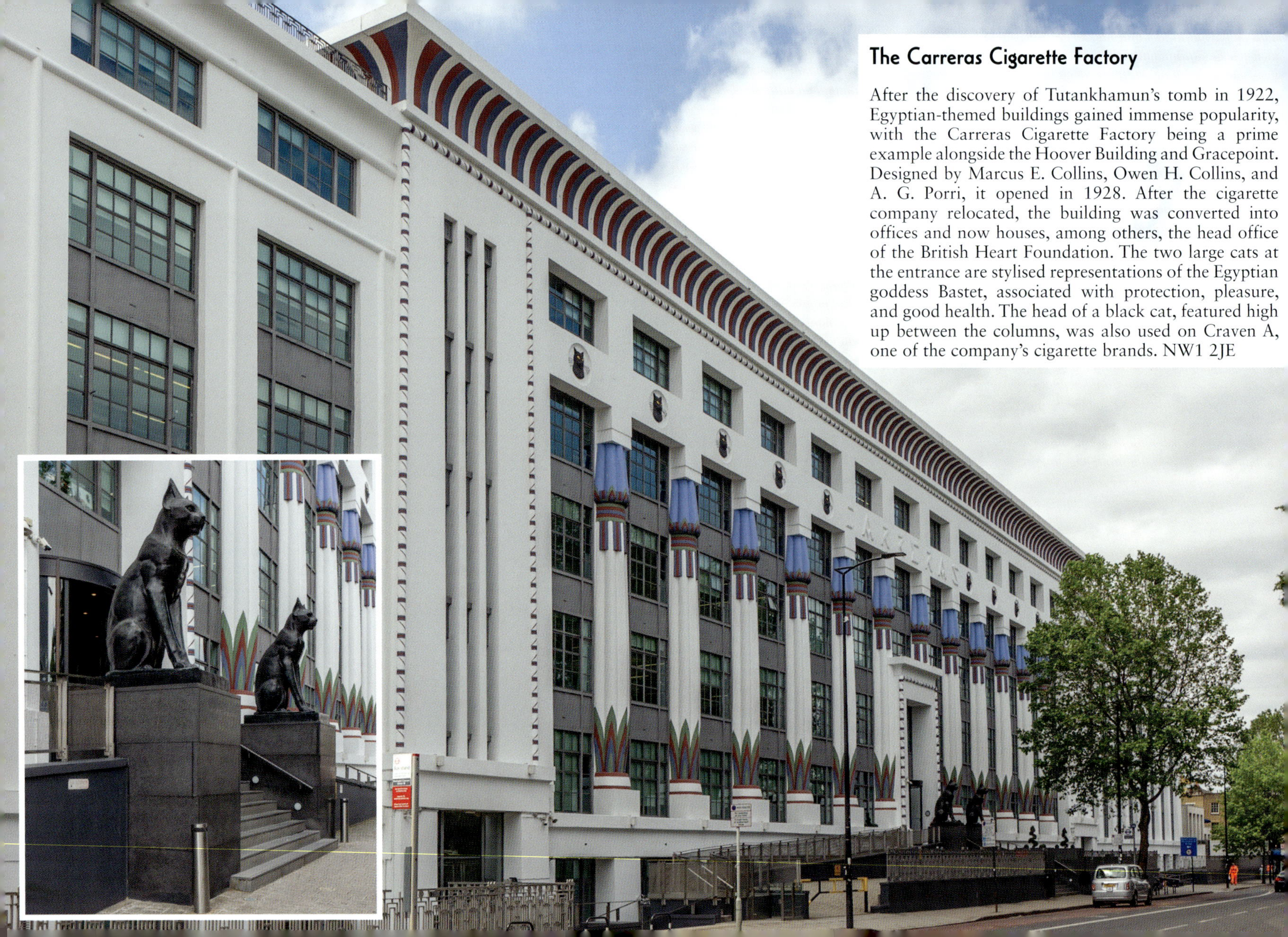

The Carreras Cigarette Factory

After the discovery of Tutankhamun's tomb in 1922, Egyptian-themed buildings gained immense popularity, with the Carreras Cigarette Factory being a prime example alongside the Hoover Building and Gracepoint. Designed by Marcus E. Collins, Owen H. Collins, and A. G. Porri, it opened in 1928. After the cigarette company relocated, the building was converted into offices and now houses, among others, the head office of the British Heart Foundation. The two large cats at the entrance are stylised representations of the Egyptian goddess Bastet, associated with protection, pleasure, and good health. The head of a black cat, featured high up between the columns, was also used on Craven A, one of the company's cigarette brands. NW1 2JE

Isokon Flats

Jack and Molly Pritchard commissioned architect Wells Coates to design the first International Style apartment building in Britain. Originally called Lawn Road Flats, now known as Isokon Flats, the building was completed in 1934 with thirty-two flats (now thirty-six), of which twenty-three were 'minimum' flats. These minimum flats featured tiny kitchens, complemented by access to a larger communal kitchen. The concept behind the building was to prioritise living over domestic chores, with services like cleaning and cooking provided. In its early days, it housed many émigré architects fleeing the Nazi regime, as well as artists, writers (including Agatha Christie), and a series of Russian spies. NW3 2XD

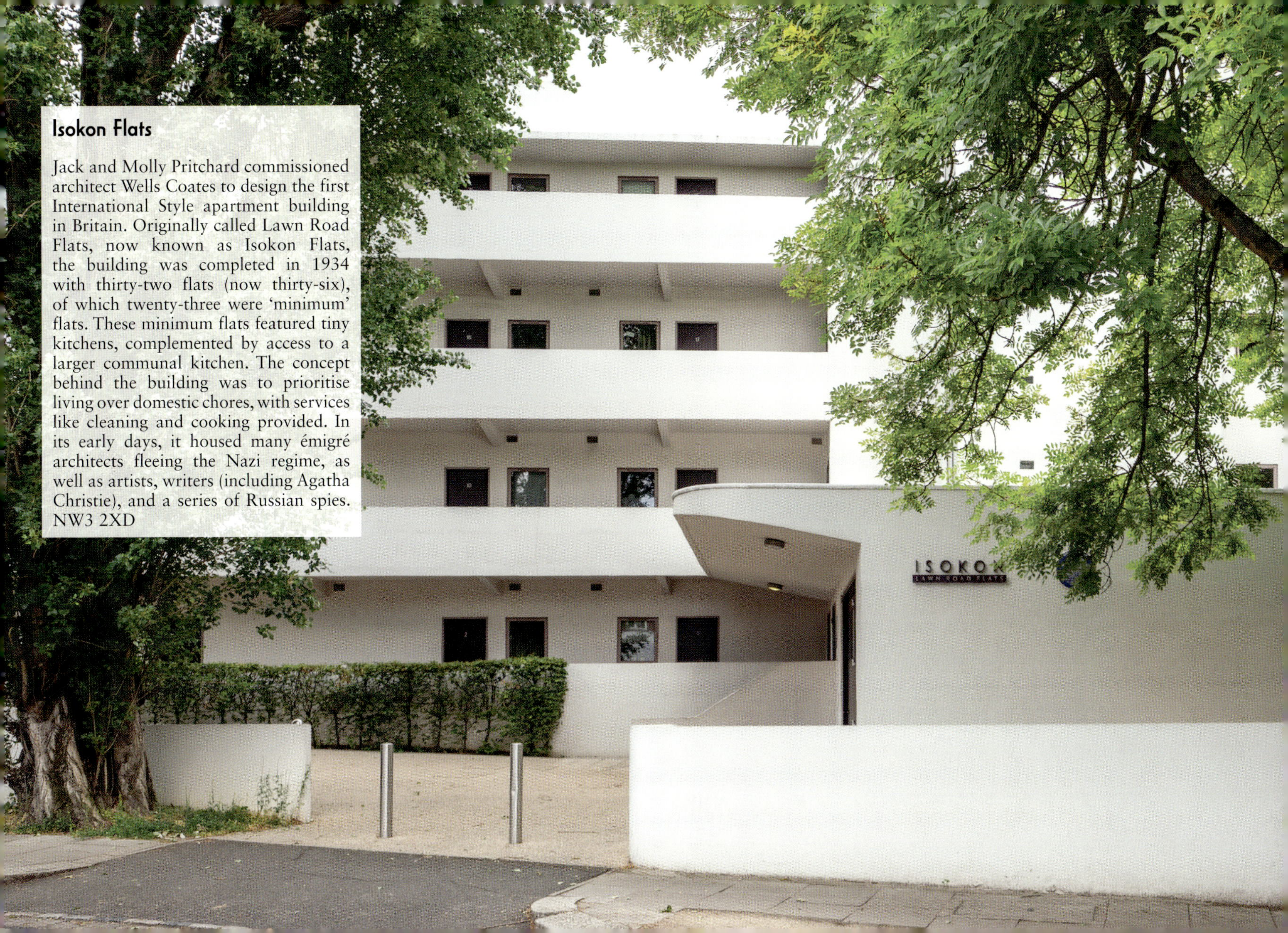

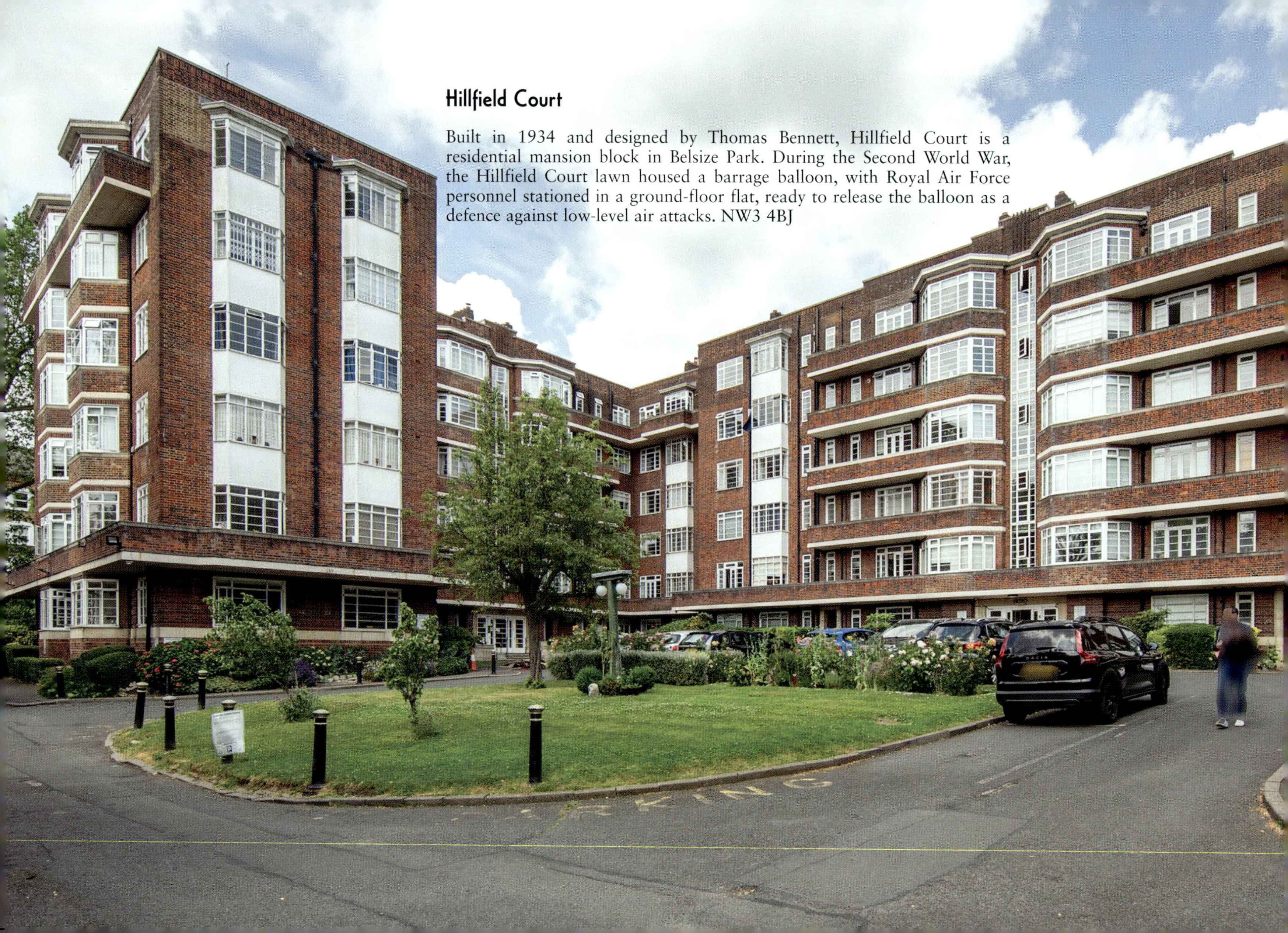

Hillfield Court

Built in 1934 and designed by Thomas Bennett, Hillfield Court is a residential mansion block in Belsize Park. During the Second World War, the Hillfield Court lawn housed a barrage balloon, with Royal Air Force personnel stationed in a ground-floor flat, ready to release the balloon as a defence against low-level air attacks. NW3 4BJ

O2 Forum Kentish Town

The Grade II listed O2 Forum, designed by J. Stanley Beard and W. R. Bennett, originally opened its doors in 1934 as the Forum Cinema. Throughout its colourful history, it transformed into an Irish dance hall, a bingo hall, and later served as a live music venue under various ownerships. Today, it stands as a well-established live venue with a capacity of 2300, hosting a diverse array of performances. NW5 1JY

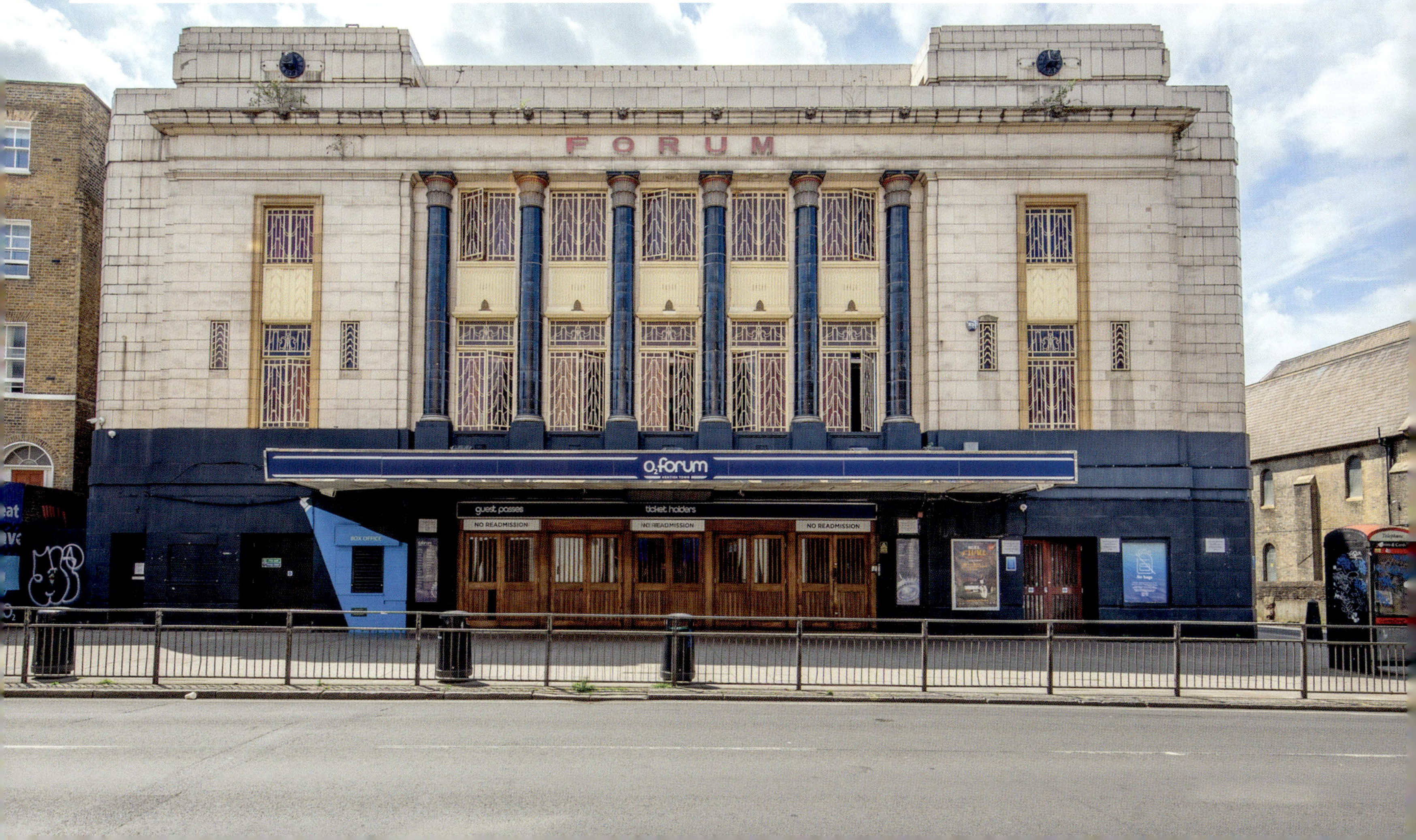

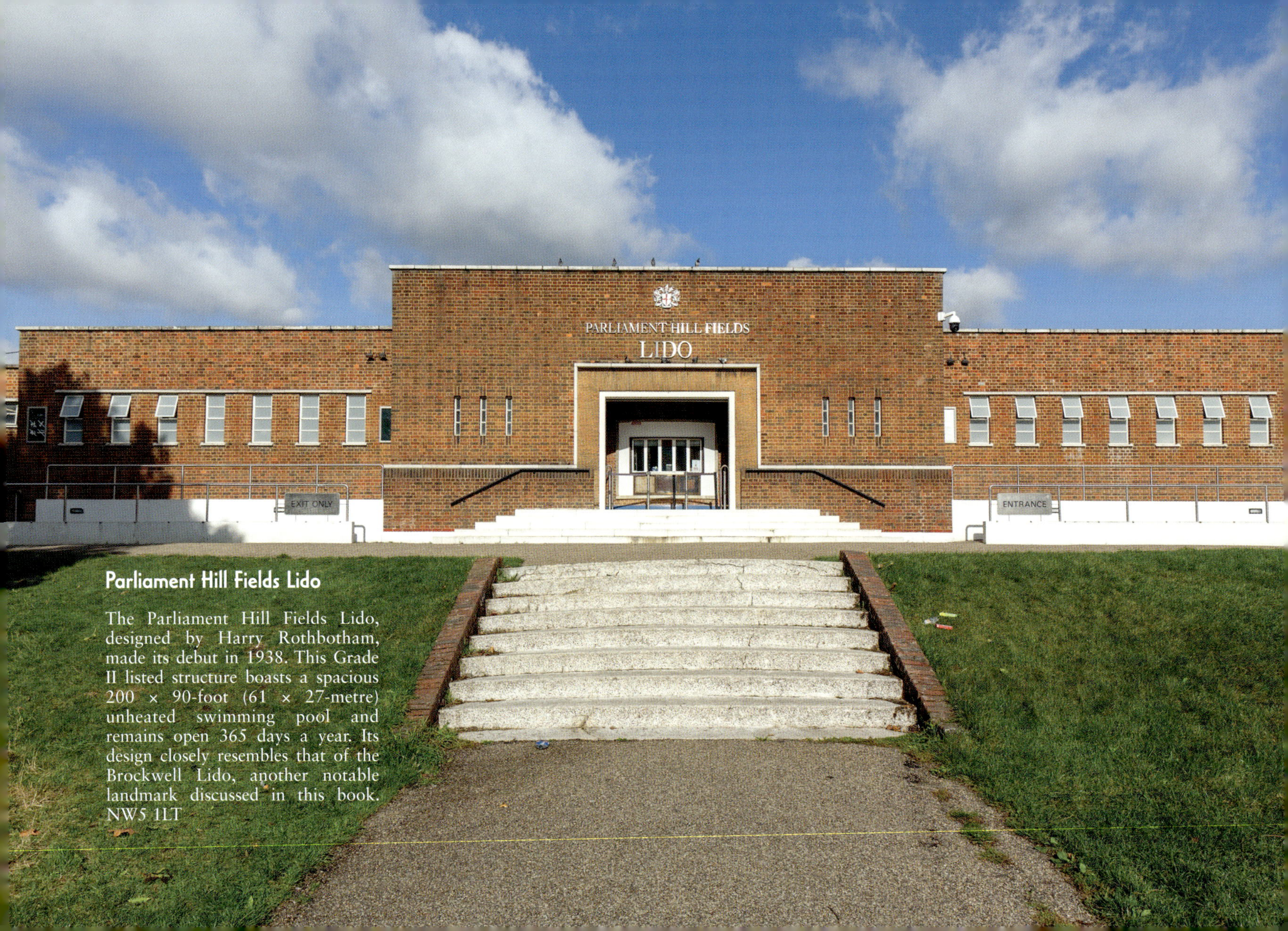

Parliament Hill Fields Lido

The Parliament Hill Fields Lido, designed by Harry Rothbotham, made its debut in 1938. This Grade II listed structure boasts a spacious 200 × 90-foot (61 × 27-metre) unheated swimming pool and remains open 365 days a year. Its design closely resembles that of the Brockwell Lido, another notable landmark discussed in this book. NW5 1LT

Ruach City Church

Originally designed by George Coles, the building now housing the Ruach City Church served as the Gaumont State Cinema in 1937. The inclusion of 'State' in its name paid tribute to the iconic Empire State Building in New York. Over the years, it hosted various concerts, featuring legendary acts such as the Rolling Stones and The Who. Later, it transitioned into a bingo hall, earning Grade II* listed status as the Mecca Bingo, before finding its current purpose as a church. NW6 7HY

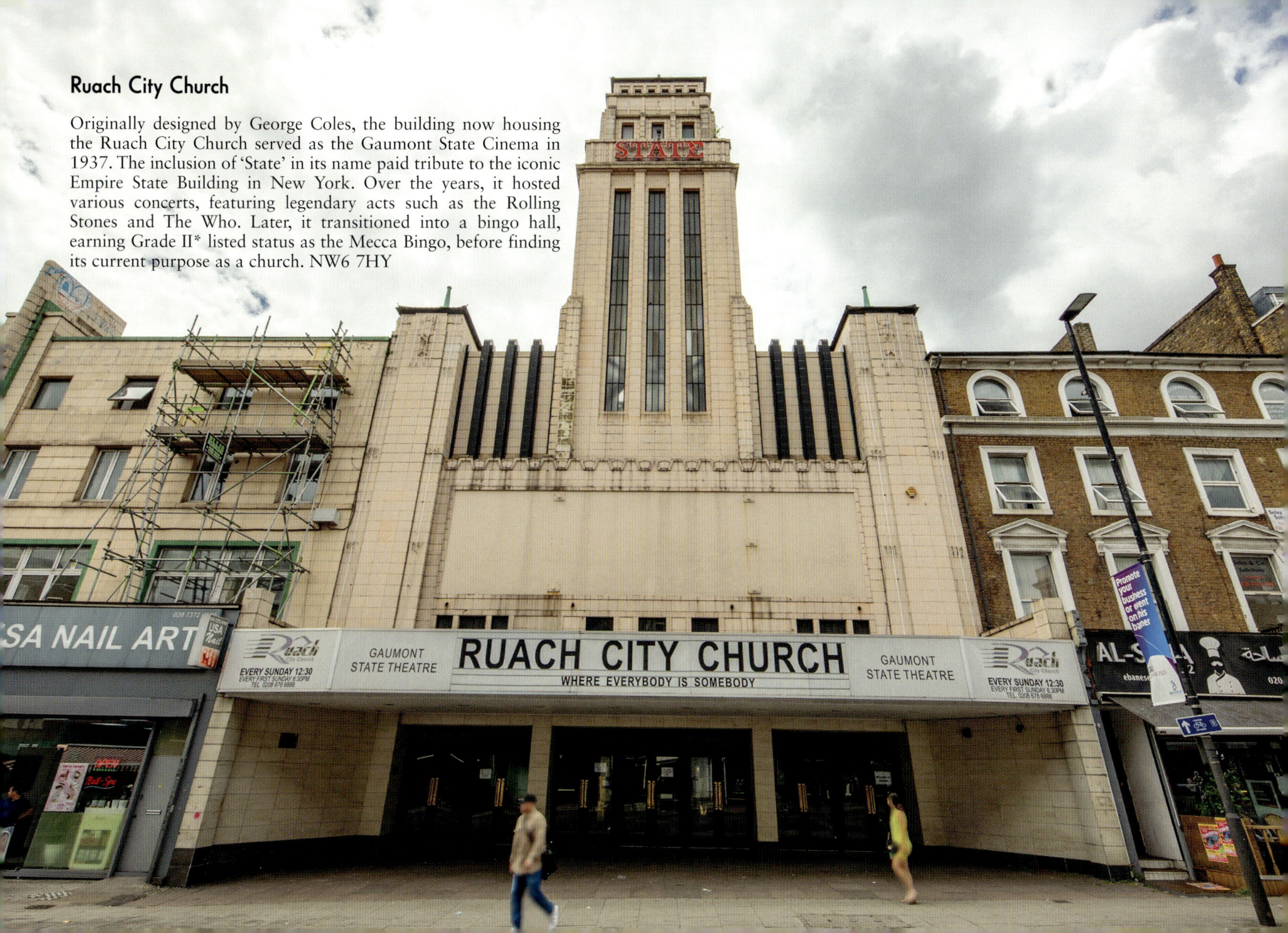

St Olaf House

Constructed around 1931 by architect Harry Stuart Goodhart-Rendel, St Olaf House, with its distinctive T-shaped design, served as the headquarters of the Hay's Wharf Company. In 1980, the Grade II* listed building was acquired by the neighbouring London Bridge Hospital and has since become an integral part of the hospital. The building is named after King Olaf II of Norway (995–1030), who among other things seems to have been responsible for the destruction of London Bridge (in order to divide the Danes who were on both sides of the river). SE1 2PR

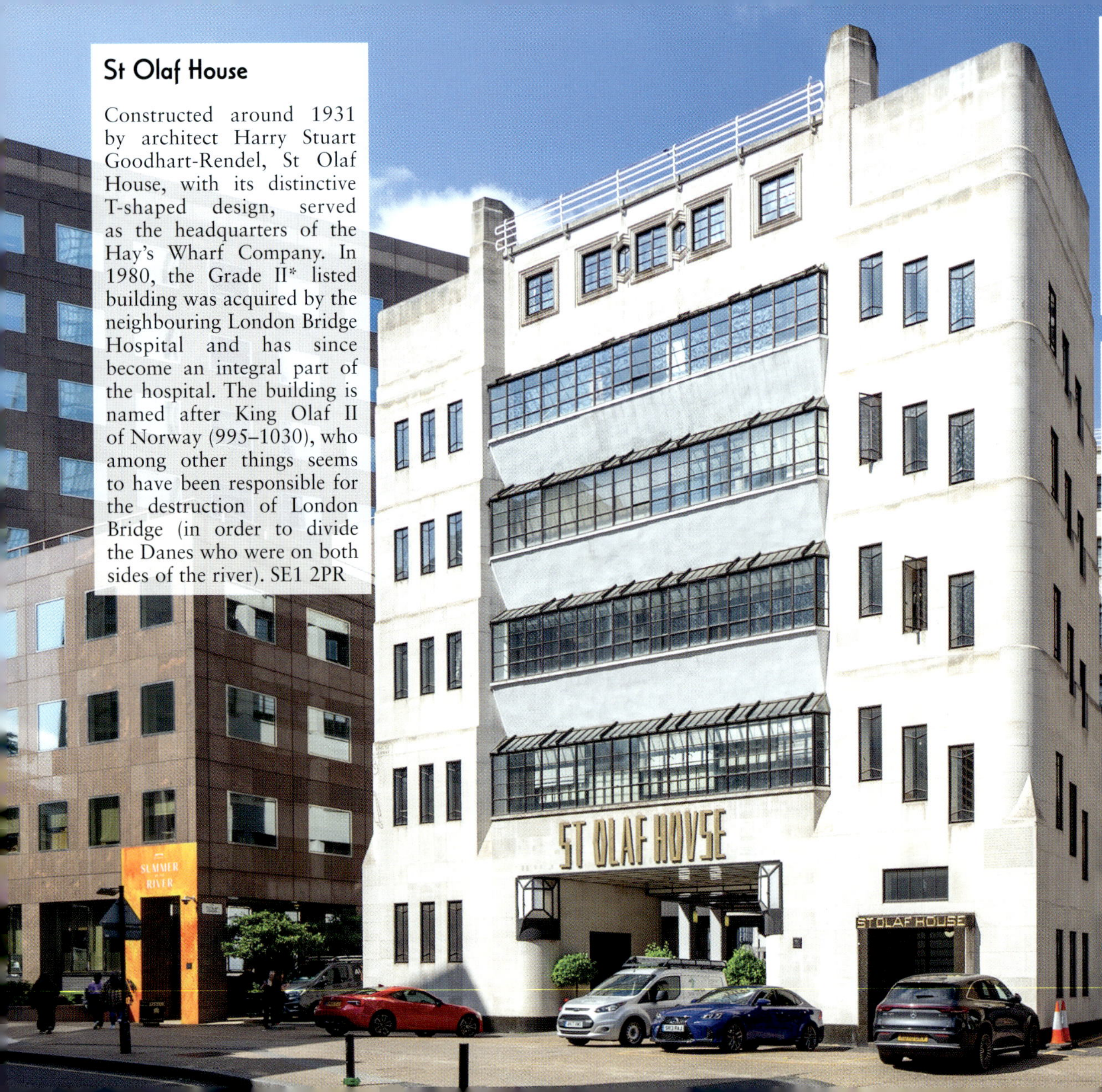

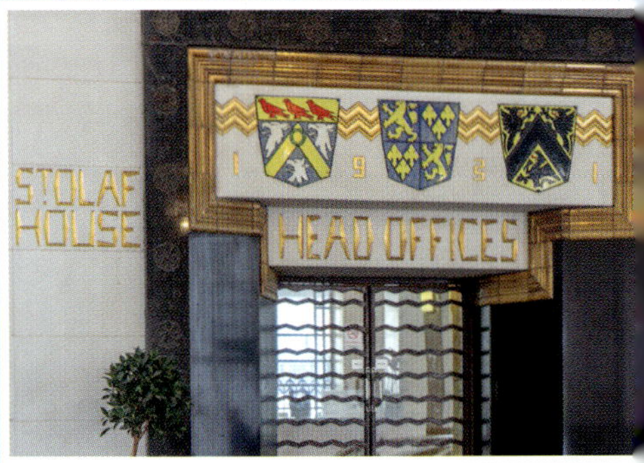

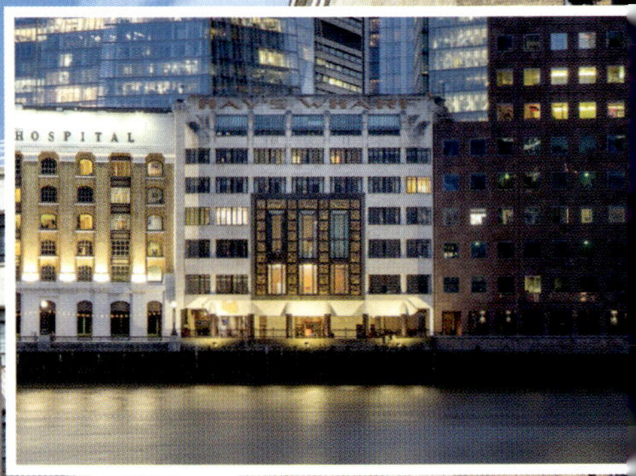

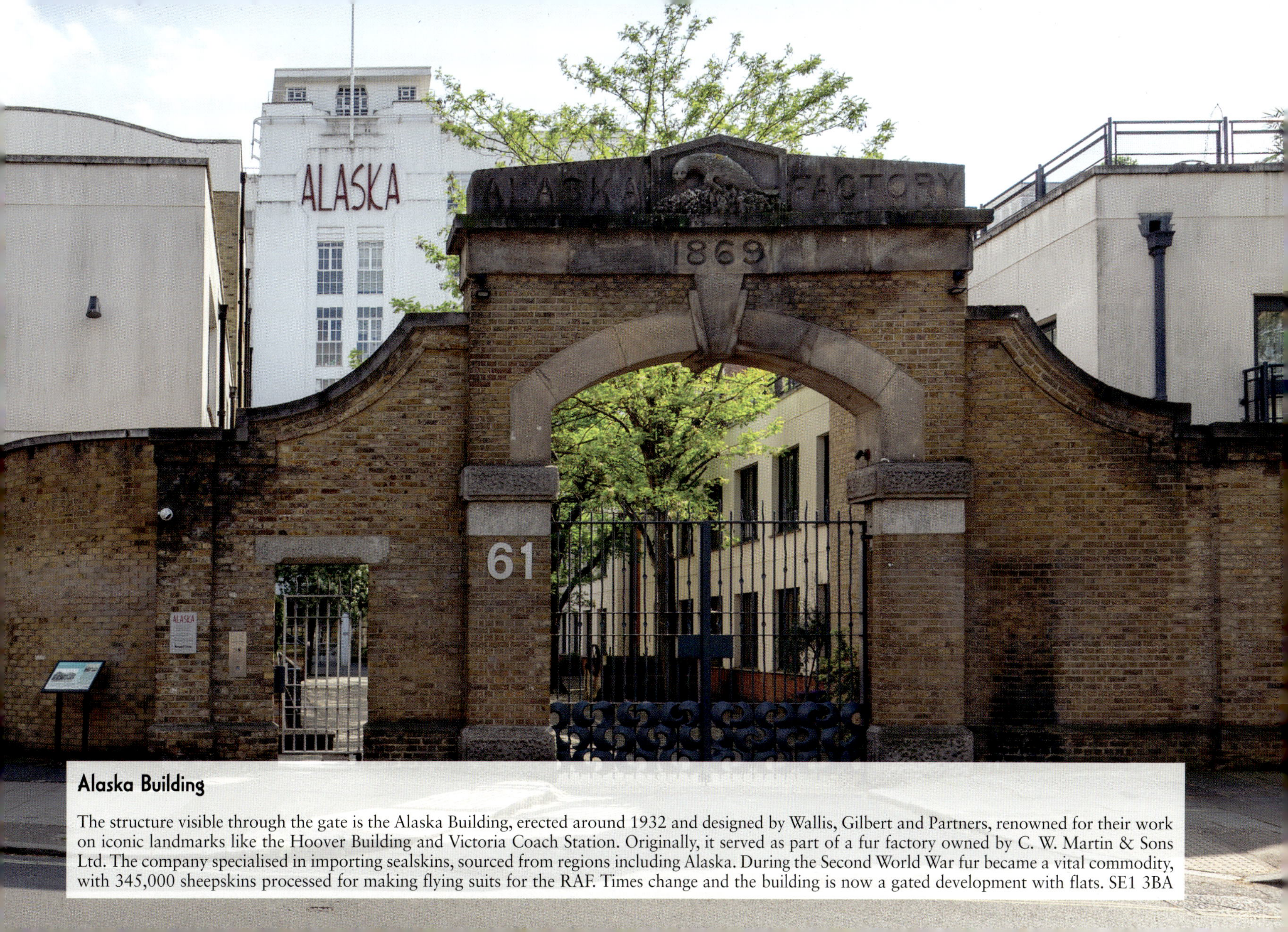

Alaska Building

The structure visible through the gate is the Alaska Building, erected around 1932 and designed by Wallis, Gilbert and Partners, renowned for their work on iconic landmarks like the Hoover Building and Victoria Coach Station. Originally, it served as part of a fur factory owned by C. W. Martin & Sons Ltd. The company specialised in importing sealskins, sourced from regions including Alaska. During the Second World War fur became a vital commodity, with 345,000 sheepskins processed for making flying suits for the RAF. Times change and the building is now a gated development with flats. SE1 3BA

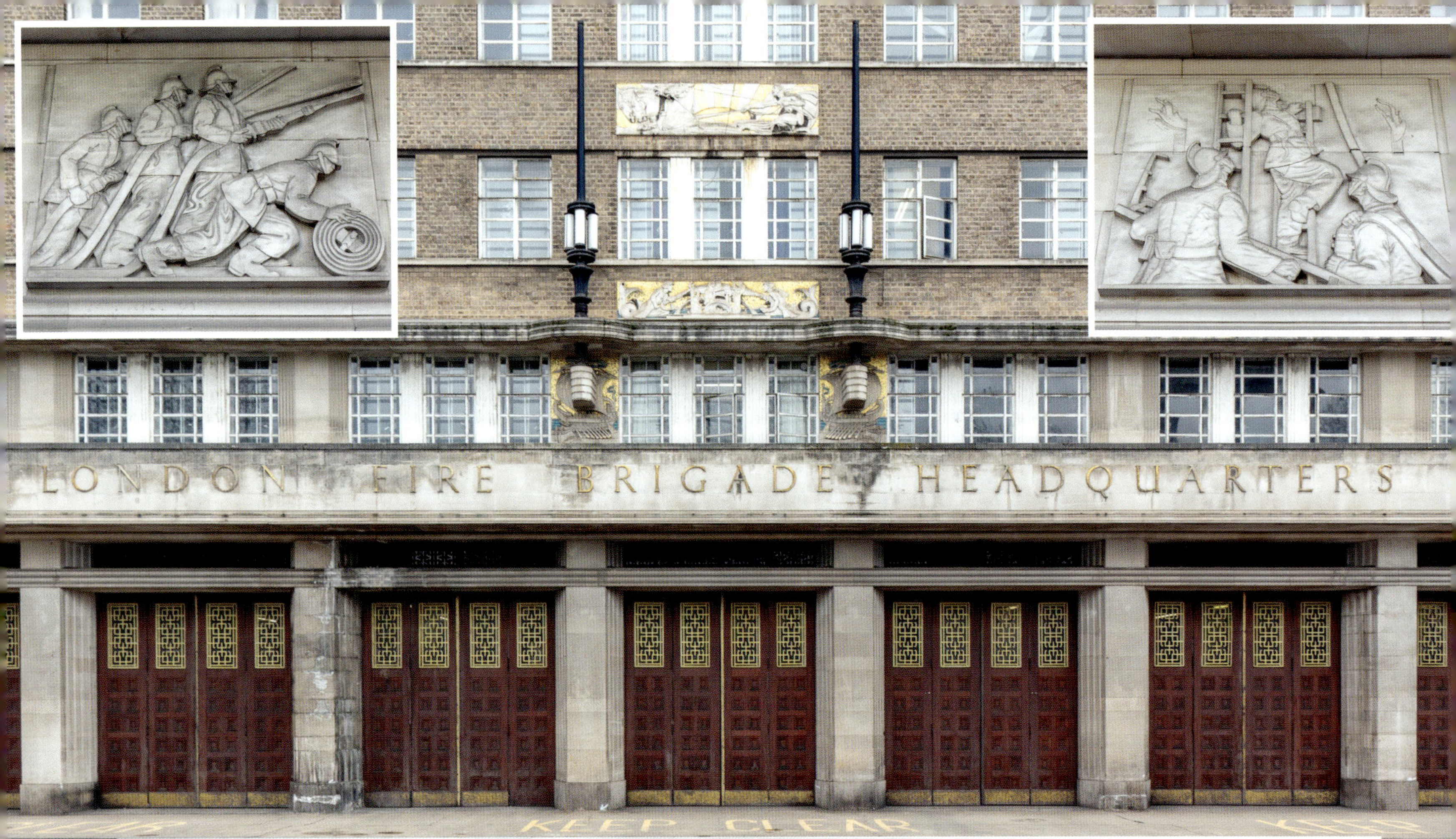

Lambeth Fire Station

The Lambeth Fire Station, formerly the headquarters of the London Fire Brigade, holds a significant historical legacy. This Grade II listed building, inaugurated in 1937 by King George VI, served as the focal point for London's firefighting efforts during the Second World War. Designed by E. P. Wheeler FRIBA, with assistance from G. Weald FRIBA, its striking Art Deco features include reliefs attributed to Gilbert Bayes, S. N. Babb, and F. P. Morton. SE1 7SD

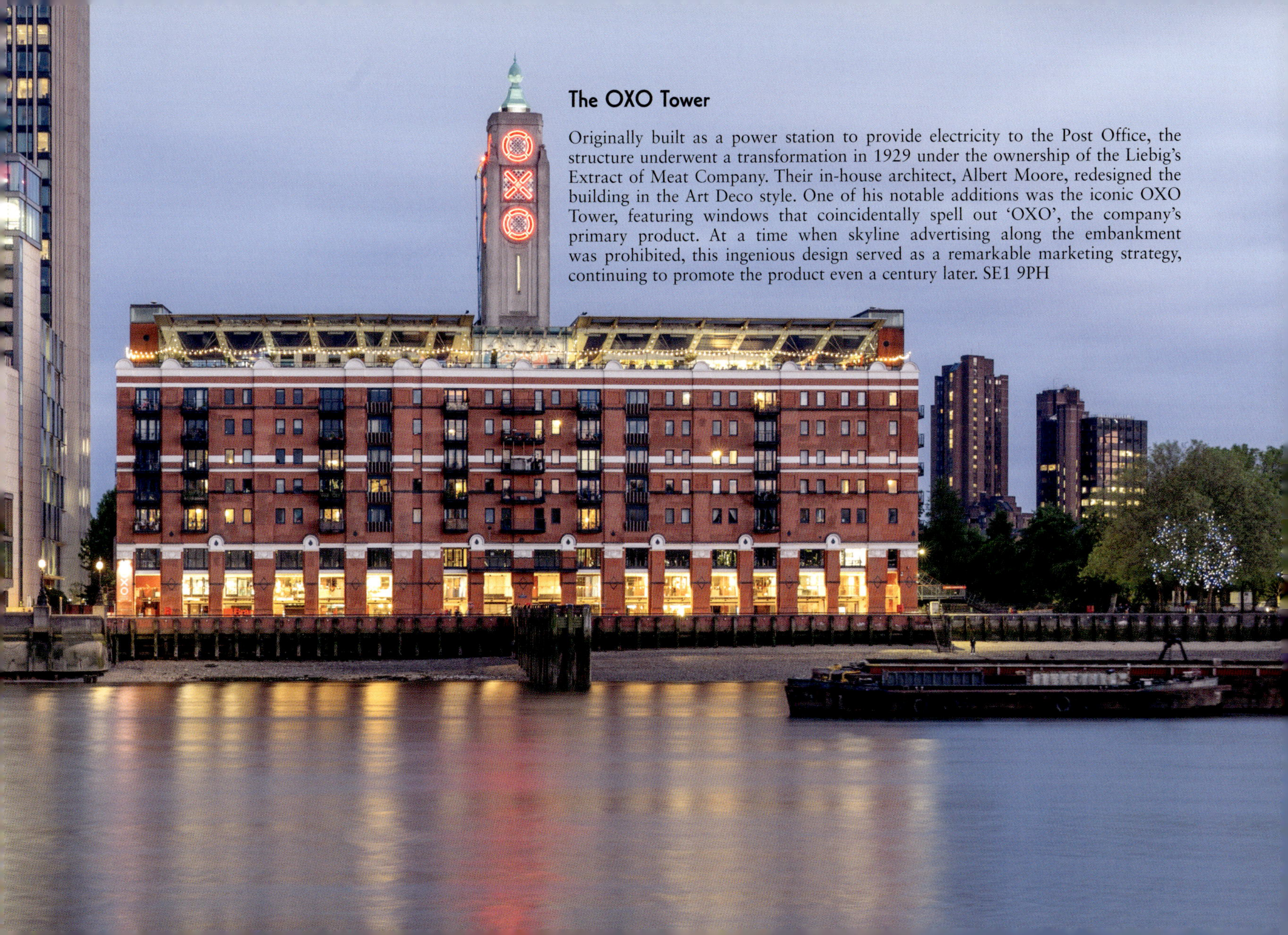

The OXO Tower

Originally built as a power station to provide electricity to the Post Office, the structure underwent a transformation in 1929 under the ownership of the Liebig's Extract of Meat Company. Their in-house architect, Albert Moore, redesigned the building in the Art Deco style. One of his notable additions was the iconic OXO Tower, featuring windows that coincidentally spell out 'OXO', the company's primary product. At a time when skyline advertising along the embankment was prohibited, this ingenious design served as a remarkable marketing strategy, continuing to promote the product even a century later. SE1 9PH

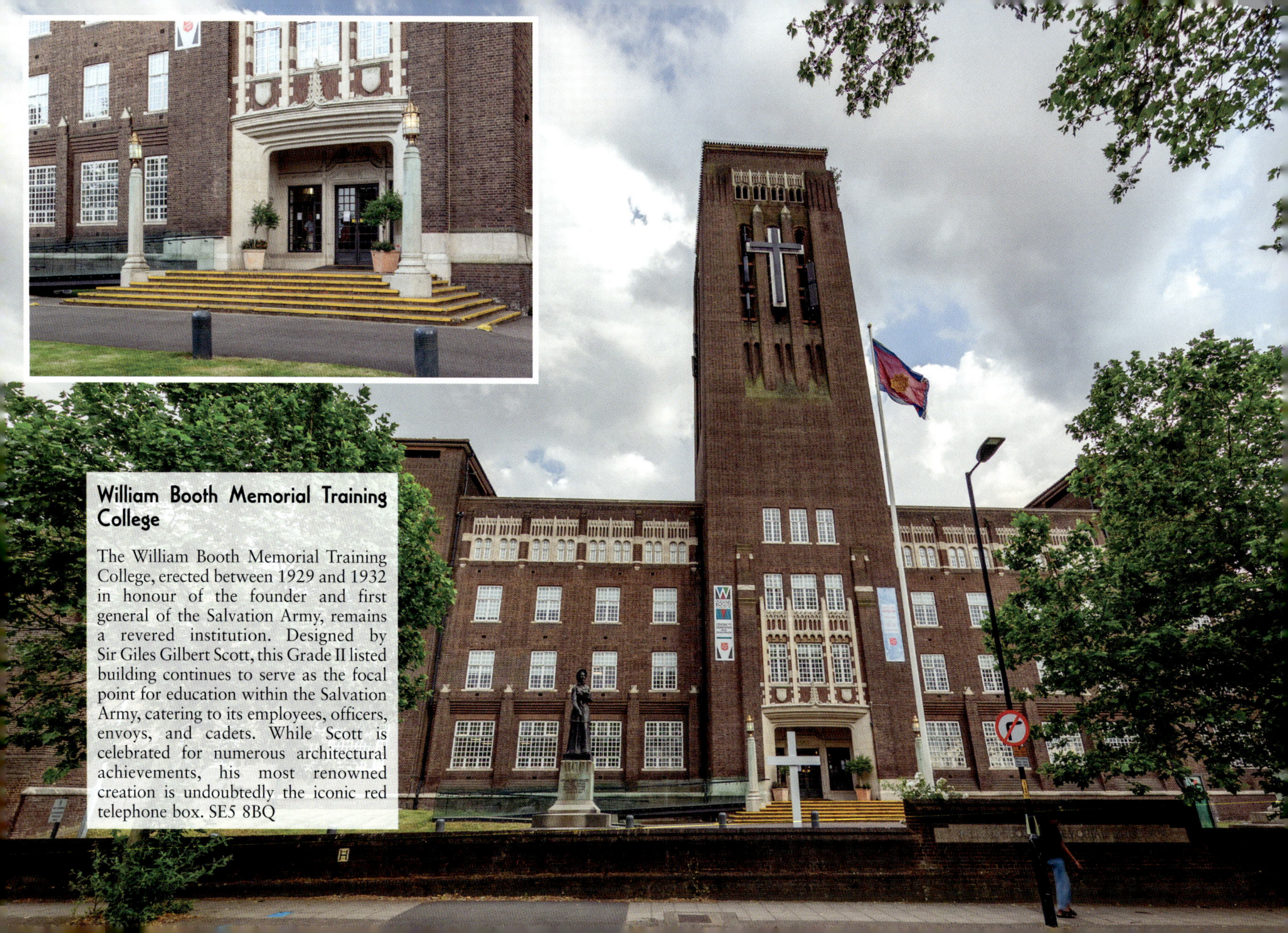

William Booth Memorial Training College

The William Booth Memorial Training College, erected between 1929 and 1932 in honour of the founder and first general of the Salvation Army, remains a revered institution. Designed by Sir Giles Gilbert Scott, this Grade II listed building continues to serve as the focal point for education within the Salvation Army, catering to its employees, officers, envoys, and cadets. While Scott is celebrated for numerous architectural achievements, his most renowned creation is undoubtedly the iconic red telephone box. SE5 8BQ

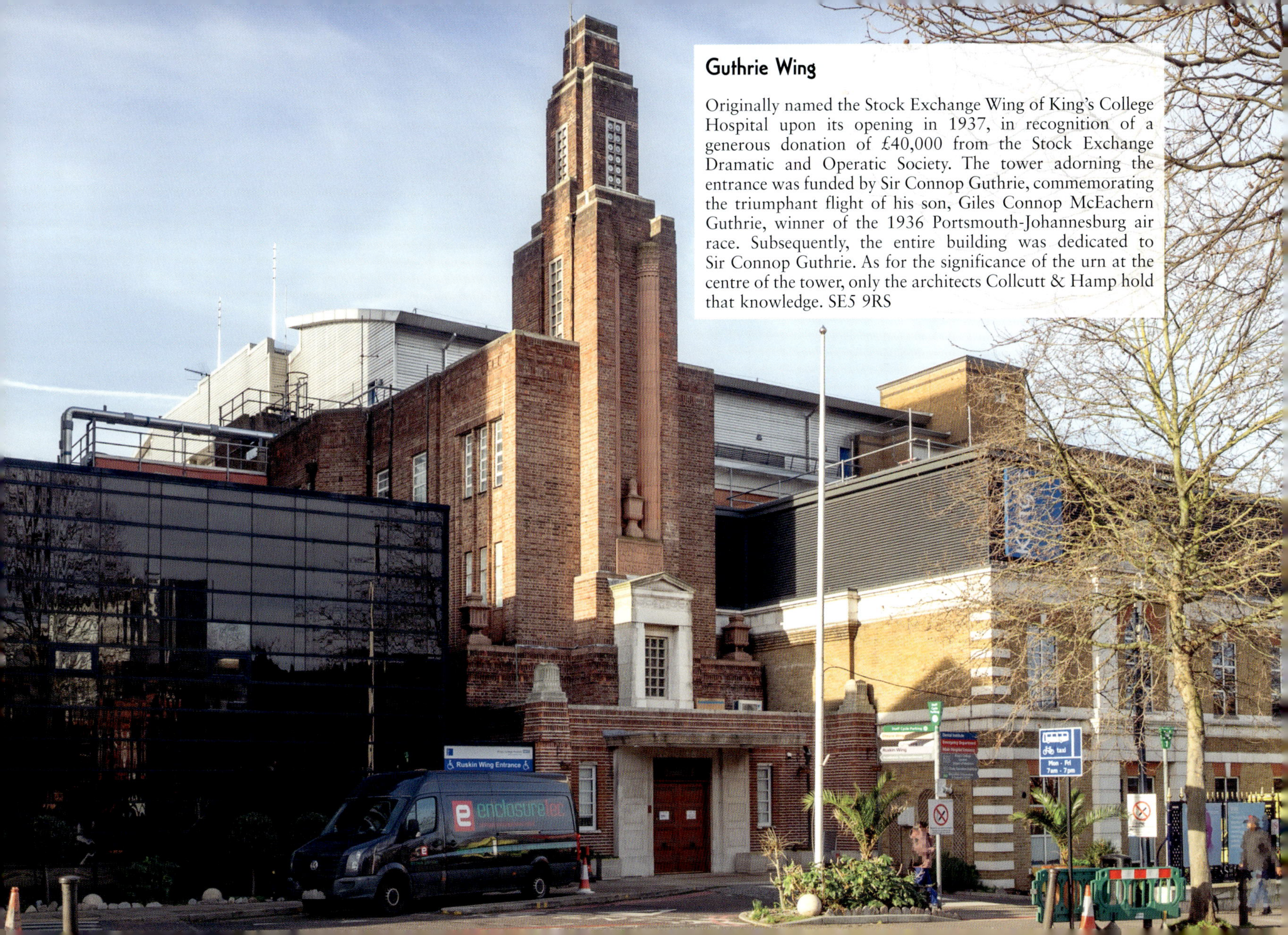

Guthrie Wing

Originally named the Stock Exchange Wing of King's College Hospital upon its opening in 1937, in recognition of a generous donation of £40,000 from the Stock Exchange Dramatic and Operatic Society. The tower adorning the entrance was funded by Sir Connop Guthrie, commemorating the triumphant flight of his son, Giles Connop McEachern Guthrie, winner of the 1936 Portsmouth-Johannesburg air race. Subsequently, the entire building was dedicated to Sir Connop Guthrie. As for the significance of the urn at the centre of the tower, only the architects Collcutt & Hamp hold that knowledge. SE5 9RS

Meridian House

Clifford Culpin envisioned the building as Greenwich Town Hall in 1939. Following the relocation of the local government, it was renamed Meridian House, acknowledging Greenwich's significant association with the Prime Meridian. Presently, the building is under the ownership of Riverlow, a real estate investment and development company. Their vision is to transform it into a multifunctional space, including flats, offices, and commercial areas. However, due to its Grade II listed status and the current shortfall in affordable housing, navigating the necessary approvals presents a few challenges. SE10 8RD

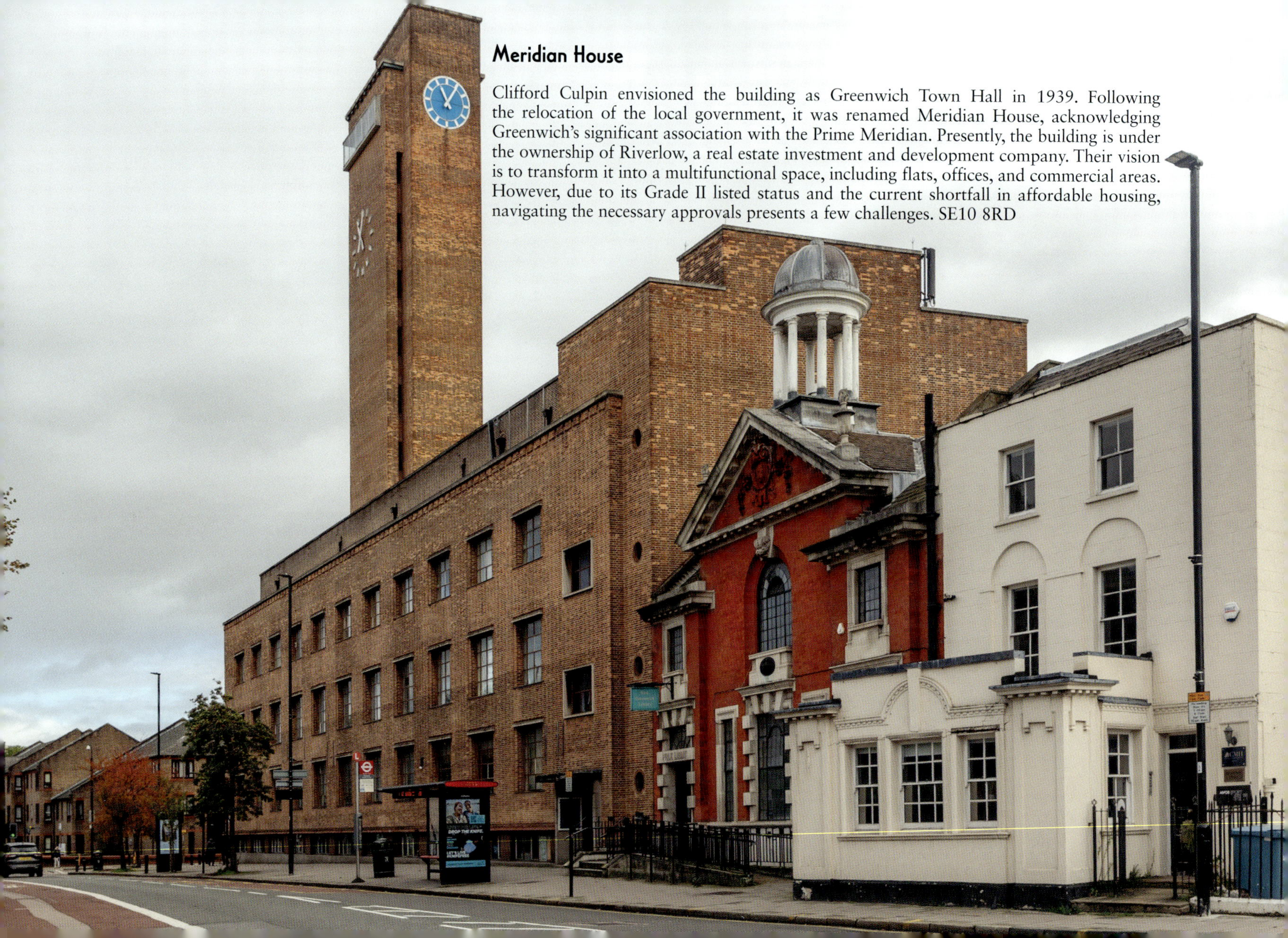

Charlton Lido

Charlton Lido, designed by Harry Rowbotham and T. L. Smithson, holds the distinction of being the final municipal pool to open in London, debuting in 1939. Unfortunately, its operation was short-lived as it closed soon after due to the outbreak of the Second World War, only to reopen its doors in 1946. Falling into disrepair in the early 2000s, the lido was fortunately restored to its former splendour ahead of the 2012 London Olympics. SE18 4LX

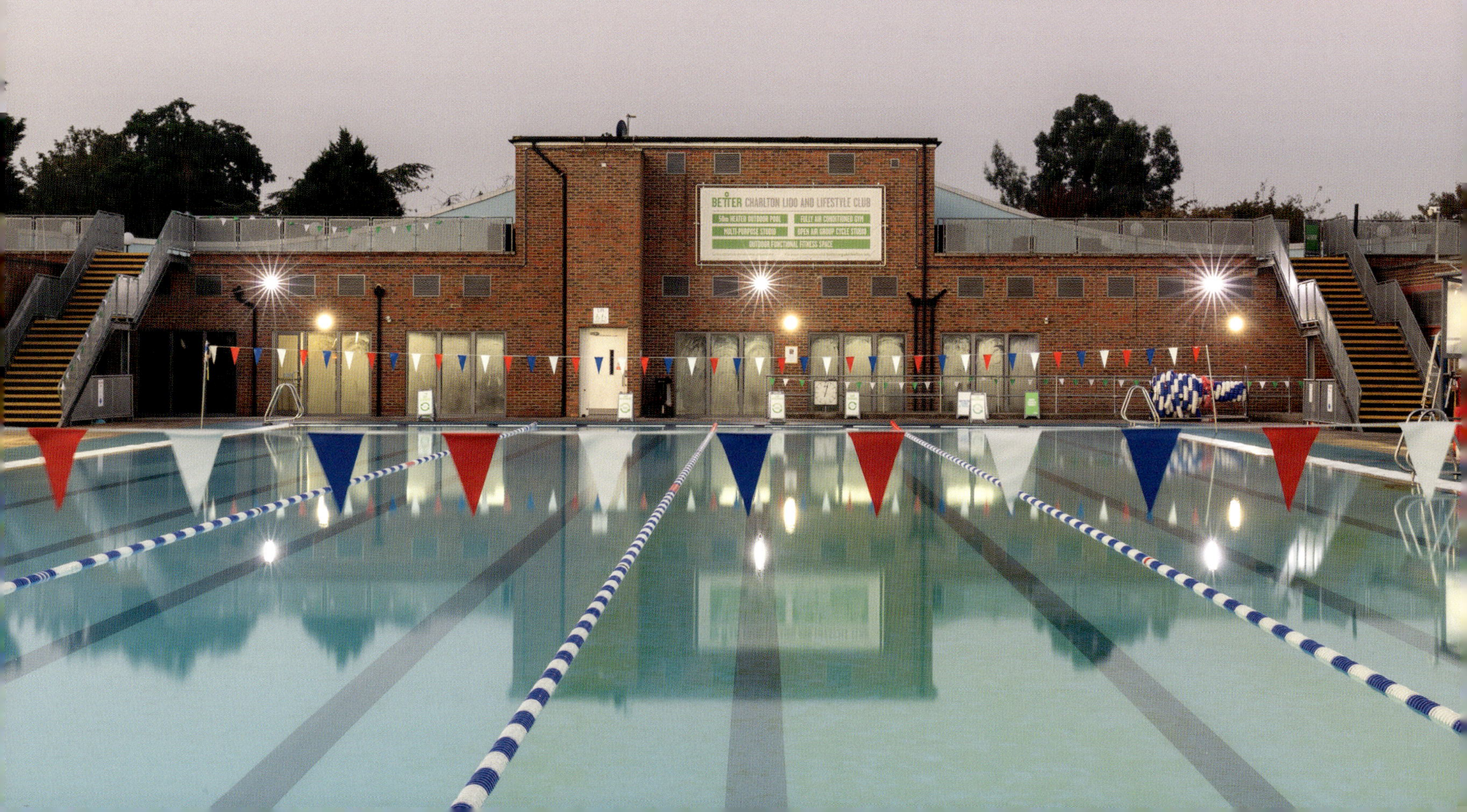

Gateway House

Gateway House, originally constructed in 1937 by George Coles as the Odeon cinema, stands as a premier example of the iconic 'Odeon' style. Now designated a Grade II listed building, it has been repurposed as the home of the New Wine Church and serves as a versatile event venue. With its stunning Art Deco rooms, it offers a unique setting for various occasions and can be hired for events. SE18 6QQ

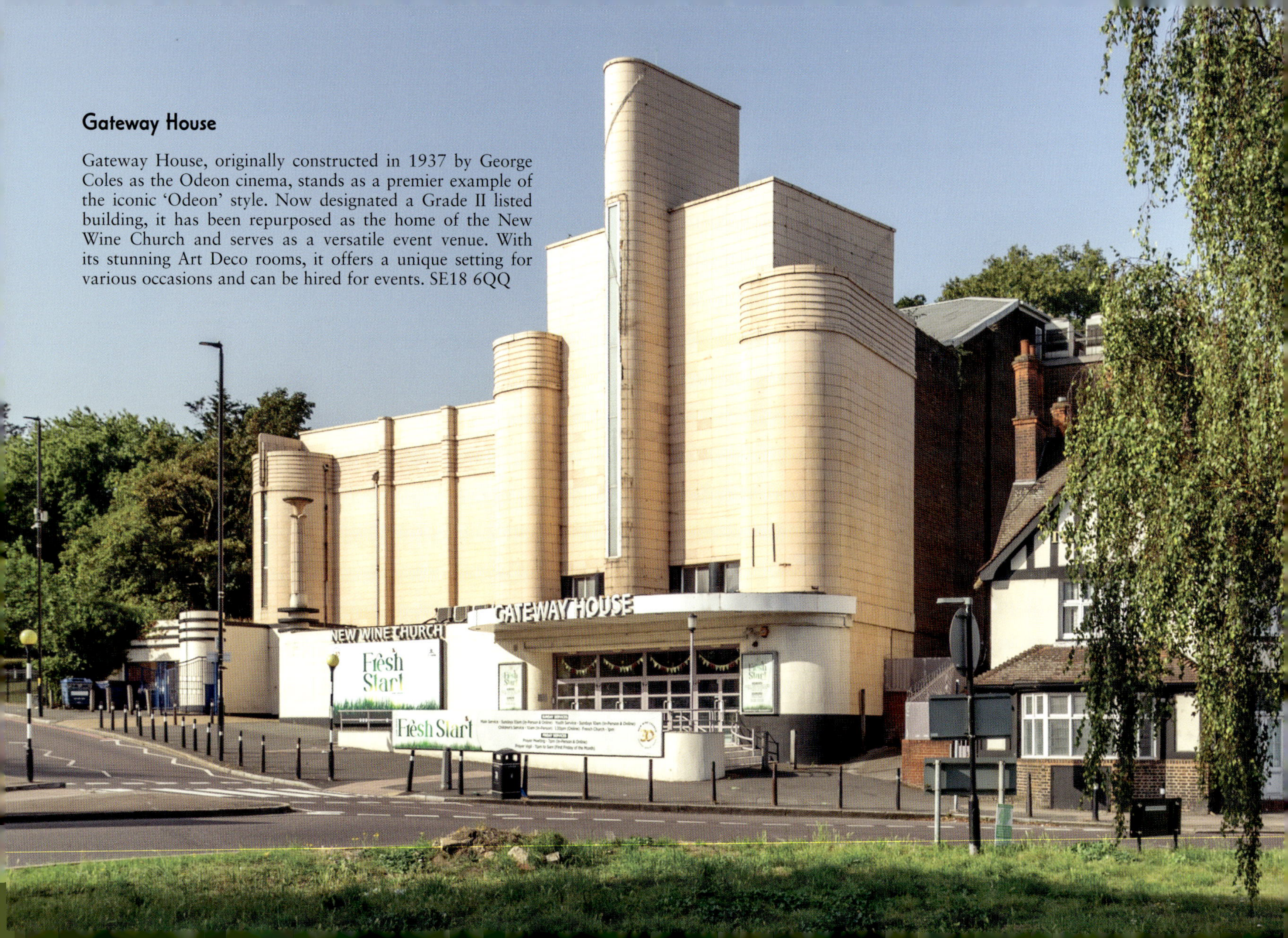

Brockwell Lido

The Brockwell Lido was designed in 1937 by Harry Rowbotham and T. L. Smithson. This Grade II listed pool is renowned for its popularity and is currently managed by Fusion Lifestyle, a sports and leisure management company. SE24 0PA

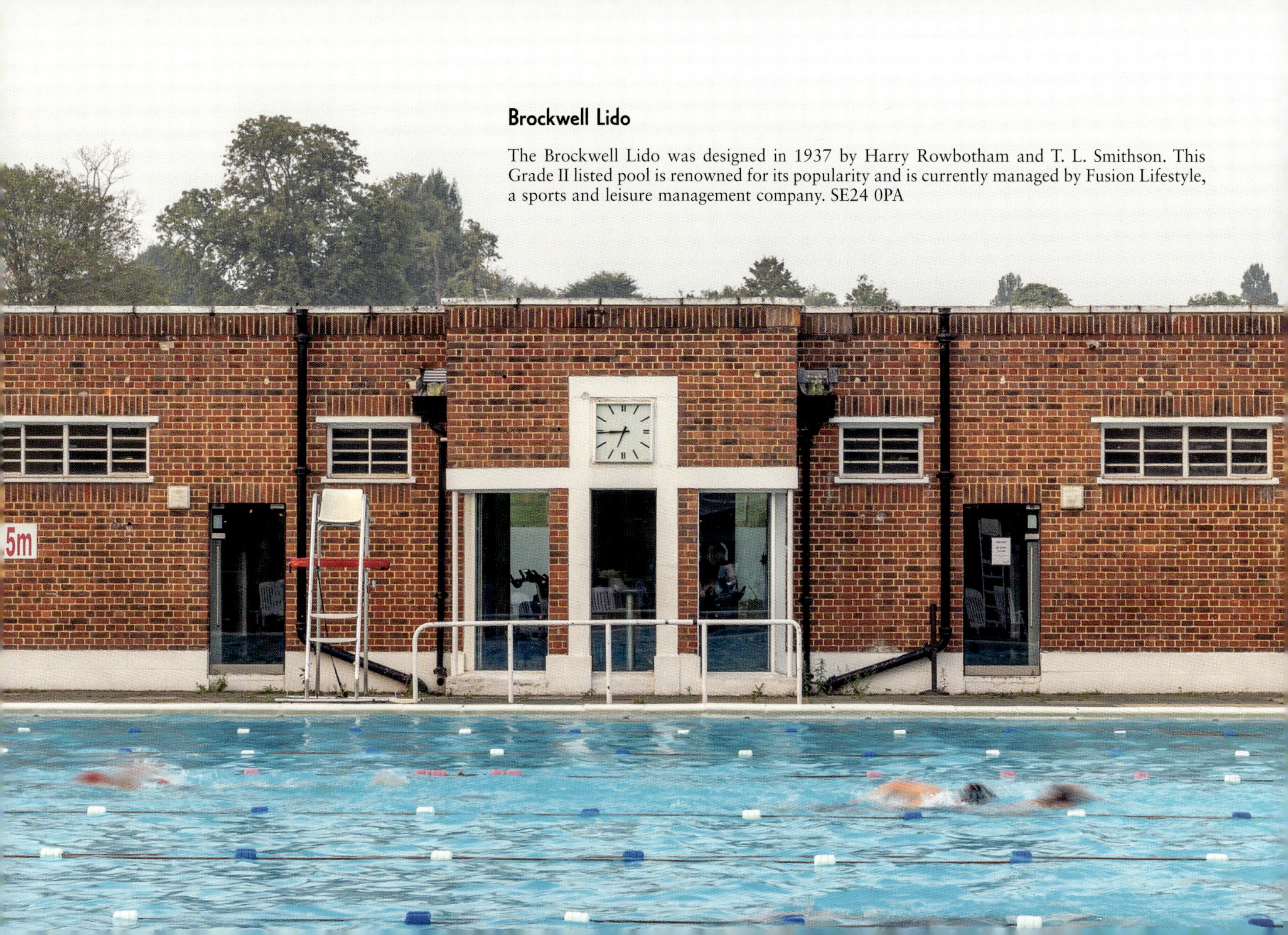

55 Broadway

55 Broadway, situated above St James's Park Station, stands as a remarkable architectural achievement, designed in 1929 by Charles Holden to serve as the headquarters for the Underground Electric Railways Company of London, which eventually evolved into Transport for London (TfL). This Grade I listed edifice once held the distinction of being the tallest office block in London. However, in 2020, TfL vacated the premises, paving the way for its transformation into a luxury hotel. Noteworthy are the various sculptures adorning the building, including one named *Day*, which was nearly excluded. Artist Jacob Epstein agreed to trim the naked penis of the sculpted boy by 1.5 inches to ensure its preservation. SW1H 0BD

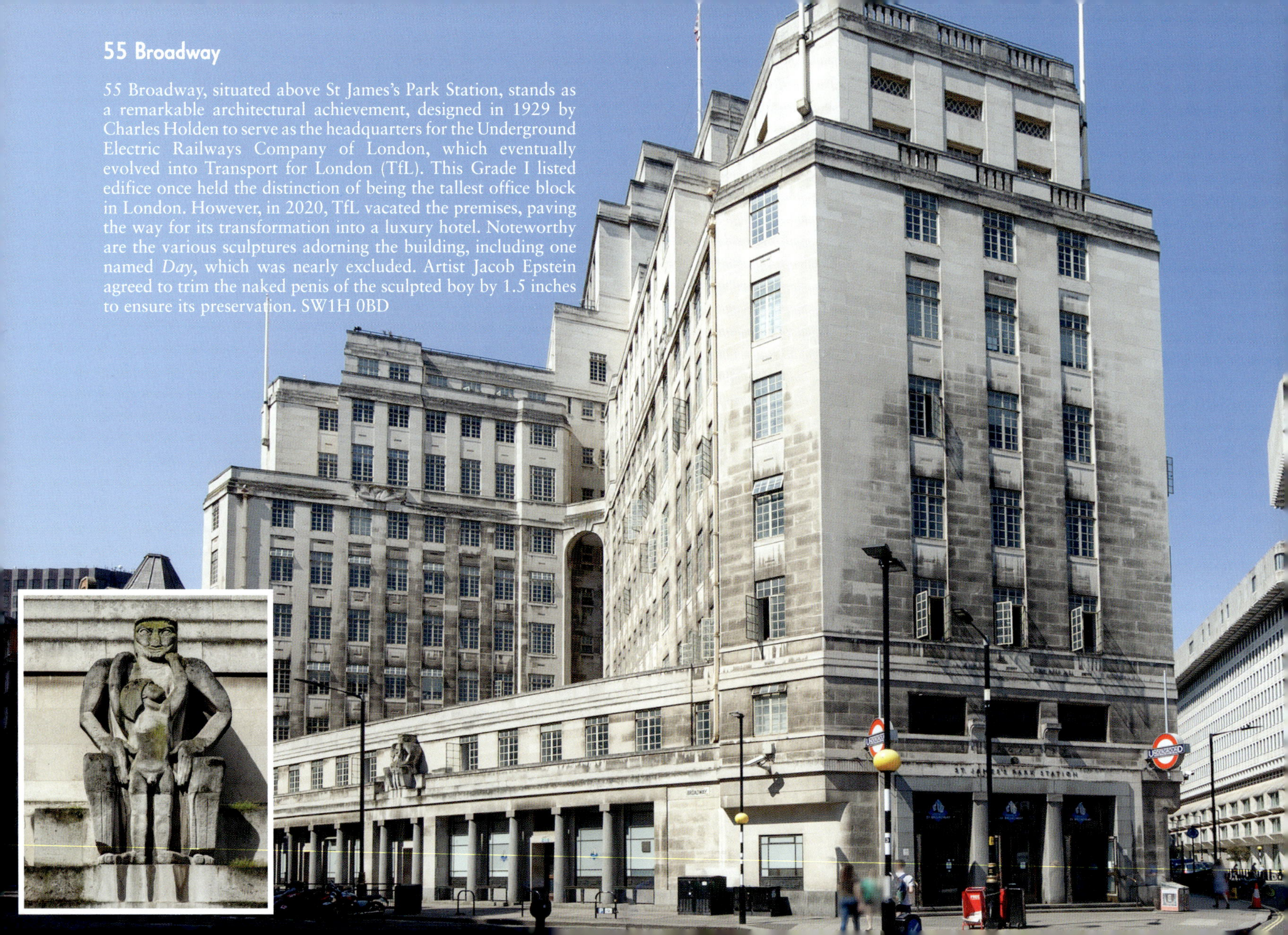

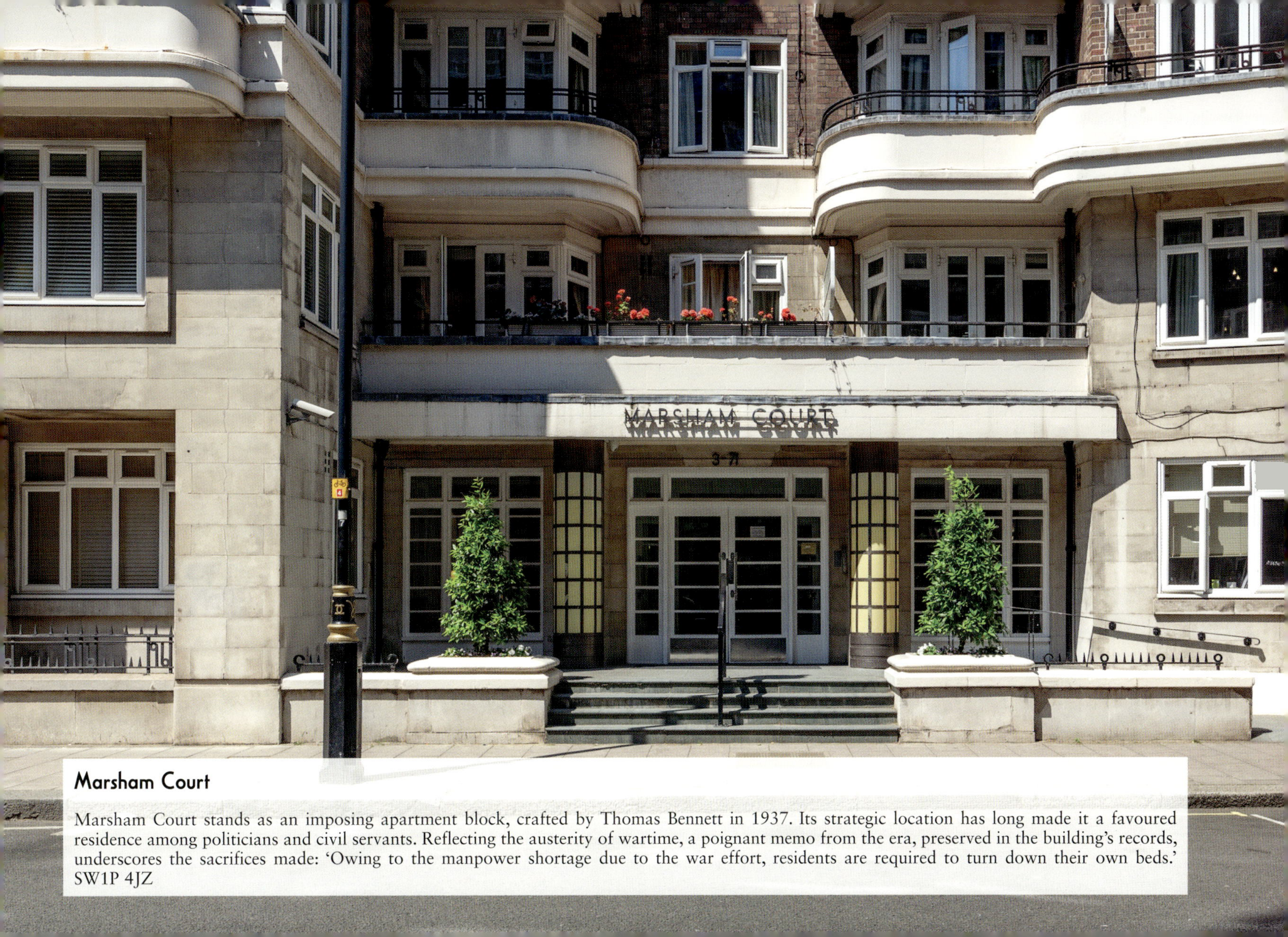

Marsham Court

Marsham Court stands as an imposing apartment block, crafted by Thomas Bennett in 1937. Its strategic location has long made it a favoured residence among politicians and civil servants. Reflecting the austerity of wartime, a poignant memo from the era, preserved in the building's records, underscores the sacrifices made: 'Owing to the manpower shortage due to the war effort, residents are required to turn down their own beds.' SW1P 4JZ

Apollo Victoria

The Apollo Victoria Theatre, originally erected in 1929 as the New Victoria Cinema by E. Wamsley Lewis and W. E. Trent, is an architectural gem that is Grade II* listed. Distinguished by its two similar entrances – one on Vauxhall Bridge Road and the other on Wilton Road – the venue has transitioned through various roles over the years. While it briefly hosted rock concerts, since the early 1980s it has been renowned as a premier stage for numerous captivating musical productions. SW1V 1LG

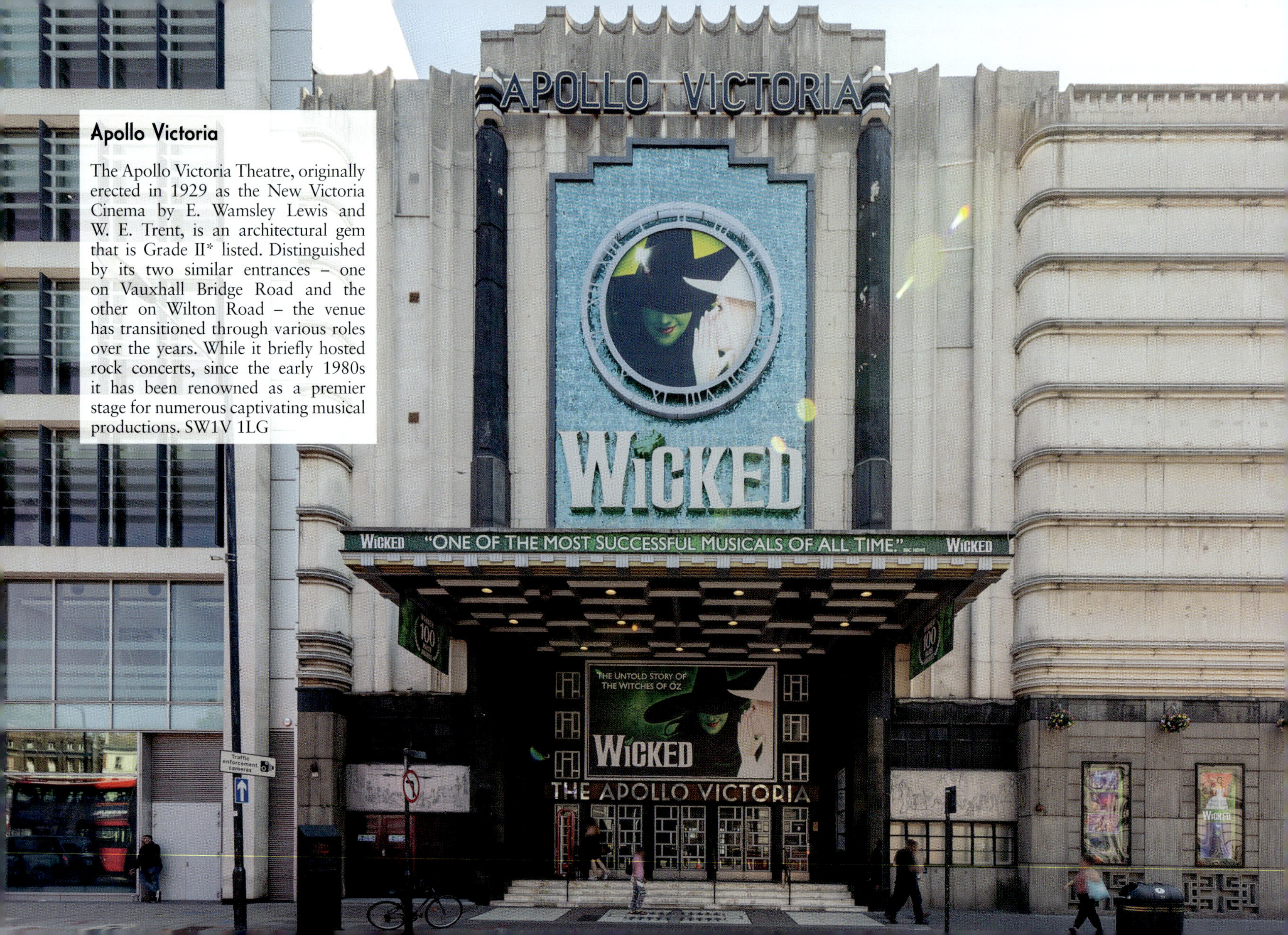

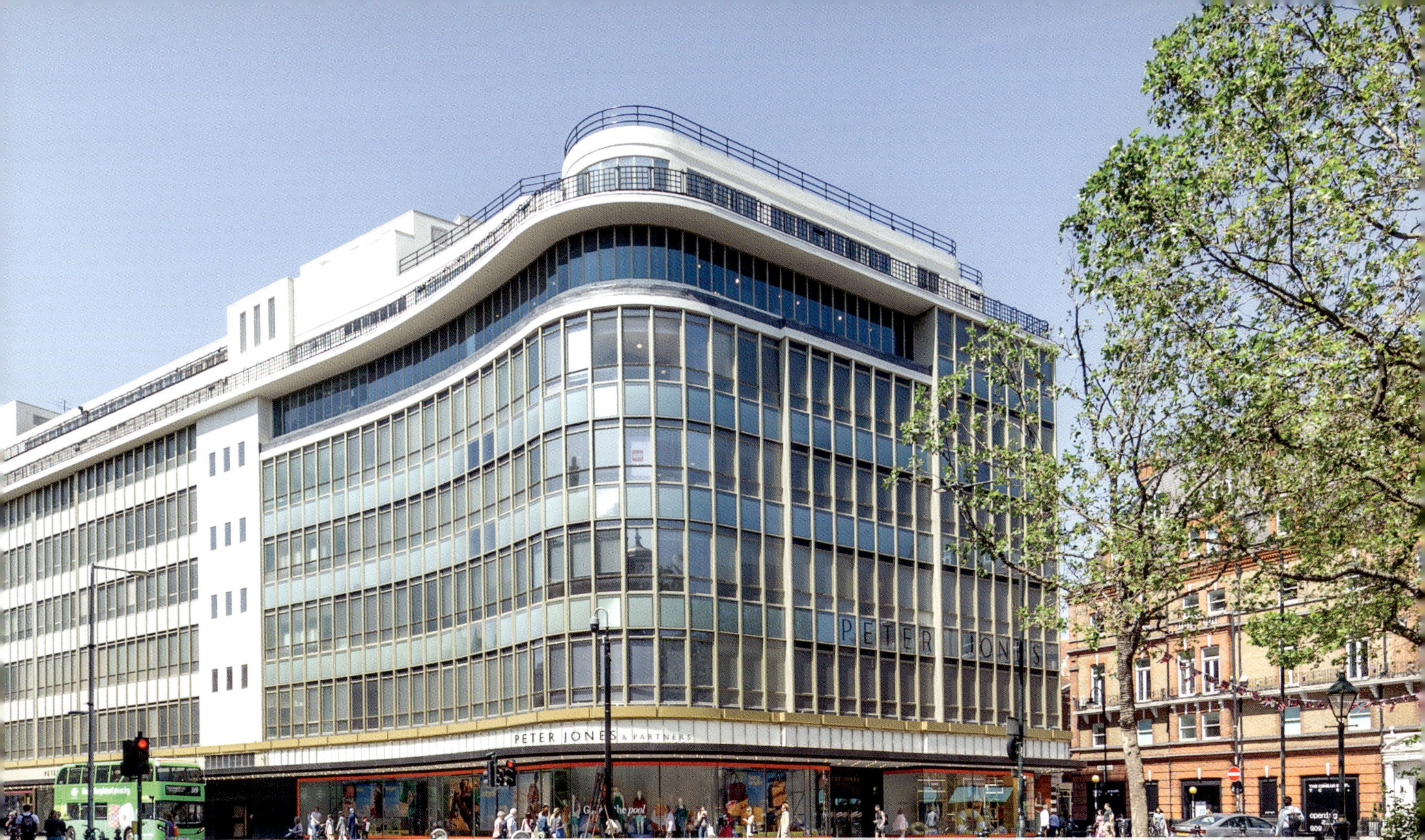

Peter Jones

Peter Jones & Partners, a renowned department store erected between 1936 and 1939, stands as a distinguished Grade II* listed building, meticulously crafted by William Crabtree in collaboration with Slater, Moberly, and Reilly. It was named after Peter Rees Jones (1842–1905) and not the TV personality (and entrepreneur) with the same name. Presently, the store is under the ownership of John Lewis & Partners, continuing its legacy as a pillar of retail excellence. SW1W 8EL

National Audit Office

Now housing the National Audit Office, this Grade II listed edifice, conceived by Albert Lakeman in 1939, once served as the Empire Terminal – a pivotal hub and passenger check-in for Imperial Airways. From this historic site, passengers embarked on journeys either to Croydon Airport or the Southampton Docks, with direct access to a platform in Victoria Station, facilitating seamless transitions onto flying boats. SW1W 9SP

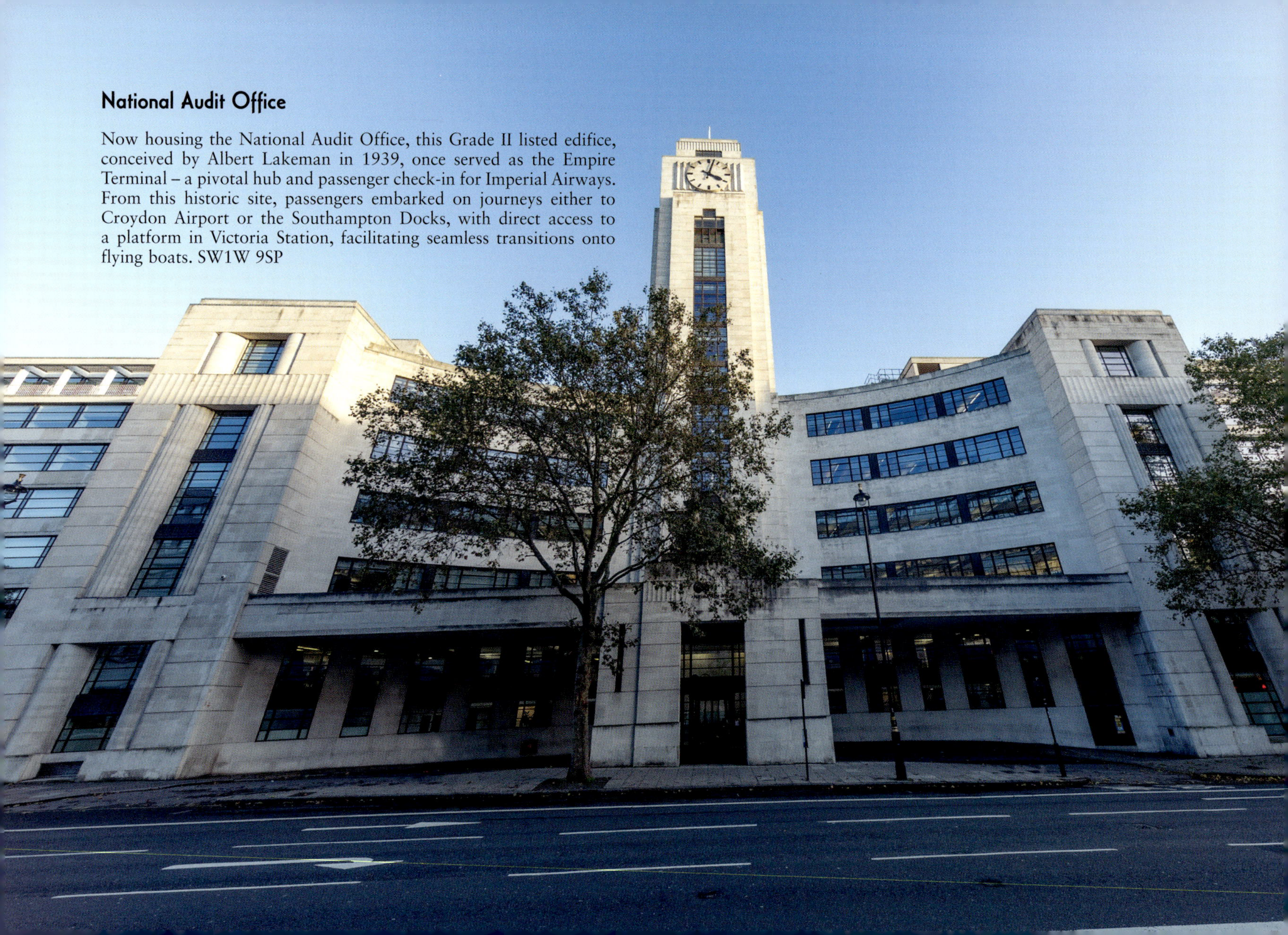

Victoria Coach Station

A standout among London's architectural marvels, the Grade II listed Victoria Coach Station embodies the essence of Art Deco aesthetics, envisioned by Wallis, Gilbert and Partners in 1932. Holding its ground as the busiest coach station in the UK, it sees a staggering influx of passengers annually, ranging from 11 million to 14.5 million departures. SW1W 9TP

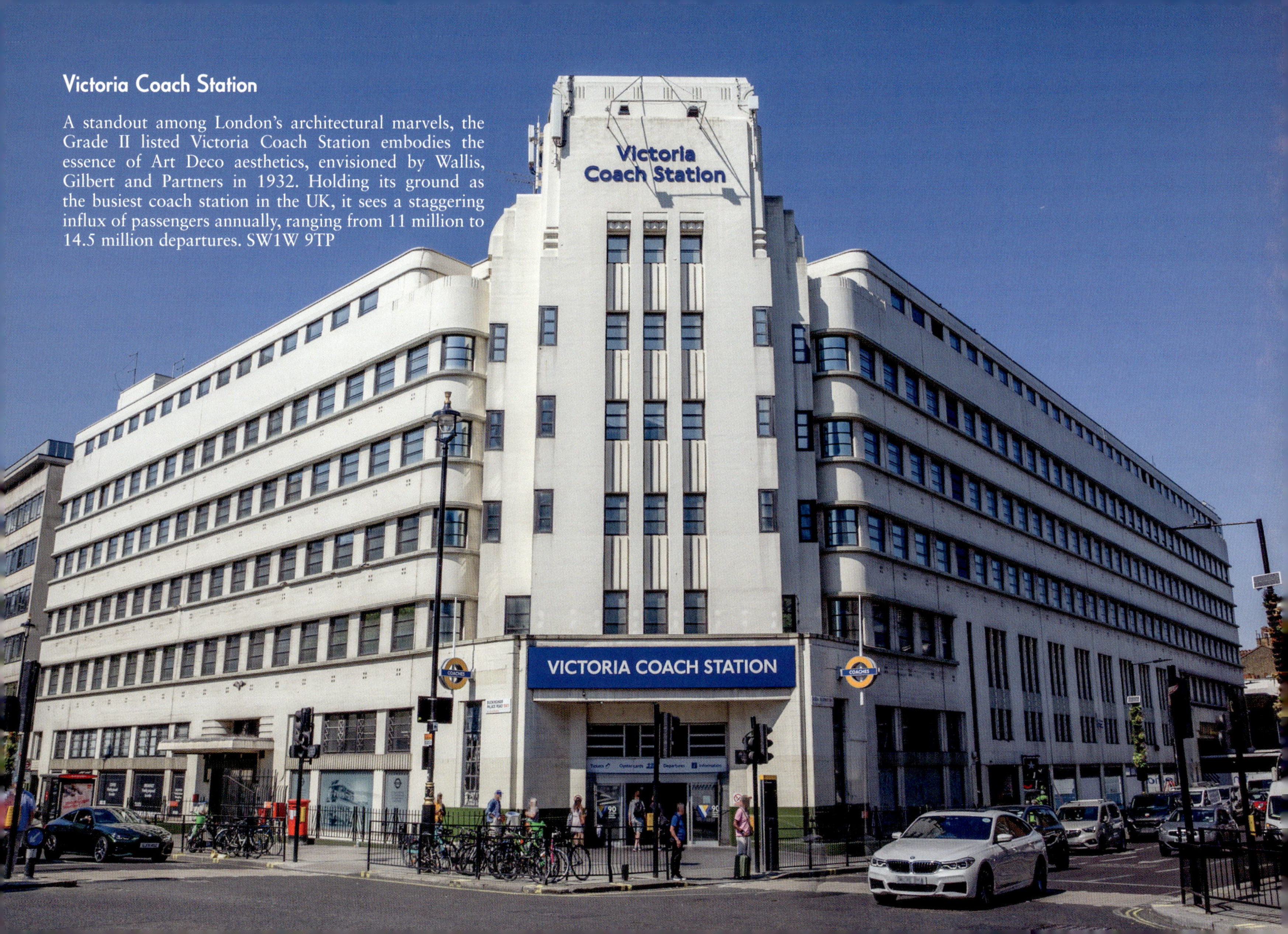

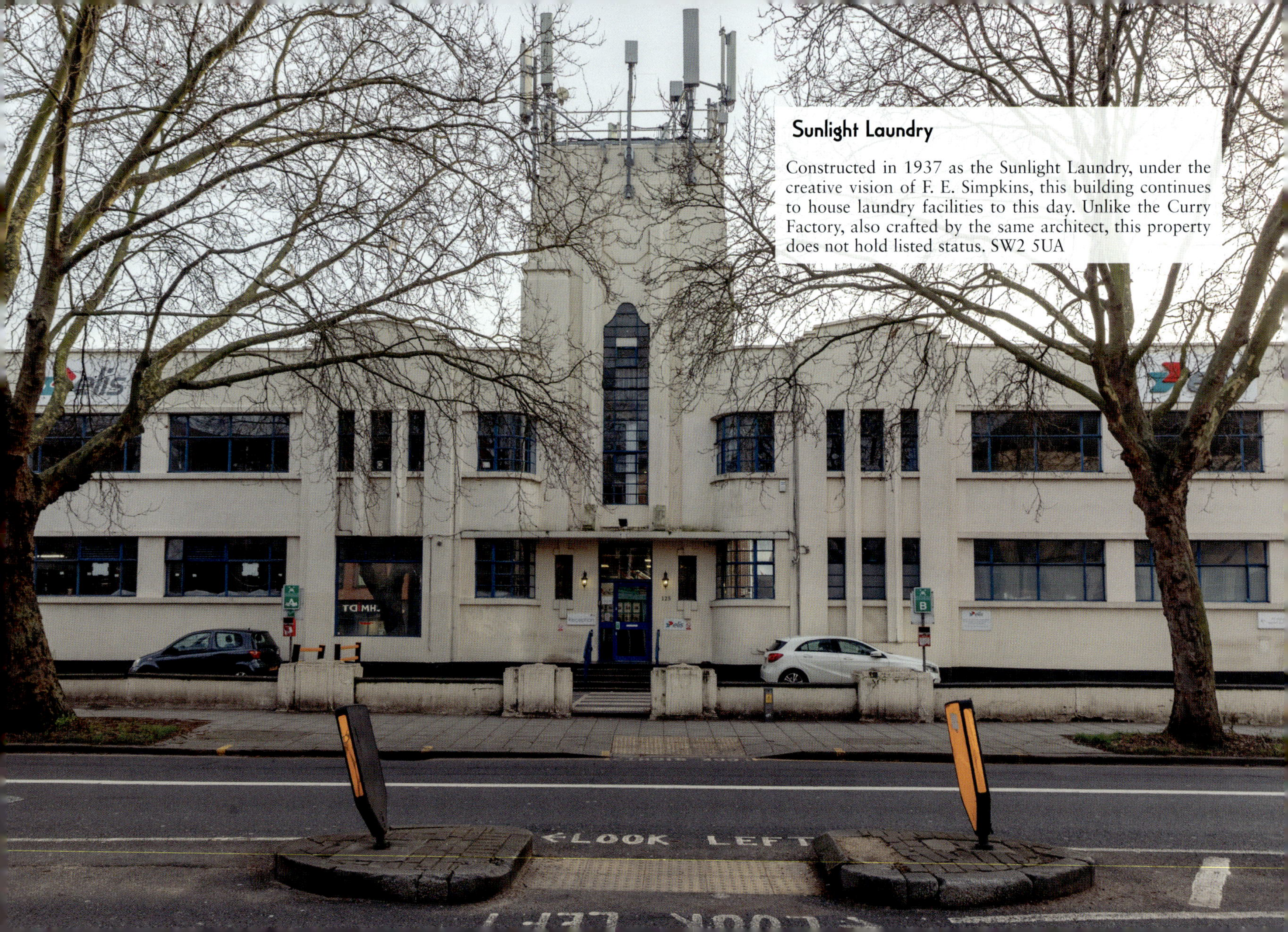

Sunlight Laundry

Constructed in 1937 as the Sunlight Laundry, under the creative vision of F. E. Simpkins, this building continues to house laundry facilities to this day. Unlike the Curry Factory, also crafted by the same architect, this property does not hold listed status. SW2 5UA

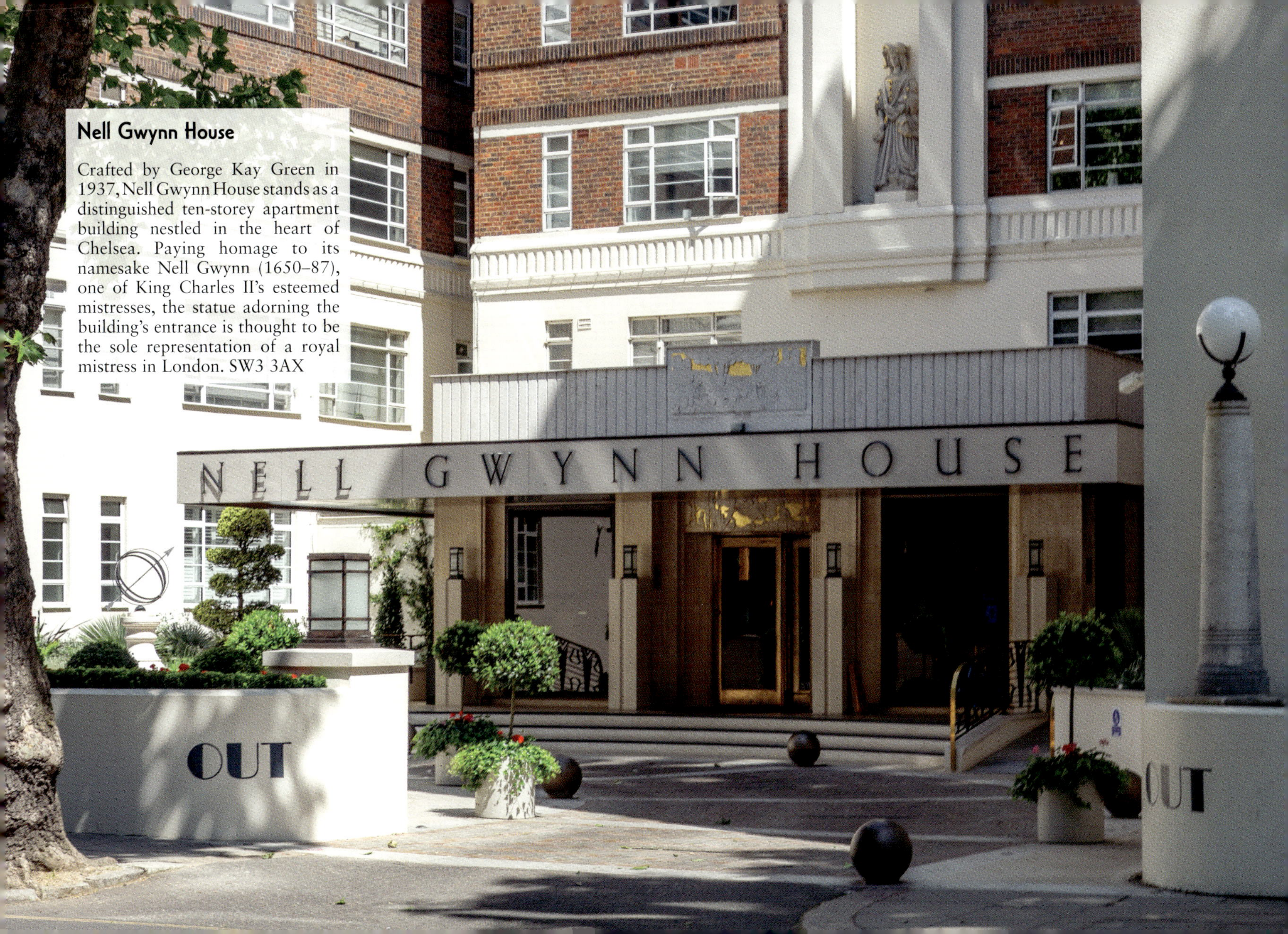

Nell Gwynn House

Crafted by George Kay Green in 1937, Nell Gwynn House stands as a distinguished ten-storey apartment building nestled in the heart of Chelsea. Paying homage to its namesake Nell Gwynn (1650–87), one of King Charles II's esteemed mistresses, the statue adorning the building's entrance is thought to be the sole representation of a royal mistress in London. SW3 3AX

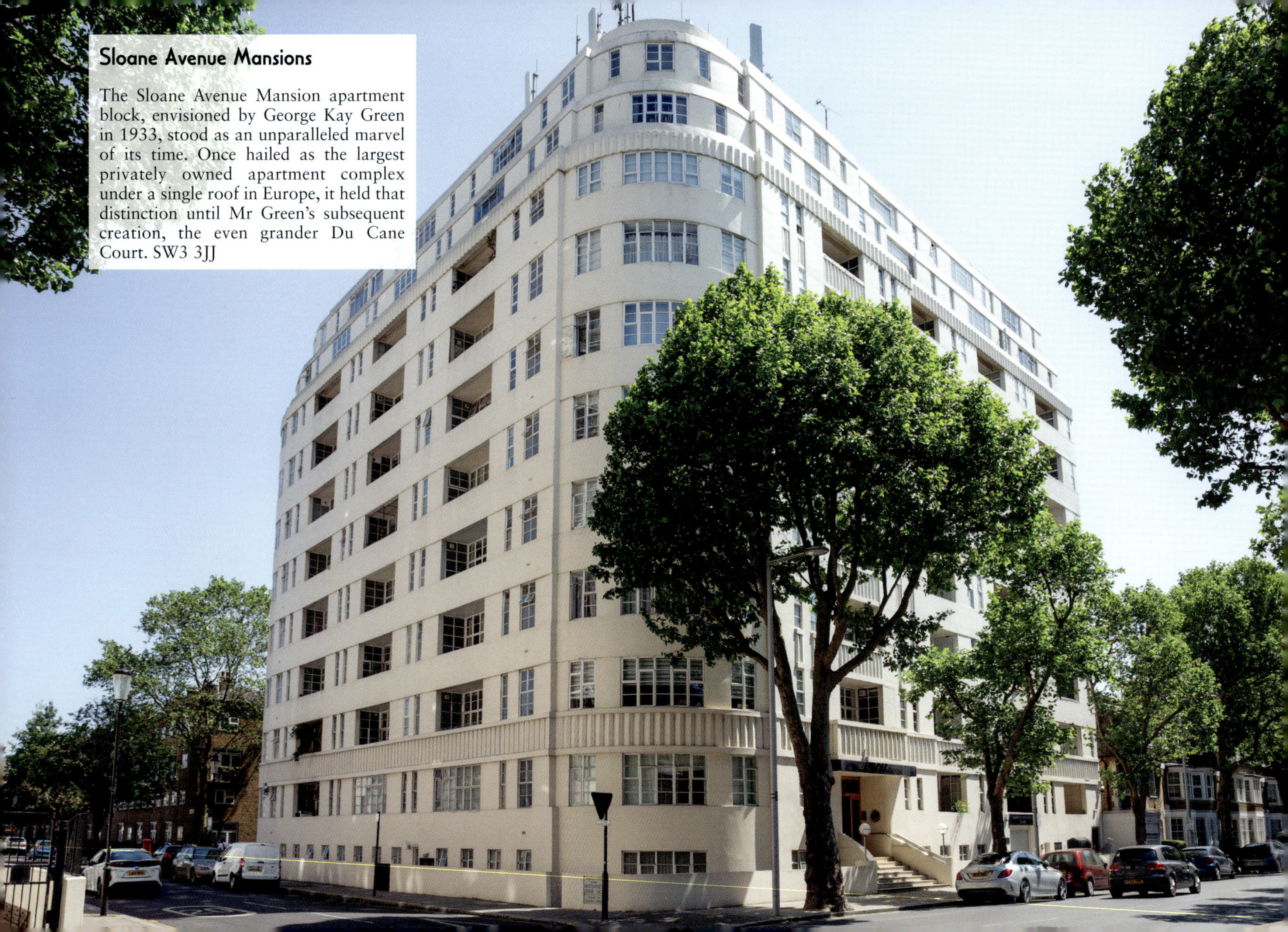

Sloane Avenue Mansions

The Sloane Avenue Mansion apartment block, envisioned by George Kay Green in 1933, stood as an unparalleled marvel of its time. Once hailed as the largest privately owned apartment complex under a single roof in Europe, it held that distinction until Mr Green's subsequent creation, the even grander Du Cane Court. SW3 3JJ

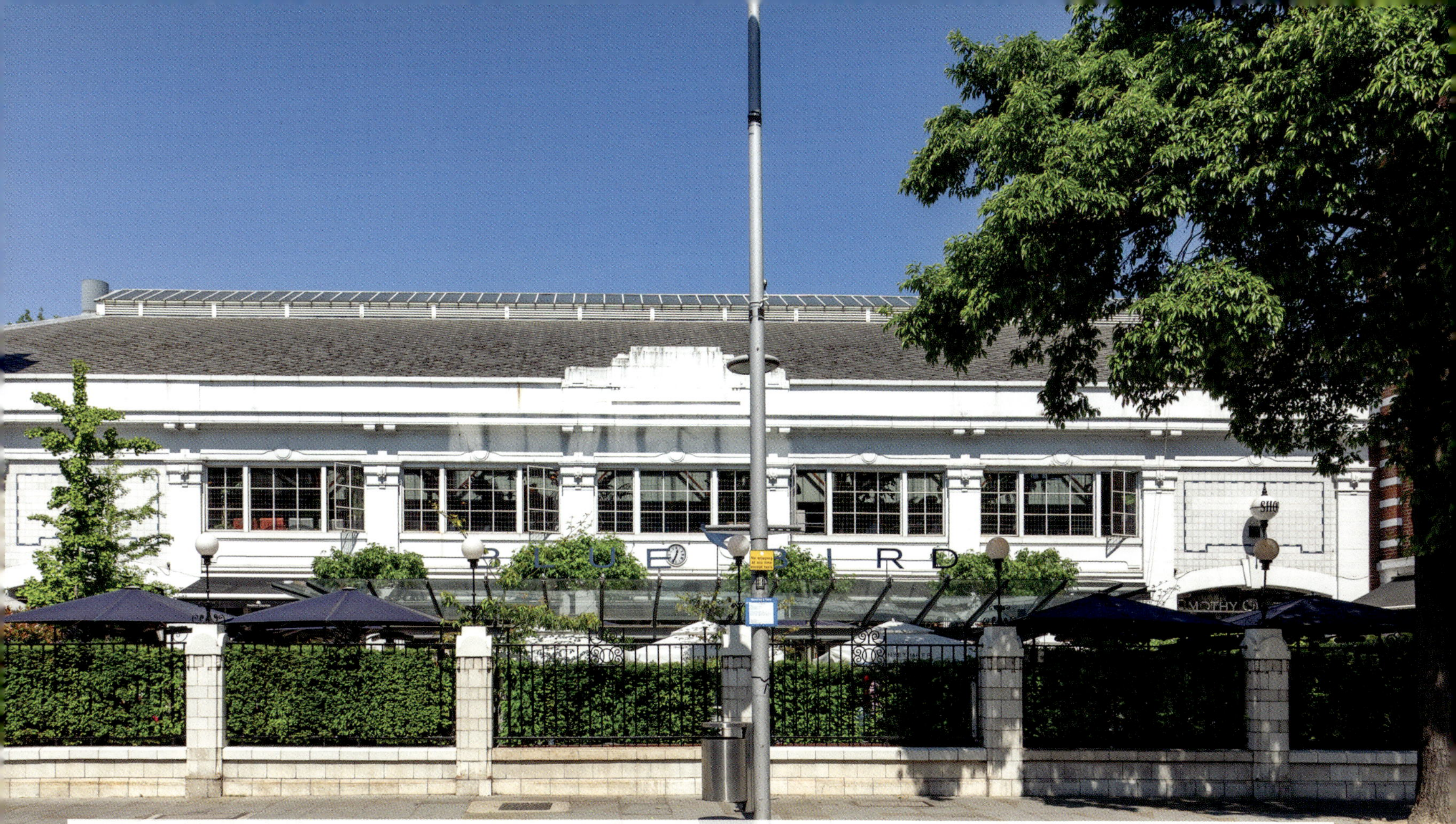

Bluebird

Designed by architect Robert Sharp in 1924, this building initially served as a garage for the esteemed Bluebird Motor Company in Chelsea, boasting the claim of being the largest of its kind in Europe at the time. Fast forward to 1997, when the Conran Group undertook a transformation, converting the Grade II listed edifice into the vibrant Bluebird Chelsea. Today, under the ownership of D&D London since 2006, it continues to thrive as a multifaceted establishment, featuring a restaurant, food stores, and private dining rooms. SW3 5UU

Michelin House

Opened in 1911, Michelin House served as the head office for the Michelin Tyre Company. Back then, it housed an impressive inventory of over 30,000 tyres within its walls. Designed by Michelin employee François Espinasse, the building epitomised the British Art Nouveau and early Art Deco styles. A true pioneer of its time, Michelin House was ahead of the curve, laying the groundwork for the Art Deco movement, despite being erected around twenty years prior. Today, it stands as a Grade II listed testament to its architectural significance. SW3 6RD

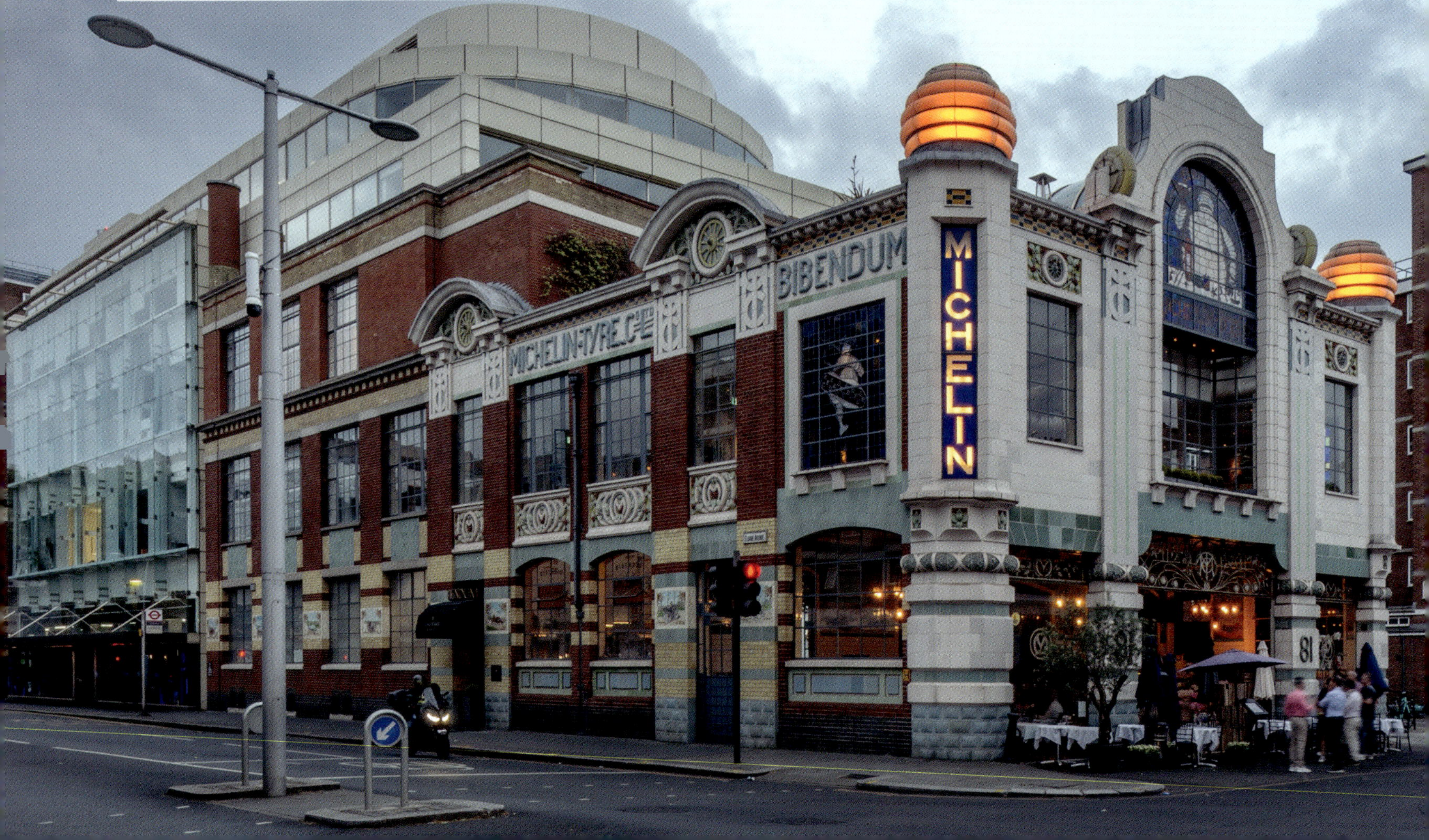

Clapham Common Underground Station

The Grade II listed entrance to Clapham Common Tube station stands as a testament to the architectural prowess of Charles Holden, completed in 1924 under his direction. Interestingly, Holden, known for his humility and commitment to collaboration, declined the offer of knighthood on two occasions. His principled stance reflected a dedication to a simple lifestyle and a belief in the collective nature of architectural creation. I think the world could benefit from more individuals embodying such virtues. SW4 7AJ

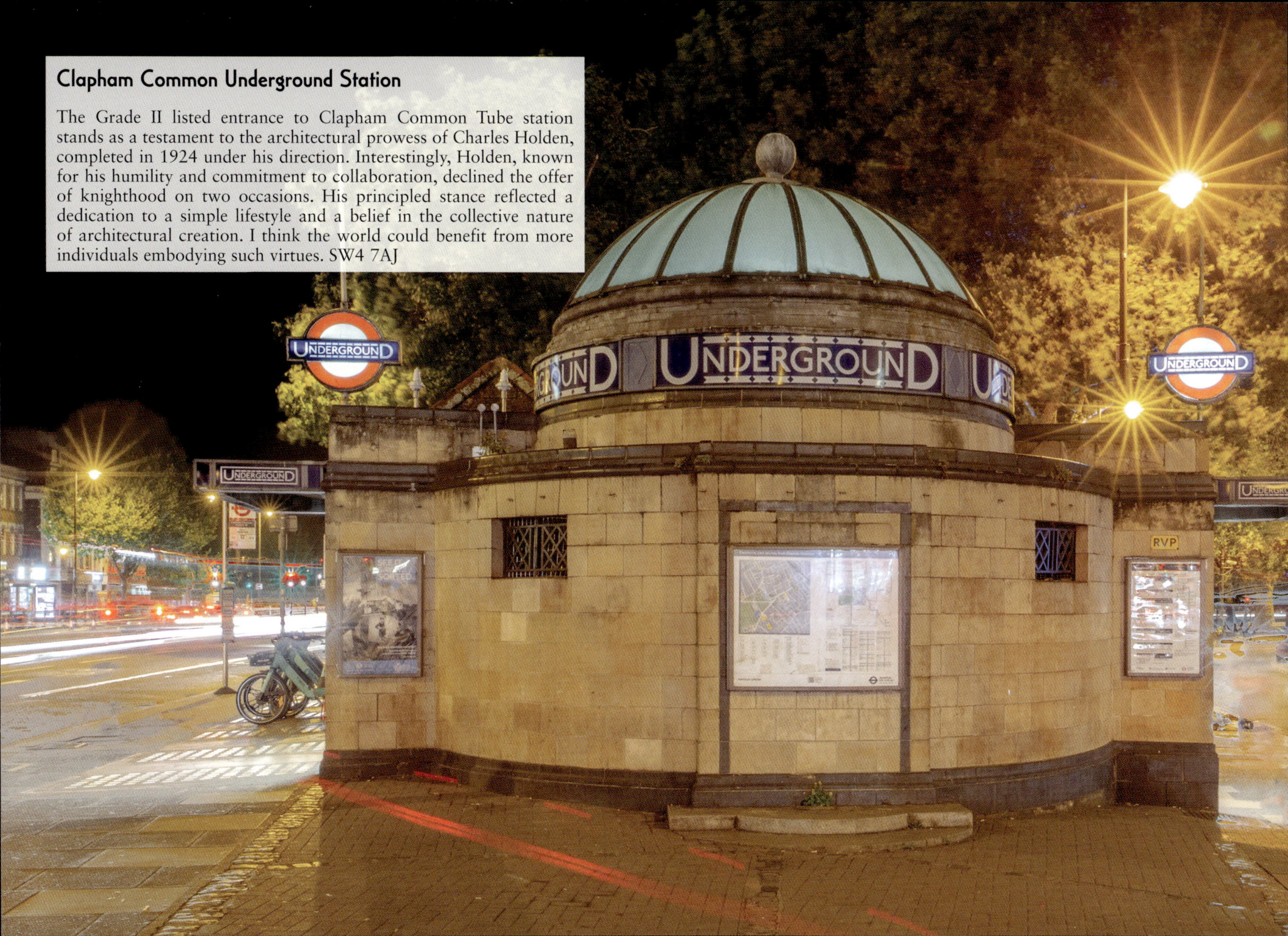

Brixton Academy

The Brixton Academy has risen to prominence as one of London's premier concert venues. Once known as the Astoria Variety Cinema, its iconic auditorium was crafted in the style of an 'atmospheric' theatre, evoking the ambiance of an Italian Renaissance garden. Designed in 1929 by Edward Stone and T. R. Somerford, the building stands as a Grade II* listed marvel, testament to its architectural significance and historical importance. SW9 9SL

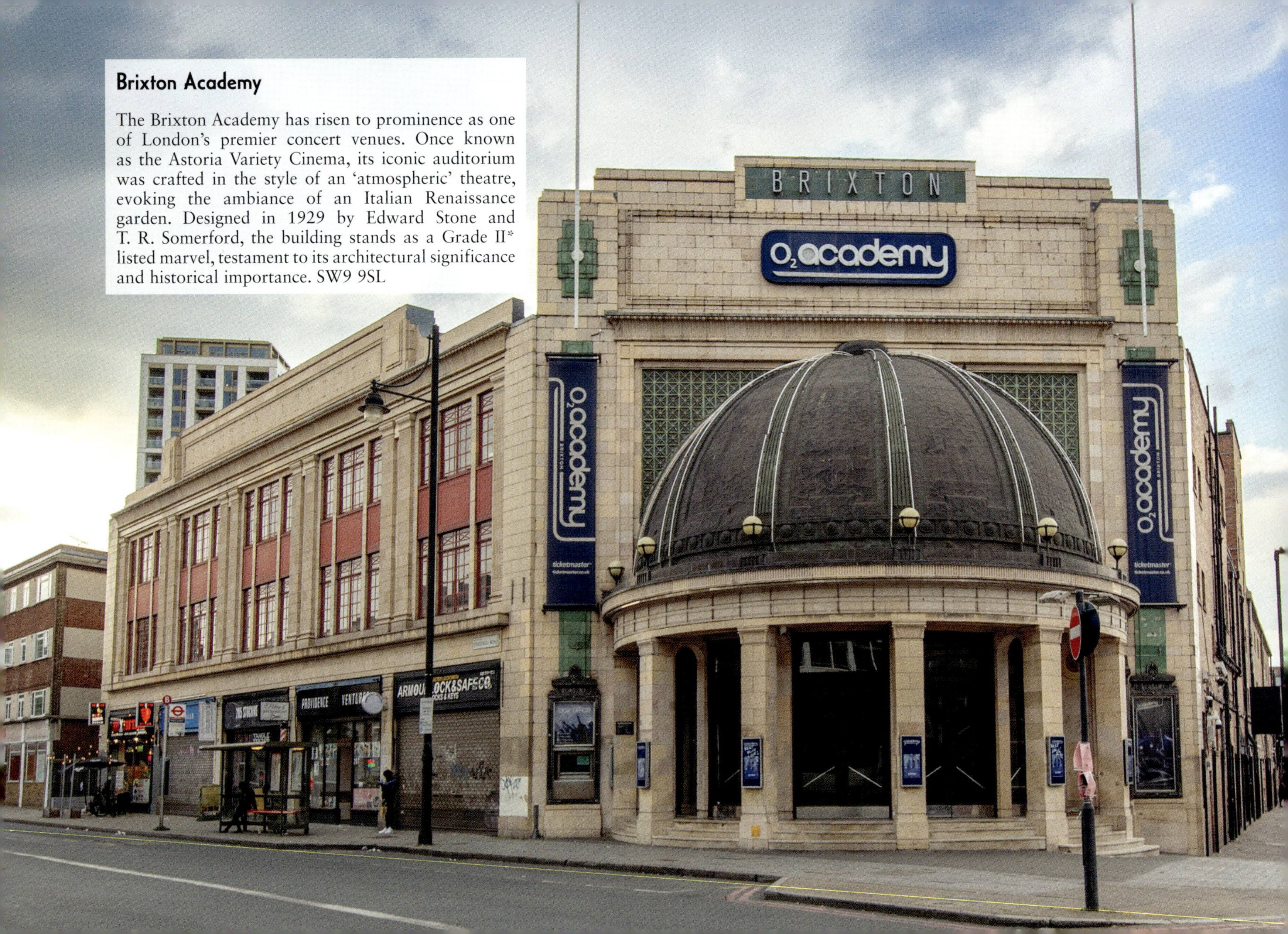

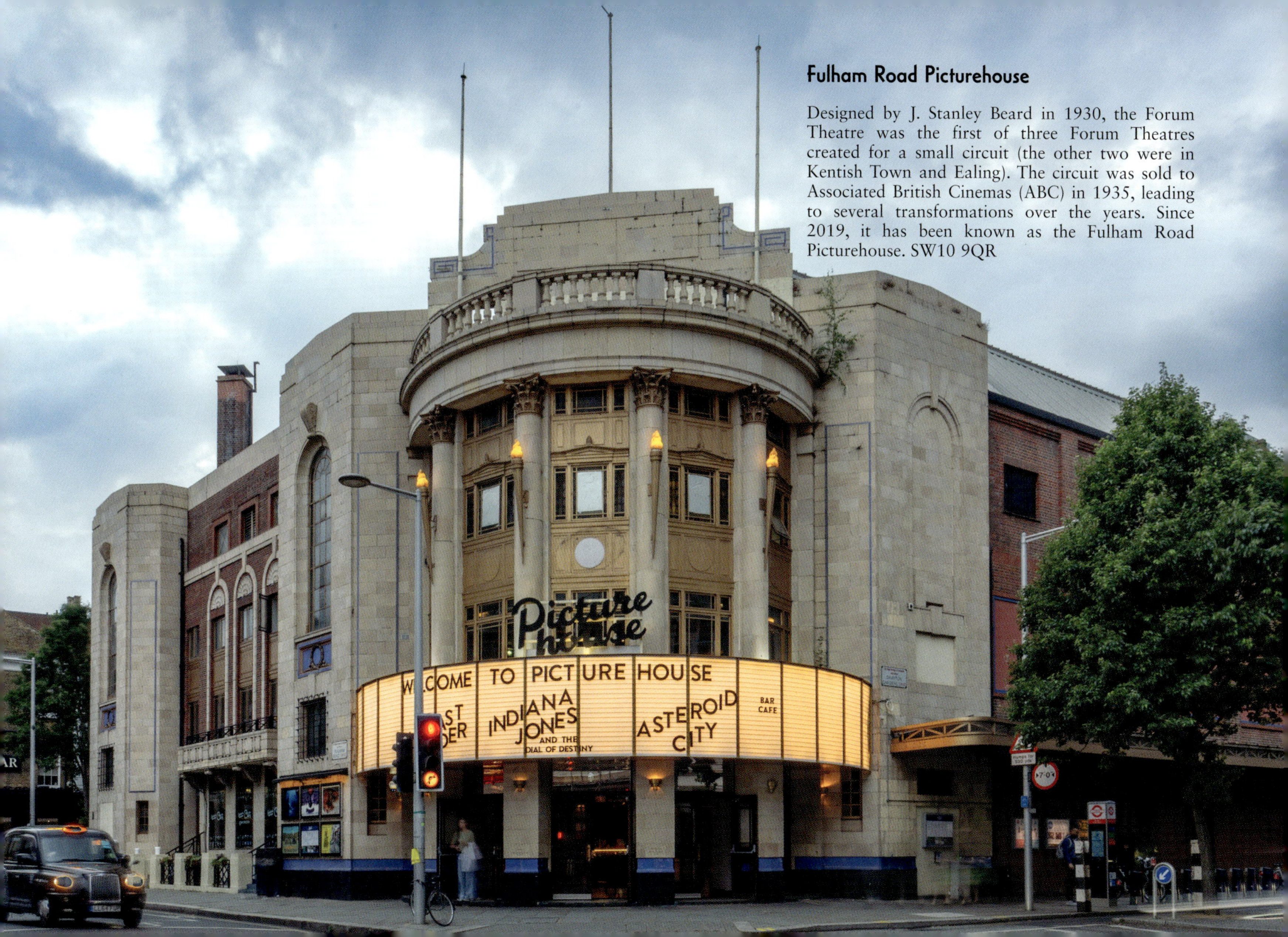

Fulham Road Picturehouse

Designed by J. Stanley Beard in 1930, the Forum Theatre was the first of three Forum Theatres created for a small circuit (the other two were in Kentish Town and Ealing). The circuit was sold to Associated British Cinemas (ABC) in 1935, leading to several transformations over the years. Since 2019, it has been known as the Fulham Road Picturehouse. SW10 9QR

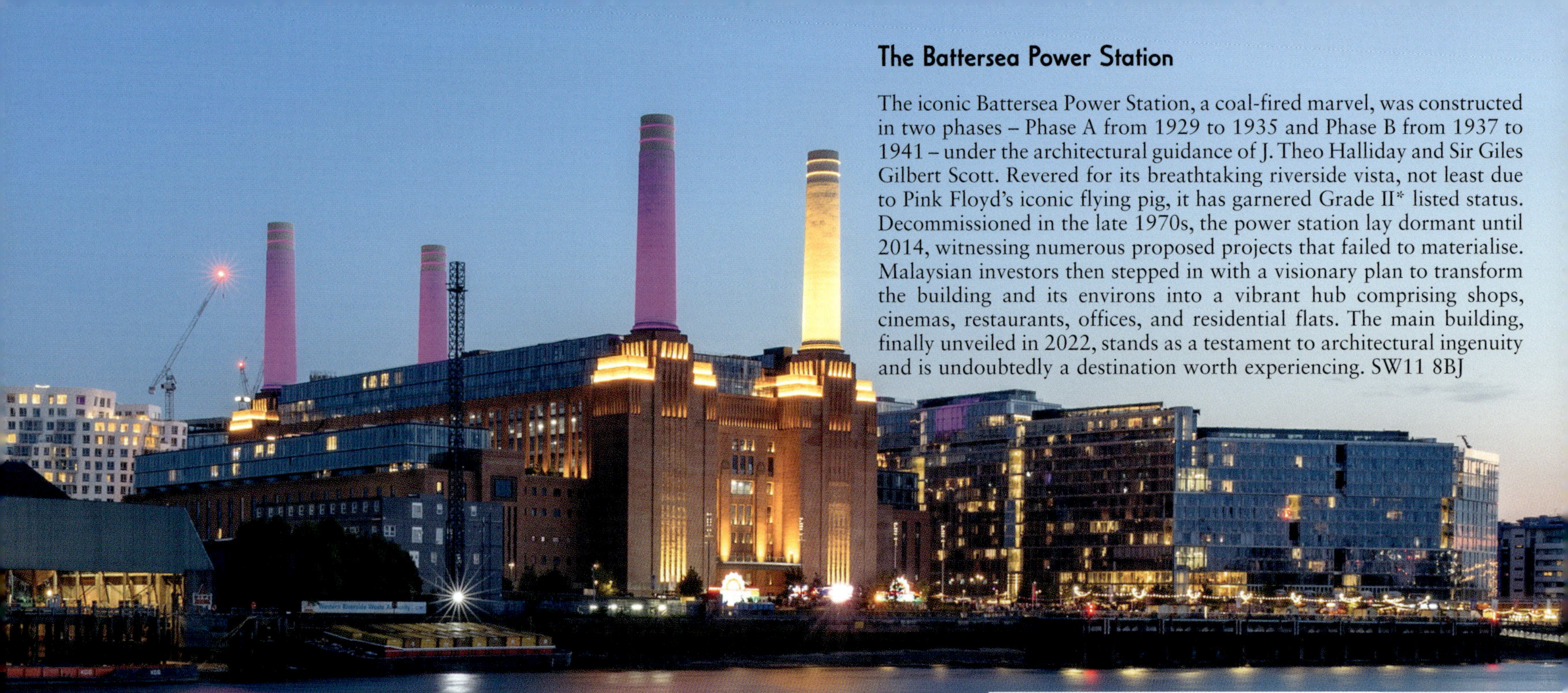

The Battersea Power Station

The iconic Battersea Power Station, a coal-fired marvel, was constructed in two phases – Phase A from 1929 to 1935 and Phase B from 1937 to 1941 – under the architectural guidance of J. Theo Halliday and Sir Giles Gilbert Scott. Revered for its breathtaking riverside vista, not least due to Pink Floyd's iconic flying pig, it has garnered Grade II* listed status. Decommissioned in the late 1970s, the power station lay dormant until 2014, witnessing numerous proposed projects that failed to materialise. Malaysian investors then stepped in with a visionary plan to transform the building and its environs into a vibrant hub comprising shops, cinemas, restaurants, offices, and residential flats. The main building, finally unveiled in 2022, stands as a testament to architectural ingenuity and is undoubtedly a destination worth experiencing. SW11 8BJ

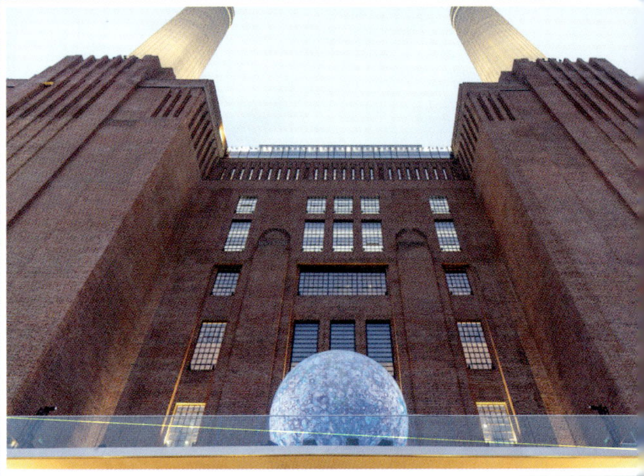

Hightrees House

Hightrees House, built in 1938, stands as a rare London project for Richard William Herbert Jones, primarily renowned for his Art Deco-style hotels and coastal commissions like the Saltdean Lido. Beyond its architectural significance, the building holds a place in legal history, notably as the focal point of the Central London Property Trust Ltd v High Trees House Ltd case, a landmark decision in English contract law rendered by the High Court. SW12 8AQ

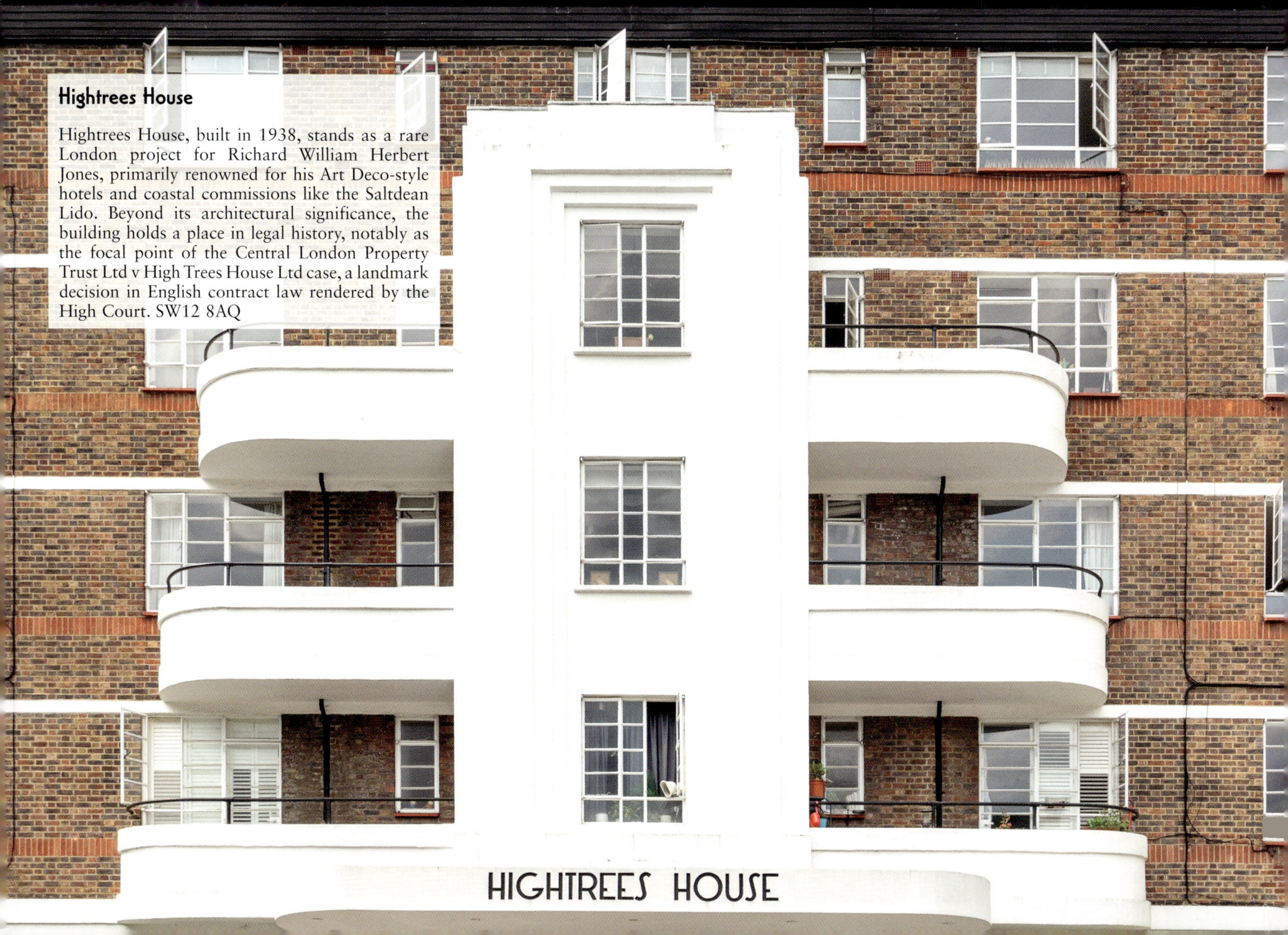

Thurleigh Court

Thurleigh Court, constructed in 1935 by architect Ernest Schaufelberg, known for his work on the Adelphi and Fortune theatres, has some notable former residents. It was once home to Malcolm McLaren, the manager of the Sex Pistols, along with fashion icon Vivienne Westwood. SW12 8AP

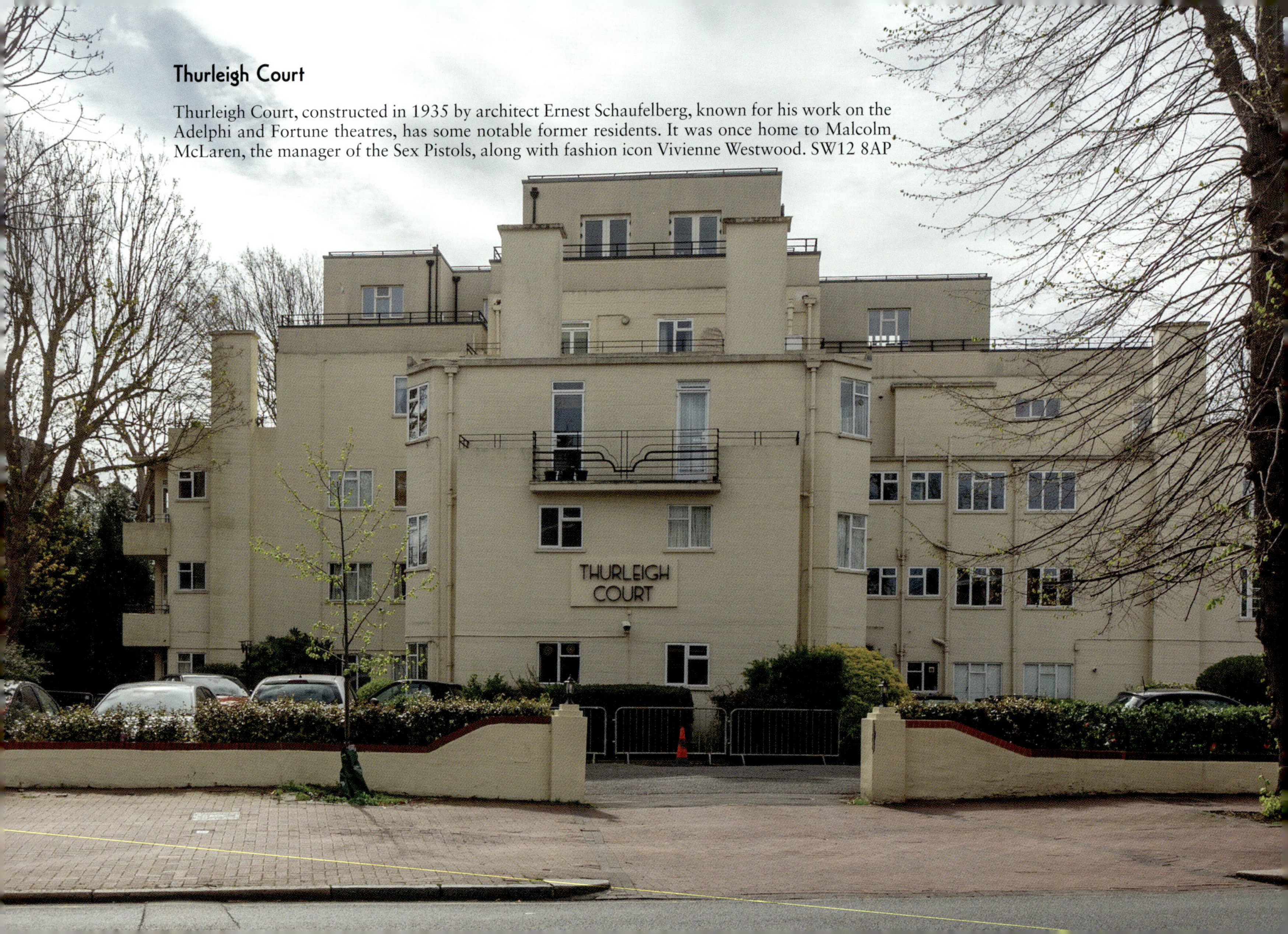

Odeon Balham

A wine shop now occupies the space once held by the Odeon cinema in Balham. I prefer that over another dodgy church any time. The Odeon was built in 1938 by Georges Coles. SW12 9EA

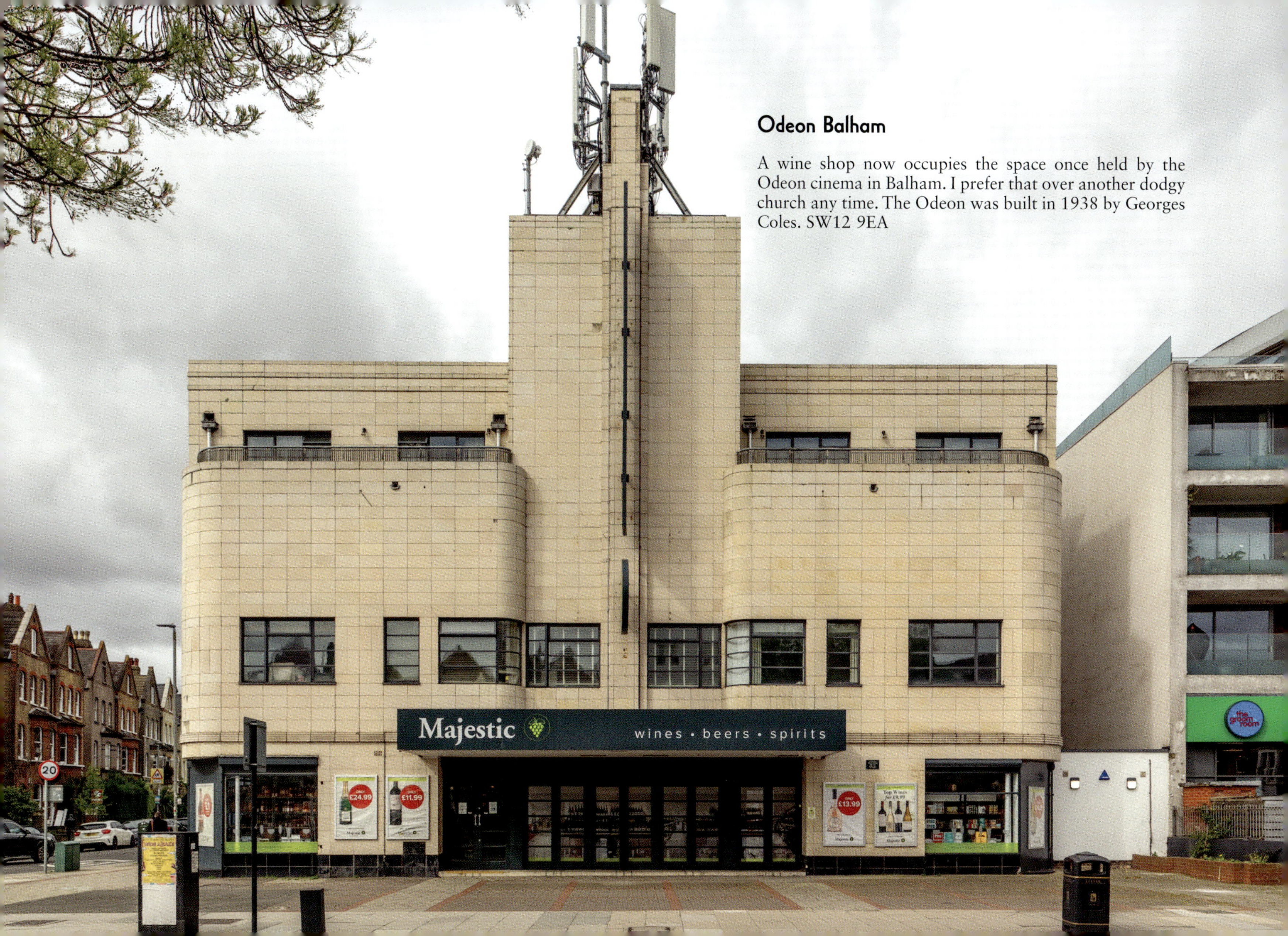

Du Cane Court

When Du Cane Court was unveiled in 1937 by George Kay Green, it claimed the title of Europe's largest privately owned apartment block, boasting an impressive 677 apartments. Following the Second World War, it earned the moniker 'Aristocrat of Apartment Houses', thanks to its prime location and luxurious amenities, which attracted a diverse array of tenants including comedians, actors, and professionals. SW17 7JZ

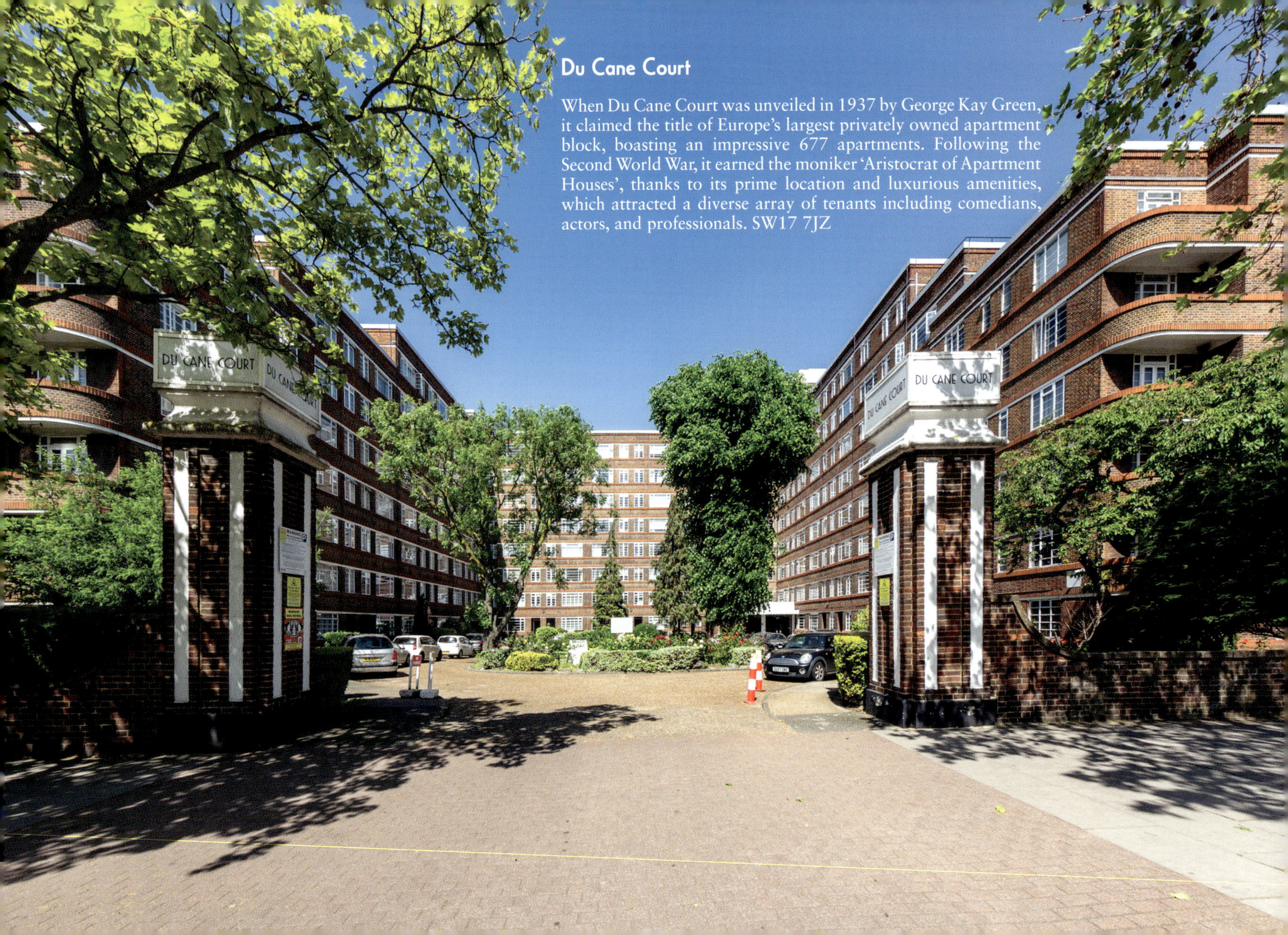

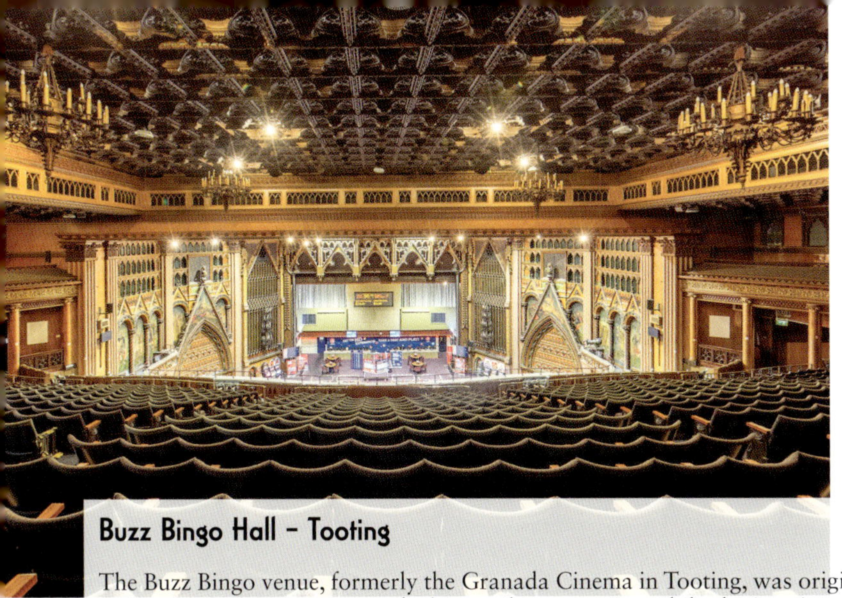

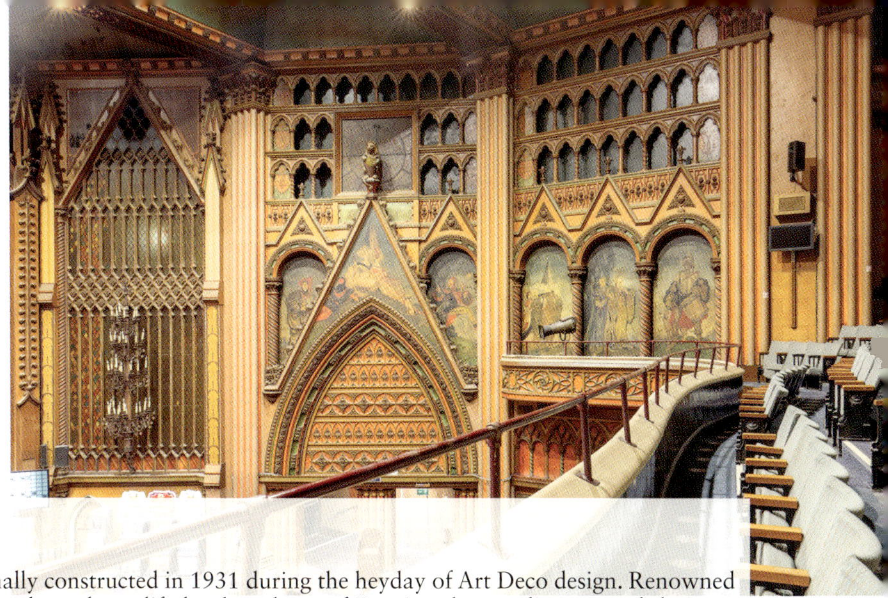

Buzz Bingo Hall – Tooting

The Buzz Bingo venue, formerly the Granada Cinema in Tooting, was originally constructed in 1931 during the heyday of Art Deco design. Renowned architect Cecil A. Massey crafted its striking exterior, while the interior was brought to life by the talents of Russian theatre director and designer Theodore Komisarjevsky. Celebrated as the most opulently adorned cinema in Great Britain, it holds the distinction of being an Asset of Community Value (ACV) and boasts a Grade I listing, highlighting its cultural significance. SW17 9NA

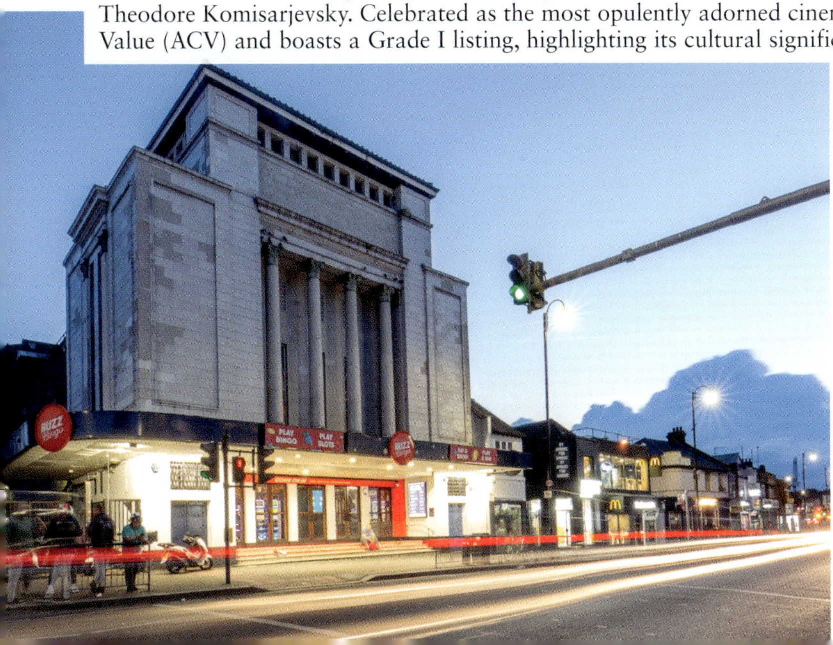

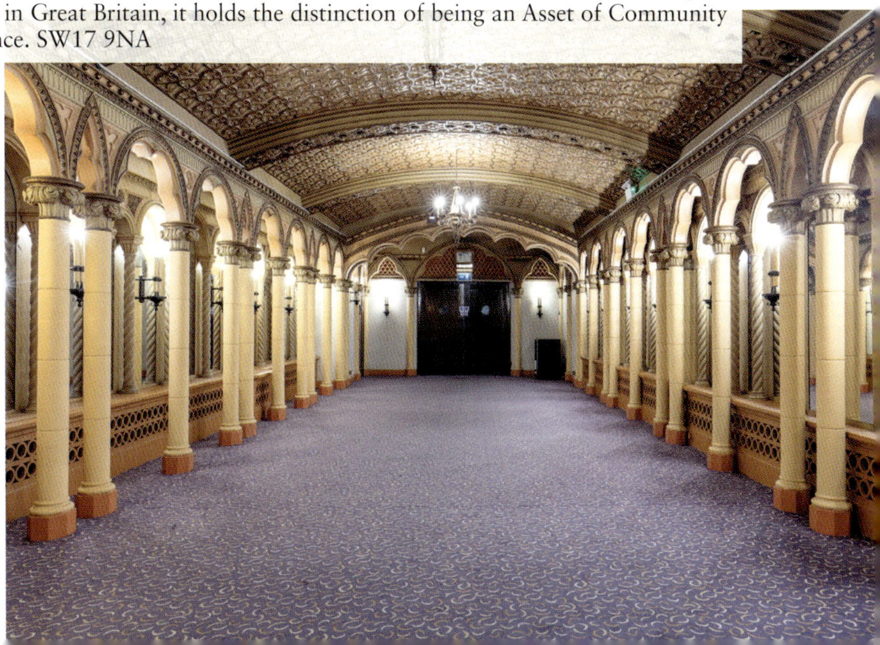

Wandsworth Town Hall

The historic Wandsworth Town Hall, which is Grade II listed, bears the architectural imprint of Edward A. Hunt, dating back to 1937. While delving into its storied past, my search for celebrity weddings yielded limited results. However, one memorable union that stands out is that of photographer Franco Pfaller and his wife Tami, who exchanged vows on 2 August 1996 and continue to share their journey together. SW18 2PU

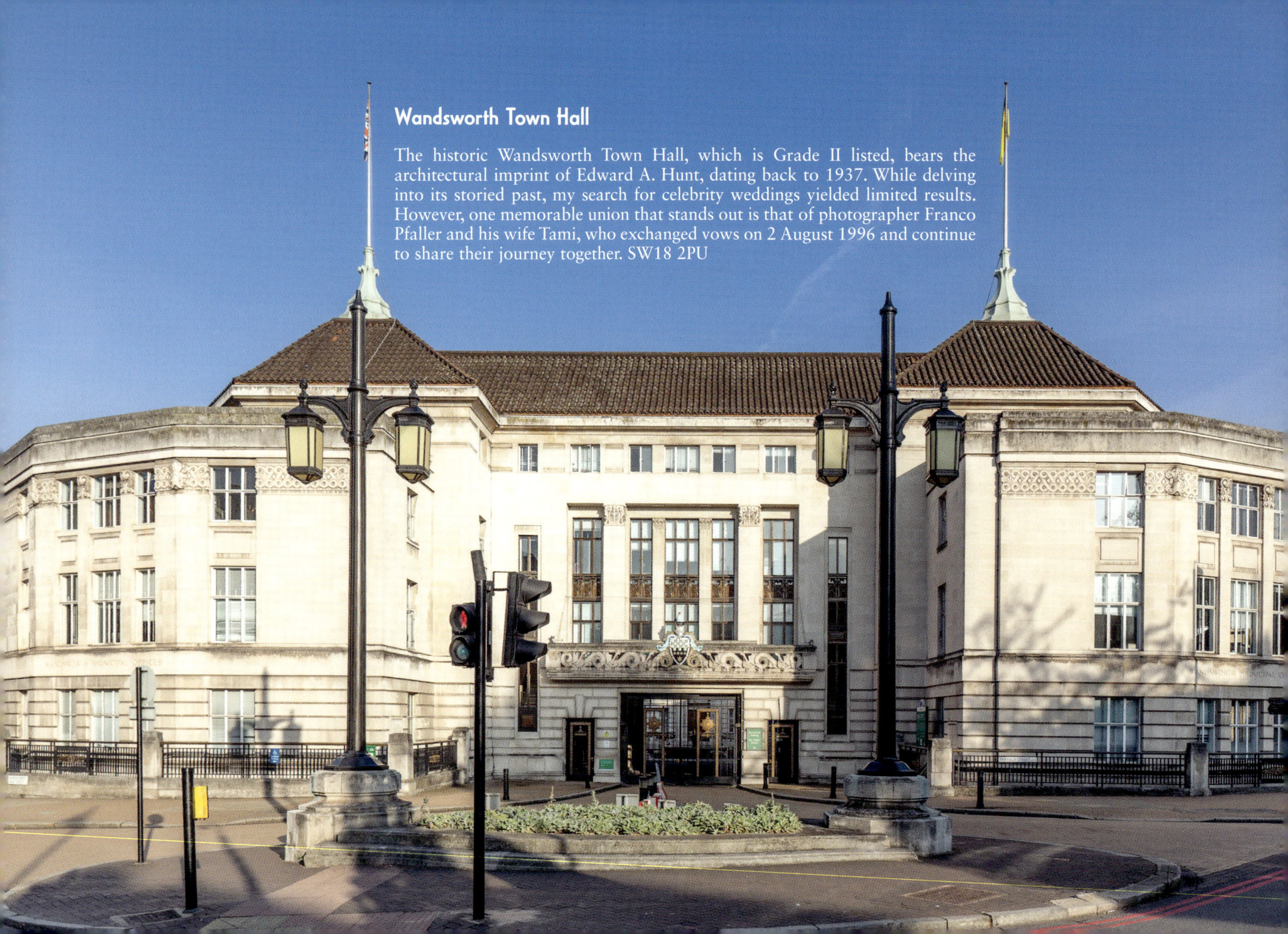

265 Merton Road

265 Merton Road, a Grade II listed building, bears the architectural imprint of Percy Sharp and was commissioned by George Mason and Co. Ltd, renowned manufacturers of OK Sauce, in 1928. Following the cessation of sauce production in 1968, the building underwent a transformation, evolving into office spaces and earning the moniker 'The Factory' through a process of rebranding. SW18 5JS

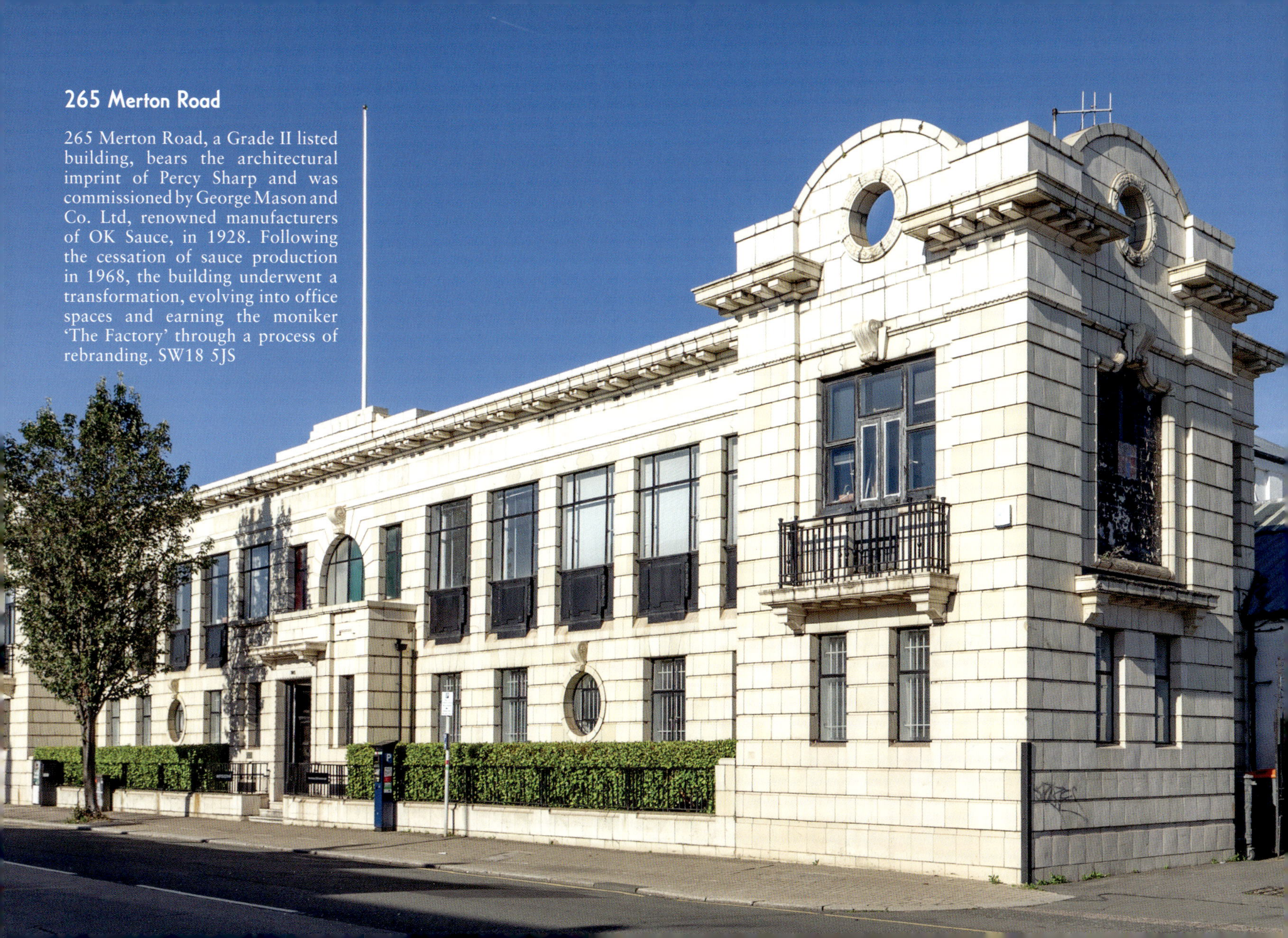

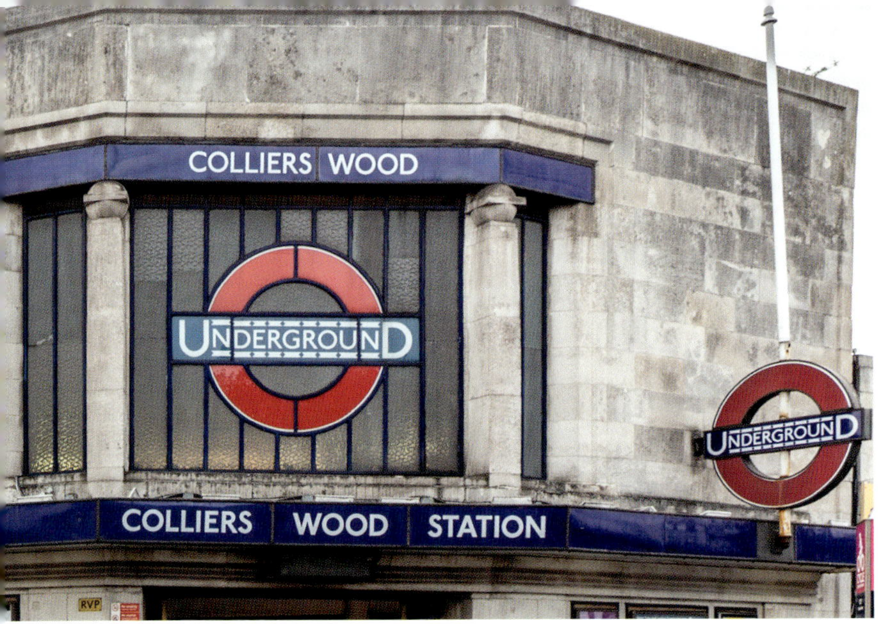

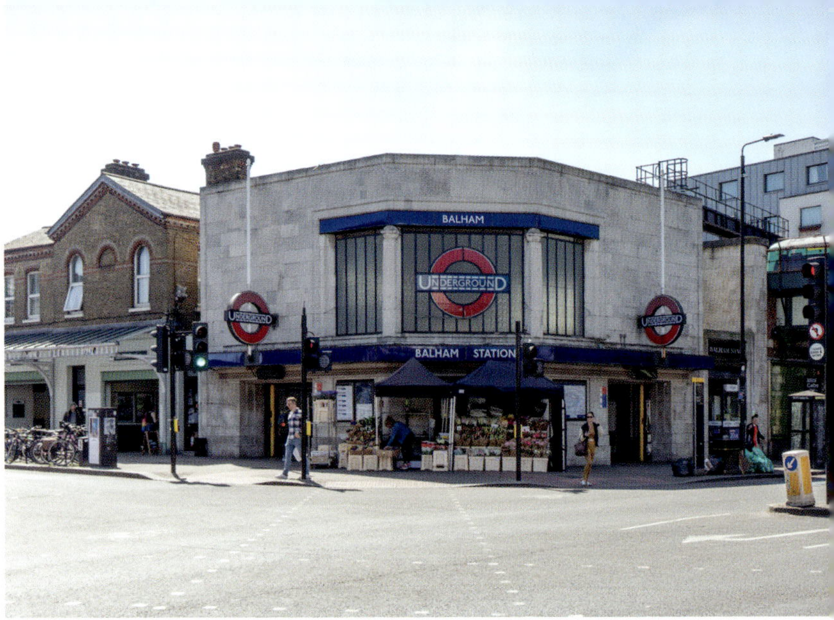

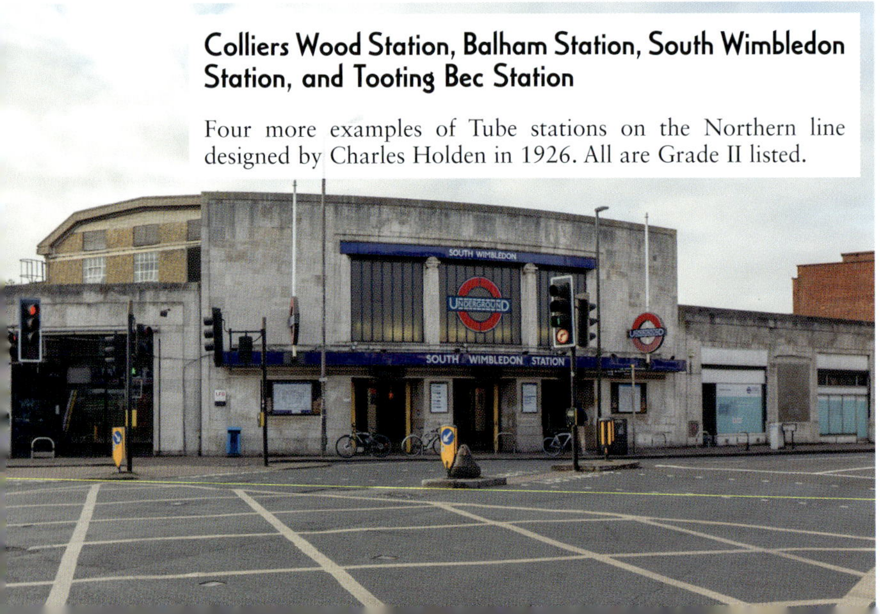

Colliers Wood Station, Balham Station, South Wimbledon Station, and Tooting Bec Station

Four more examples of Tube stations on the Northern line designed by Charles Holden in 1926. All are Grade II listed.

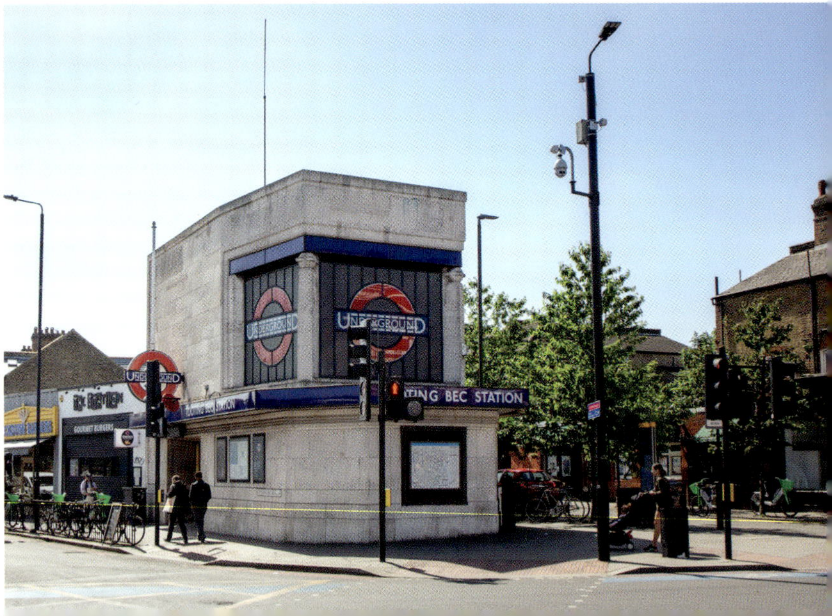

Globe Central

Though shrouded in mystery, archival records from Richmond shed light on the origins of this building. Plans submitted by Edvin Pover & Sons for Winchester Works closely resemble its current form, offering a glimpse into its early days. Historical traces reveal that the establishment was once occupied by The Thames Photographic Co. Ltd, adding another layer to its enigmatic past. TW1 1LX

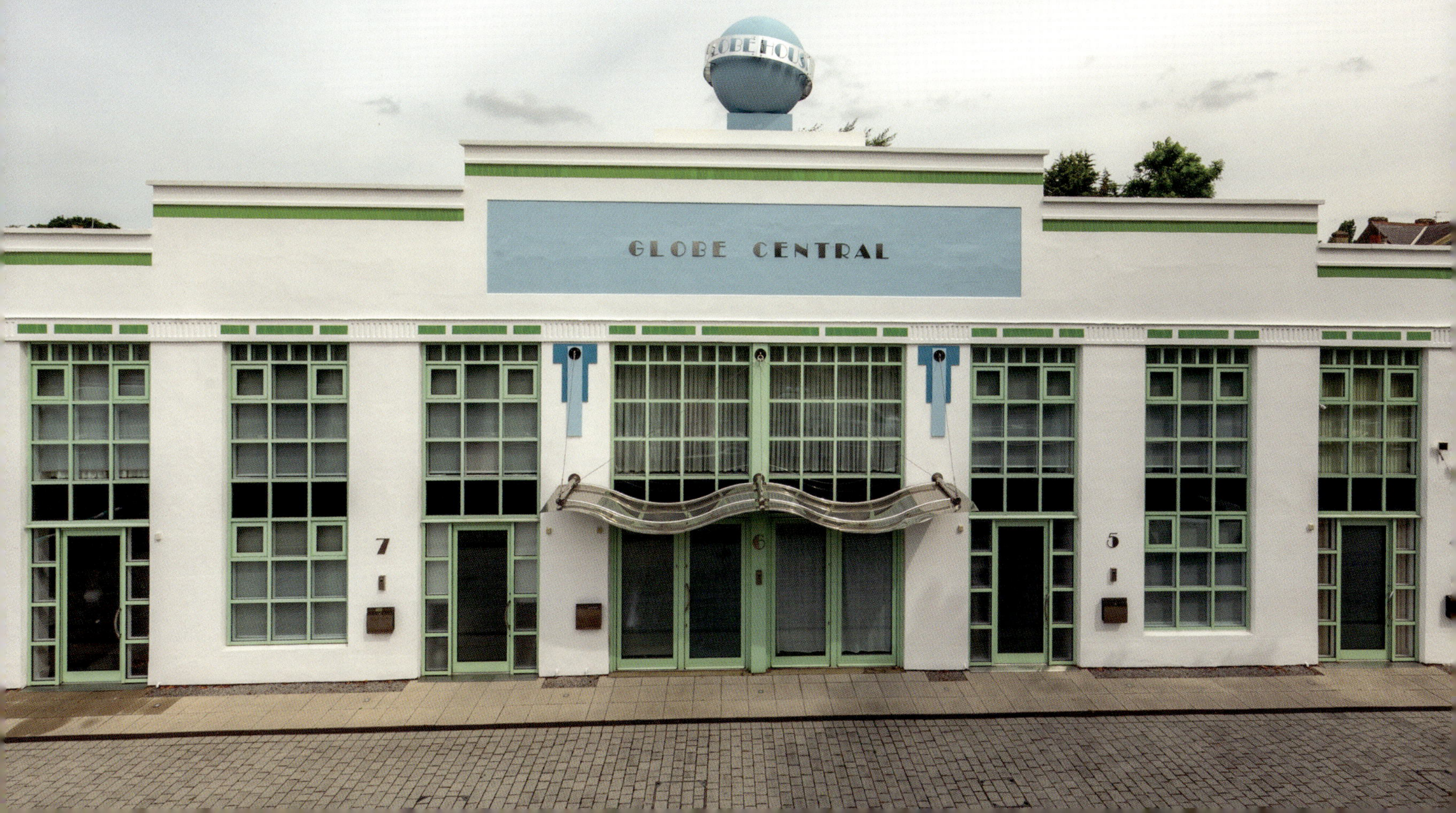

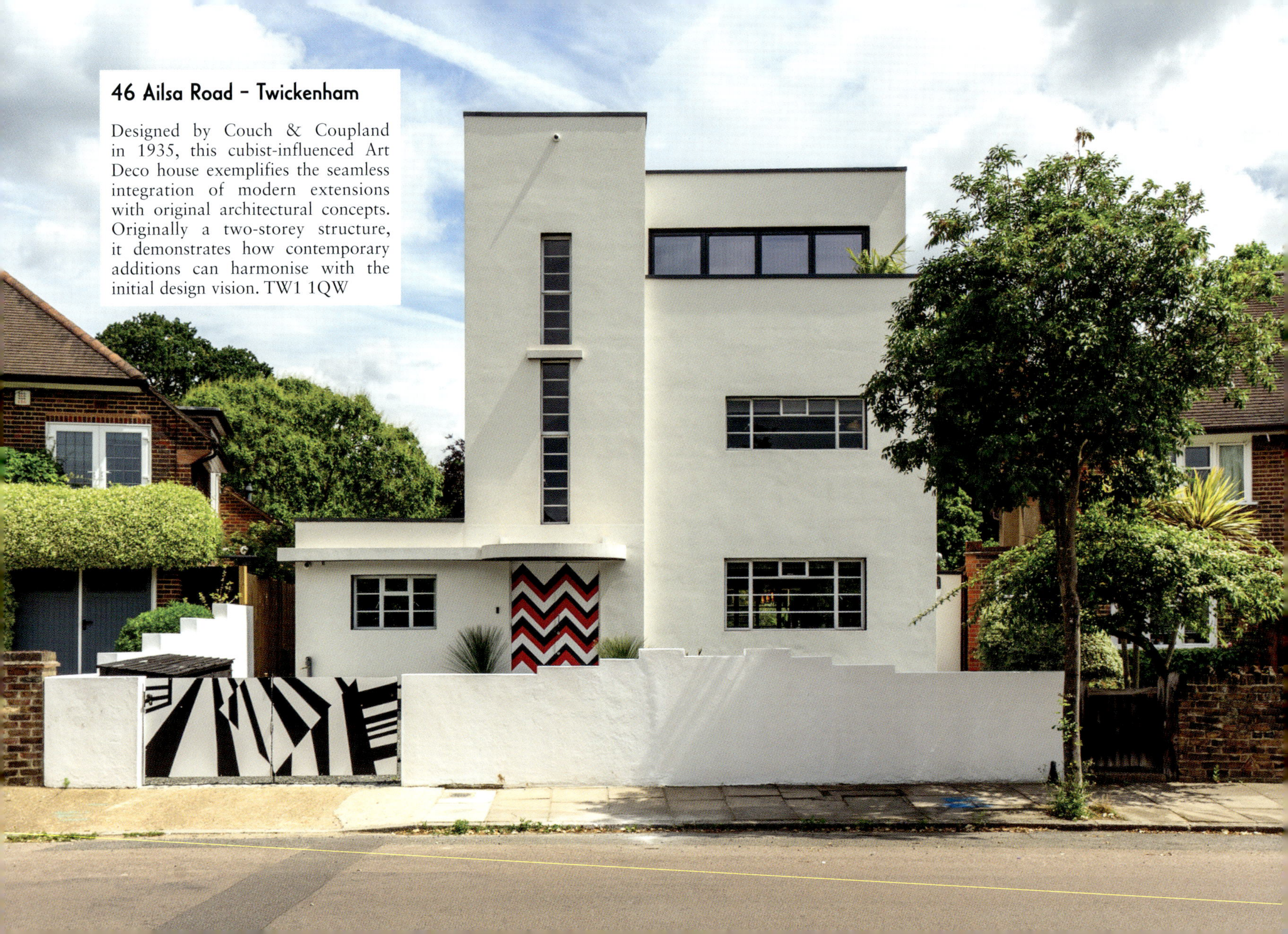

46 Ailsa Road – Twickenham

Designed by Couch & Coupland in 1935, this cubist-influenced Art Deco house exemplifies the seamless integration of modern extensions with original architectural concepts. Originally a two-storey structure, it demonstrates how contemporary additions can harmonise with the initial design vision. TW1 1QW

Pavilion & Clubhouse – Isleworth

The Pavilion & Clubhouse stands as a Grade II listed gem, a sports pavilion masterfully crafted by architects Brian L. Sutcliffe and H. Colin Farmer in 1935. Originally commissioned for the University College School Old Boys Club, it fell into disrepair over time. However, through dedicated restoration efforts, it has been revitalised to its former glory and is now a Goals Soccer Centre. TW7 5DB

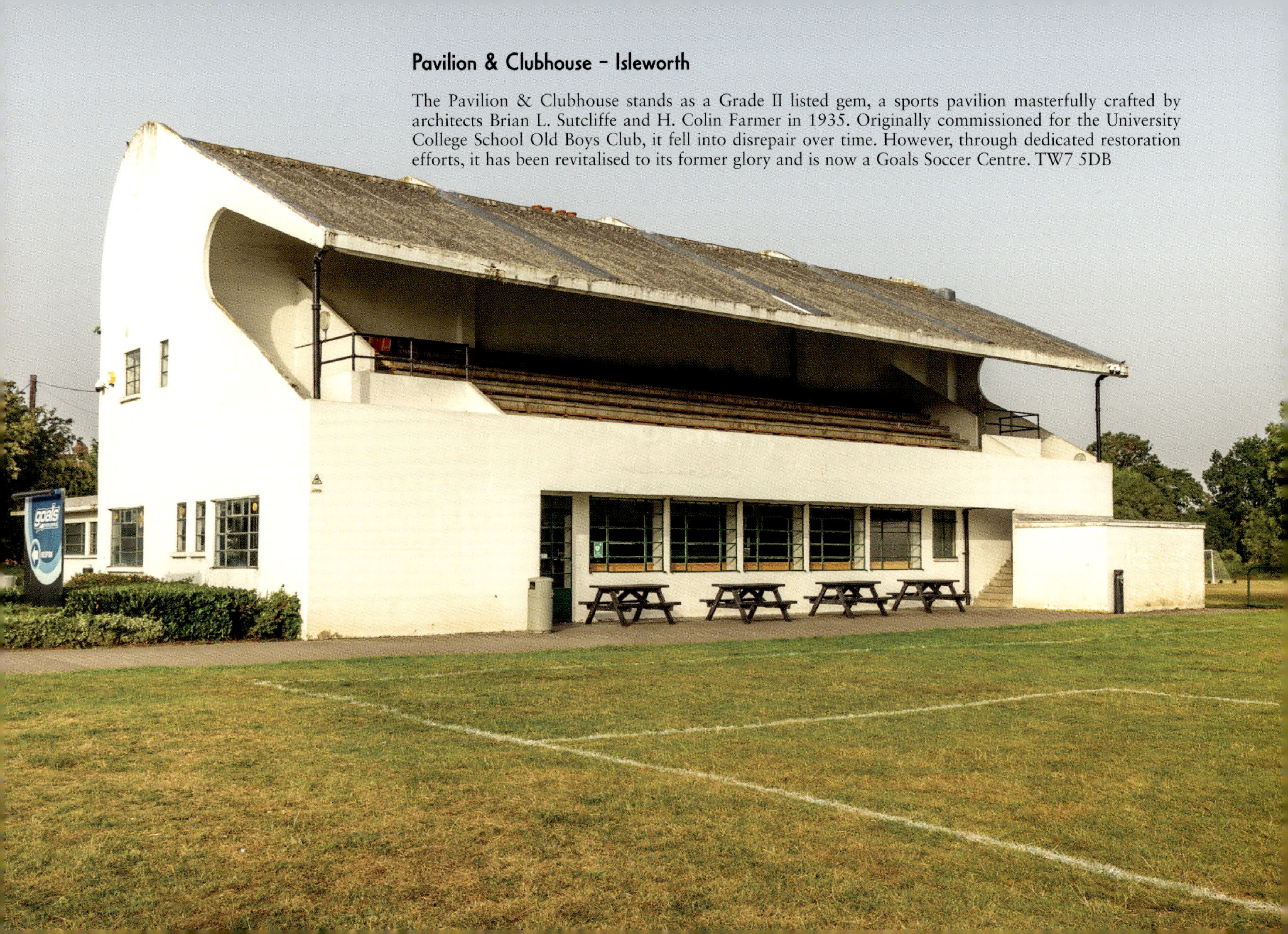

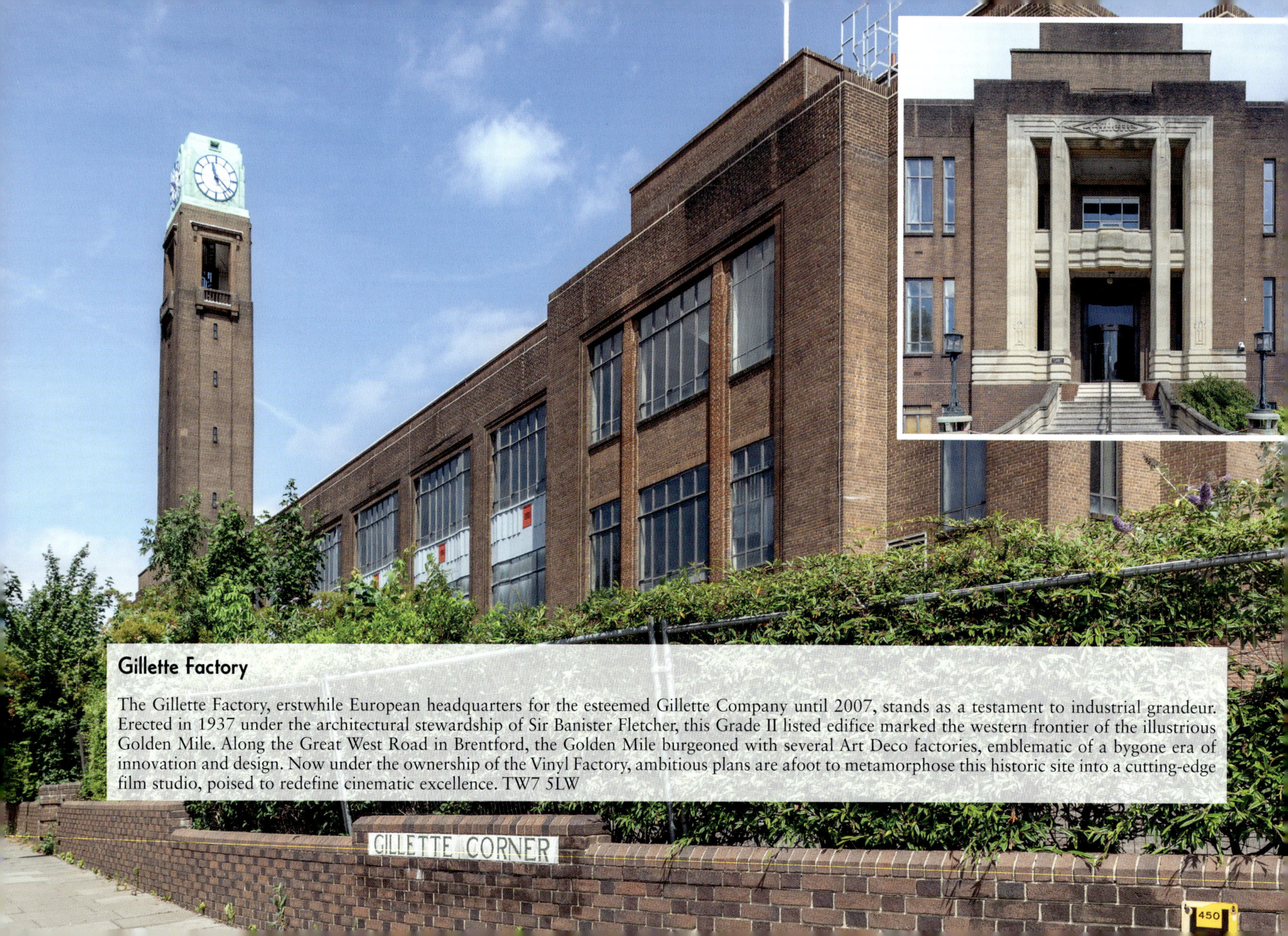

Gillette Factory

The Gillette Factory, erstwhile European headquarters for the esteemed Gillette Company until 2007, stands as a testament to industrial grandeur. Erected in 1937 under the architectural stewardship of Sir Banister Fletcher, this Grade II listed edifice marked the western frontier of the illustrious Golden Mile. Along the Great West Road in Brentford, the Golden Mile burgeoned with several Art Deco factories, emblematic of a bygone era of innovation and design. Now under the ownership of the Vinyl Factory, ambitious plans are afoot to metamorphose this historic site into a cutting-edge film studio, poised to redefine cinematic excellence. TW7 5LW

941 Great West Road – Syon Clinic

Designed by Wallis, Gilbert and Partners, this Grade II listed building was originally constructed in 1933 for the Coty Cosmetics Company. Today, it houses the Syon Clinic, a private outpatient facility located on the iconic Golden Mile. TW8 9DU

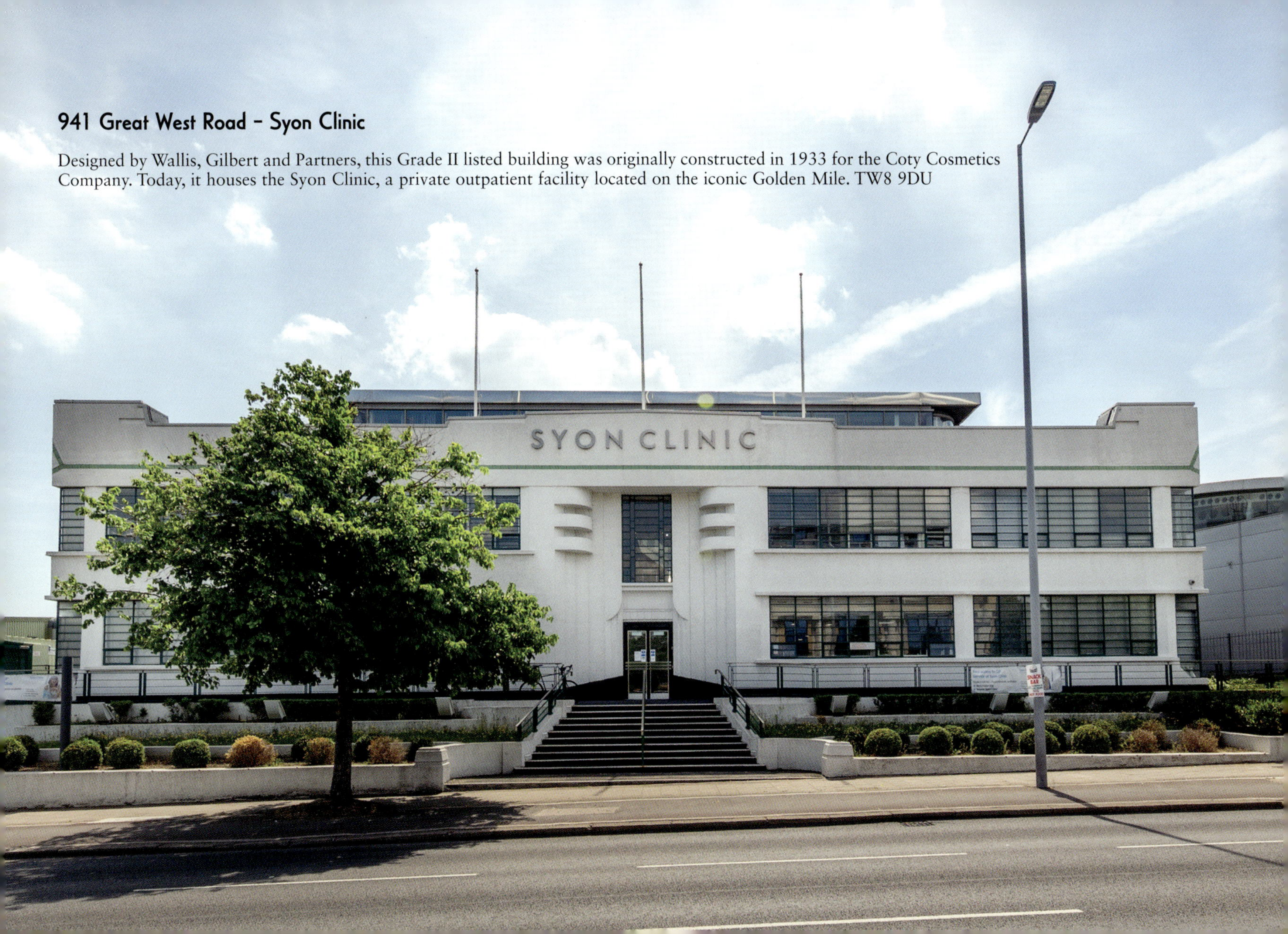

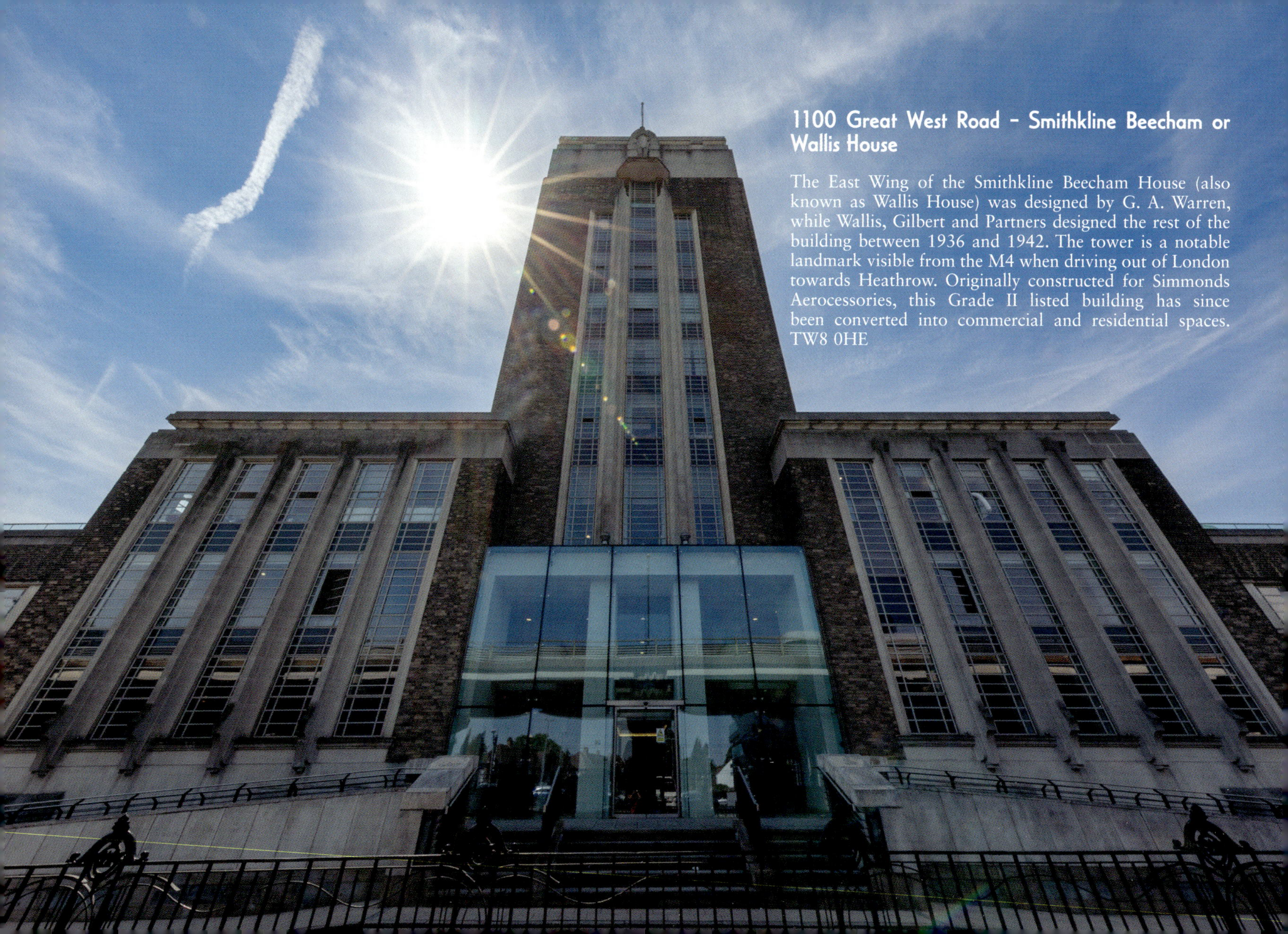

1100 Great West Road – Smithkline Beecham or Wallis House

The East Wing of the Smithkline Beecham House (also known as Wallis House) was designed by G. A. Warren, while Wallis, Gilbert and Partners designed the rest of the building between 1936 and 1942. The tower is a notable landmark visible from the M4 when driving out of London towards Heathrow. Originally constructed for Simmonds Aerocessories, this Grade II listed building has since been converted into commercial and residential spaces. TW8 0HE

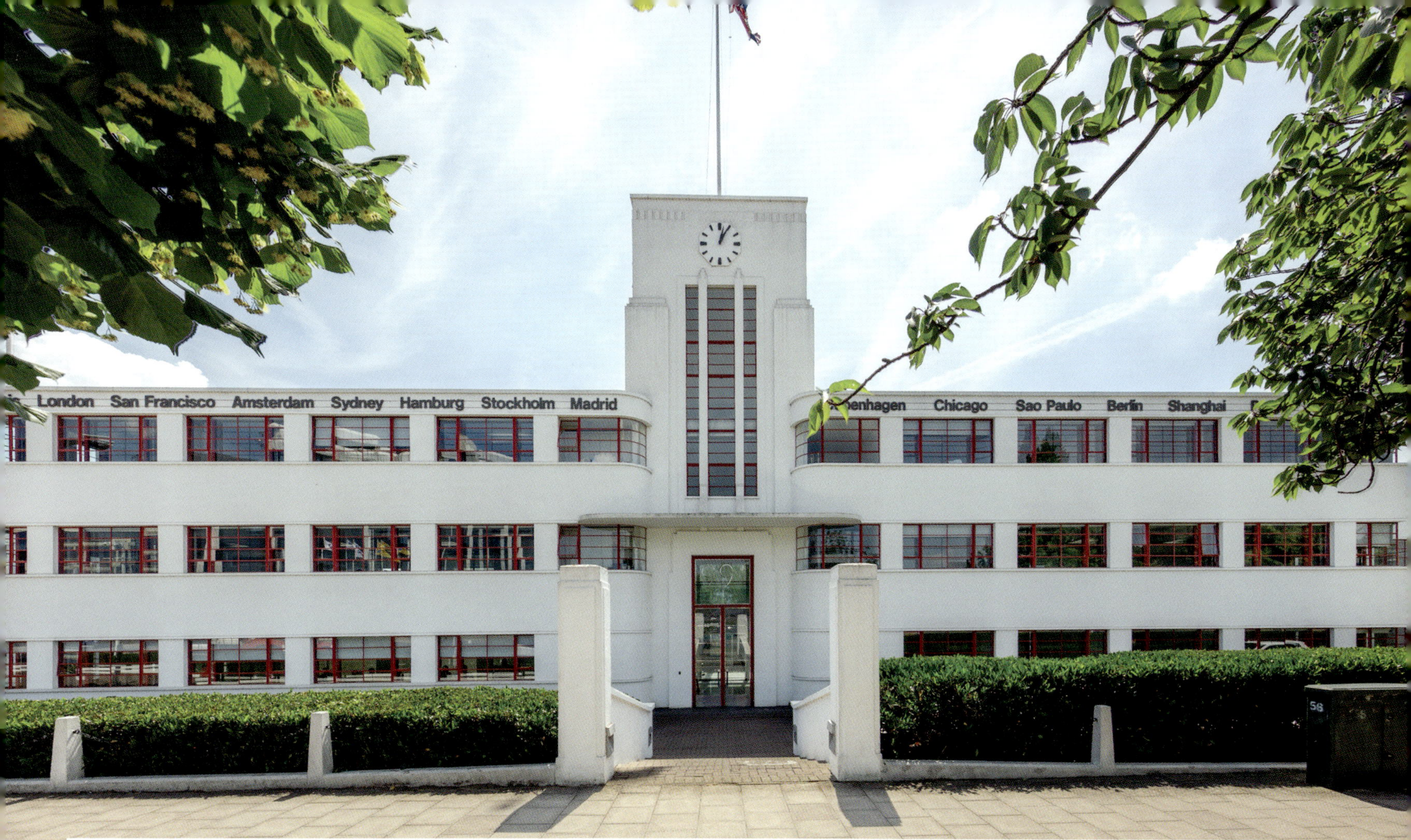

991 Great West Road – JC Decaux

Built in 1936 as a distribution centre for Currys, this Grade II listed building was designed by F. E. Simpkins. Foster and Partners restored the building for JC Decaux between 1997 and 2000. TW8 9DN

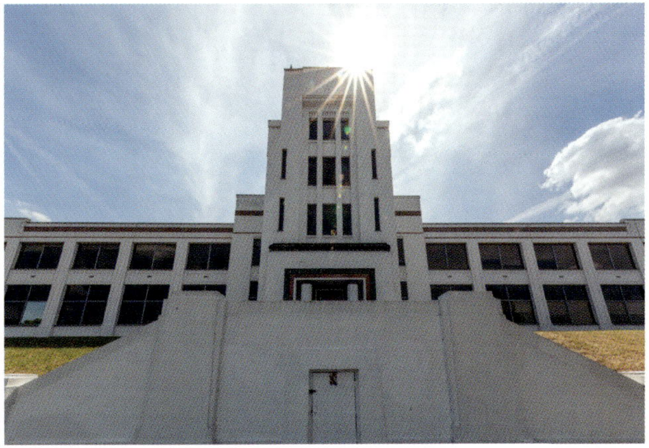

981 Great West Road – Westlink House

One of the early Art Deco buildings on the Golden Mile, this Grade II listed structure was designed by Wallis, Gilbert and Partners in 1928. Originally used by the Pyrene Company, a leader in firefighting equipment, it has since been converted into offices and is now known as Westlink House. TW8 9DN

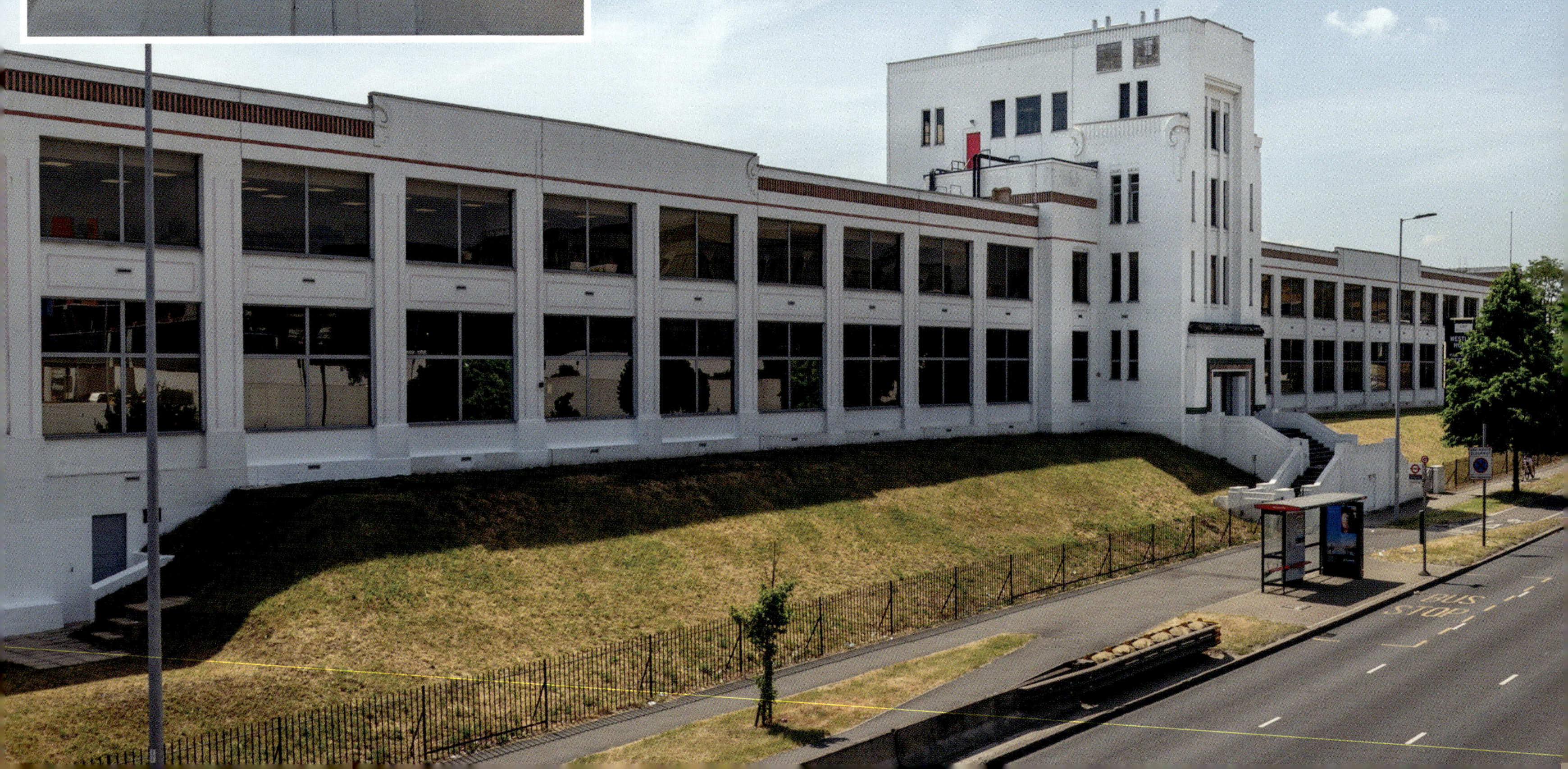

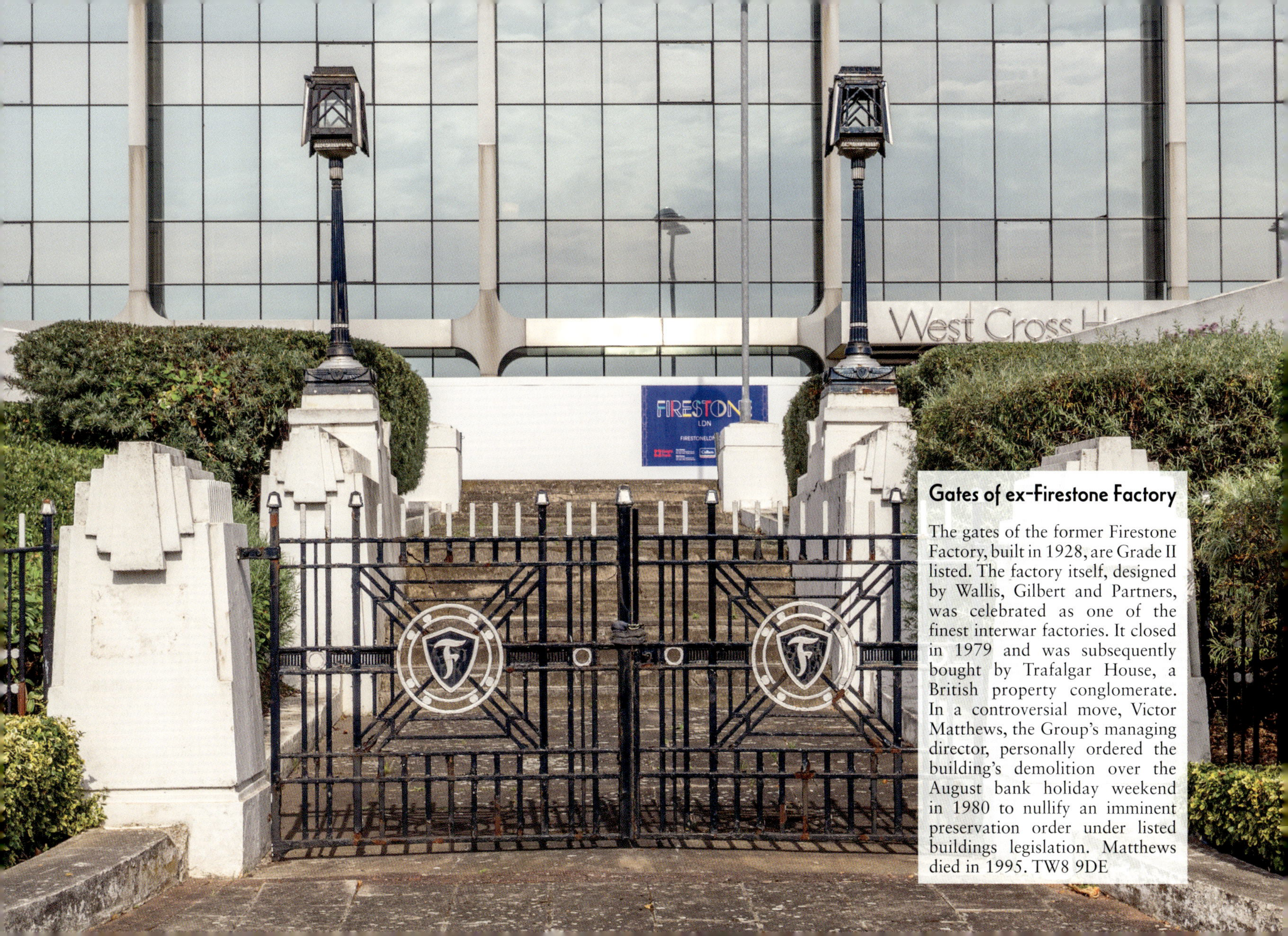

Gates of ex-Firestone Factory

The gates of the former Firestone Factory, built in 1928, are Grade II listed. The factory itself, designed by Wallis, Gilbert and Partners, was celebrated as one of the finest interwar factories. It closed in 1979 and was subsequently bought by Trafalgar House, a British property conglomerate. In a controversial move, Victor Matthews, the Group's managing director, personally ordered the building's demolition over the August bank holiday weekend in 1980 to nullify an imminent preservation order under listed buildings legislation. Matthews died in 1995. TW8 9DE

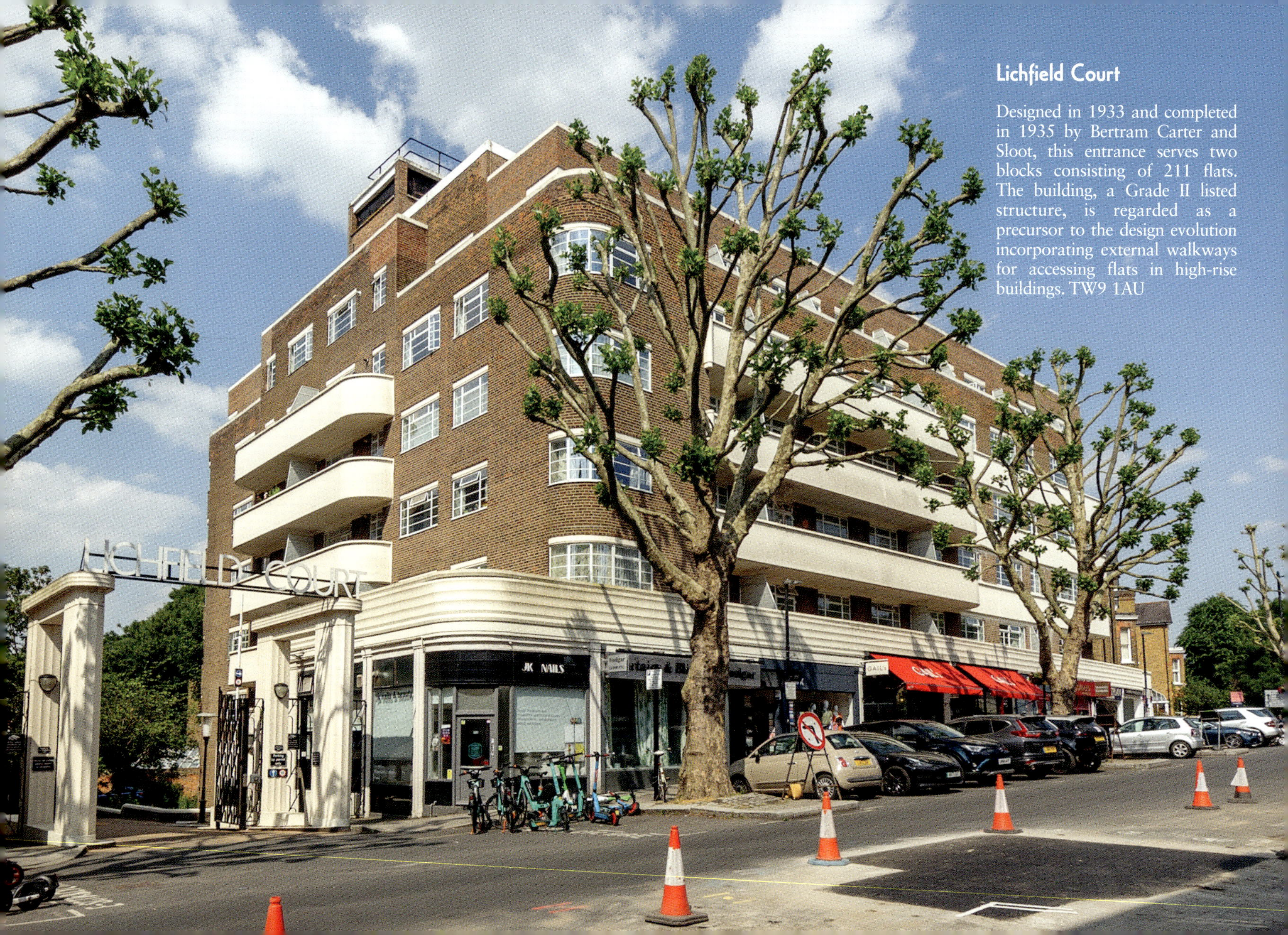

Lichfield Court

Designed in 1933 and completed in 1935 by Bertram Carter and Sloot, this entrance serves two blocks consisting of 211 flats. The building, a Grade II listed structure, is regarded as a precursor to the design evolution incorporating external walkways for accessing flats in high-rise buildings. TW9 1AU

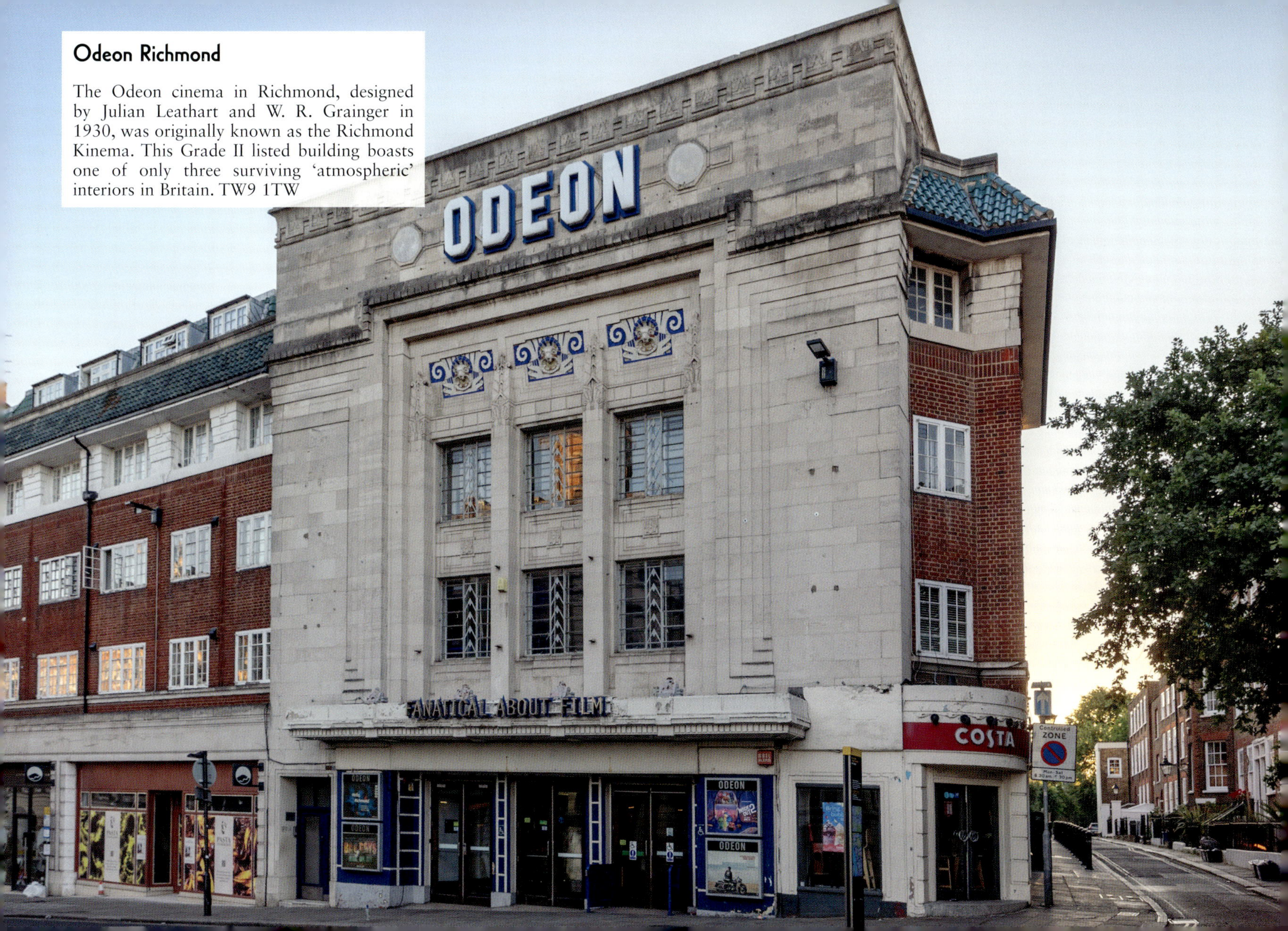

Odeon Richmond

The Odeon cinema in Richmond, designed by Julian Leathart and W. R. Grainger in 1930, was originally known as the Richmond Kinema. This Grade II listed building boasts one of only three surviving 'atmospheric' interiors in Britain. TW9 1TW

Richmond Station

Richmond Station was built in 1937, designed by James Robb Scott, the chief architect of Southern Railway. TW9 2NA

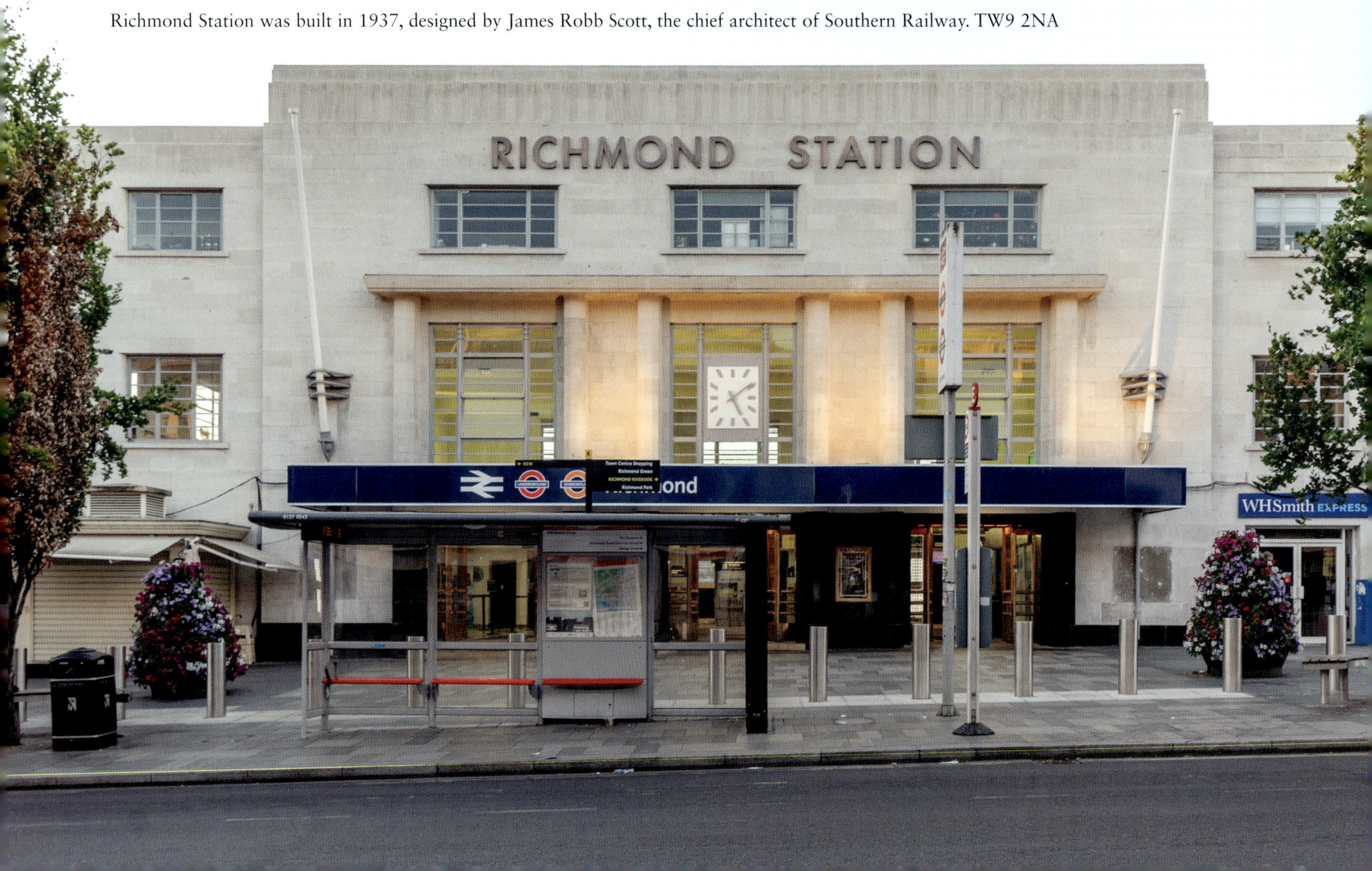

Mortlake Crematorium

Designed by F. Douglas Barton, the Grade II listed Mortlake Crematorium was inaugurated in 1939 by Lord Horder, the esteemed physician to the king and a leading figure in the medical community at the time. This establishment was the result of a collaborative effort among the boroughs of Hammersmith, Richmond, Barnes, and Acton. Among the many individuals cremated there, one notable figure is Tommy Cooper – 'just like that'. TW9 4EN

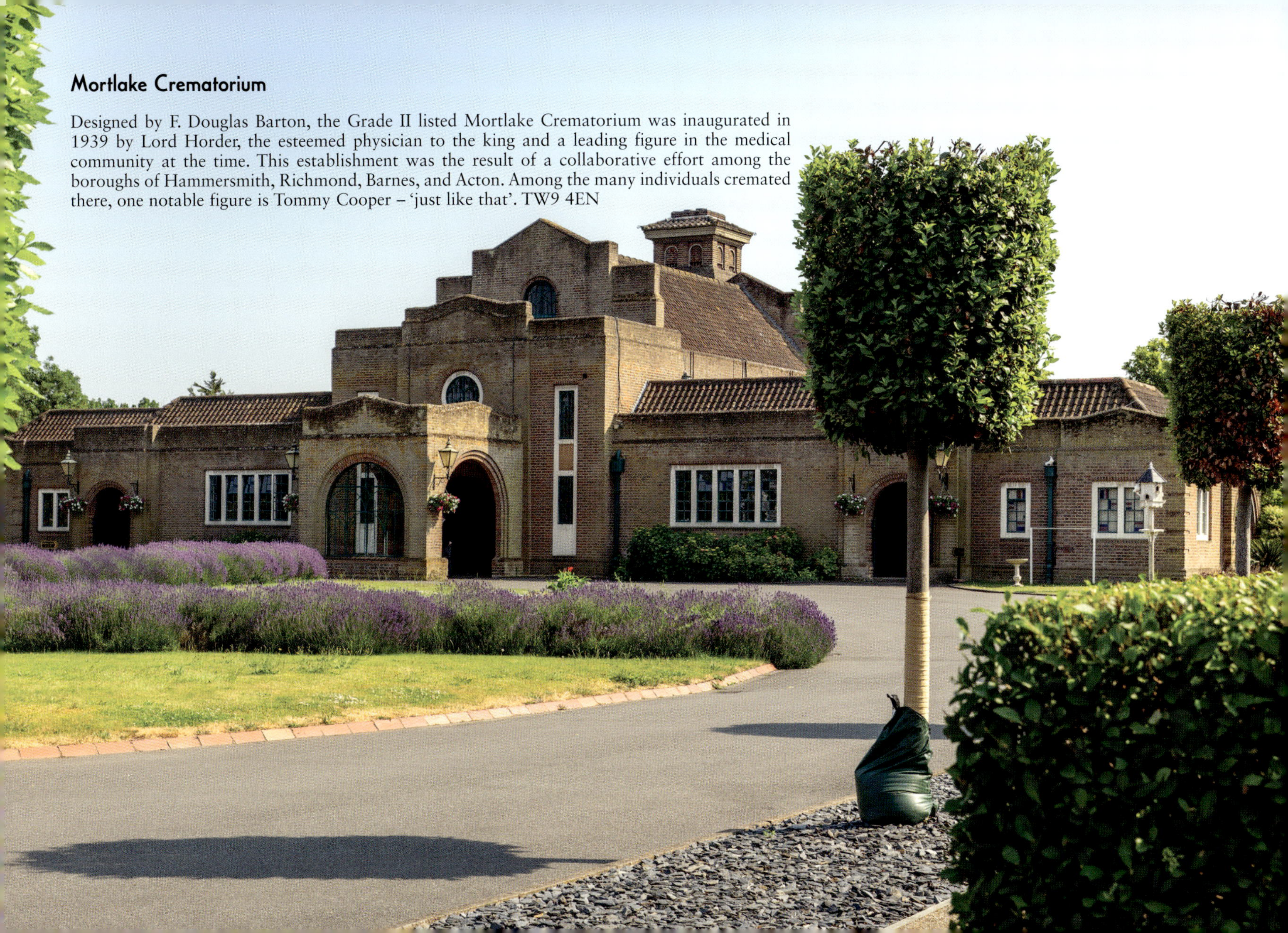

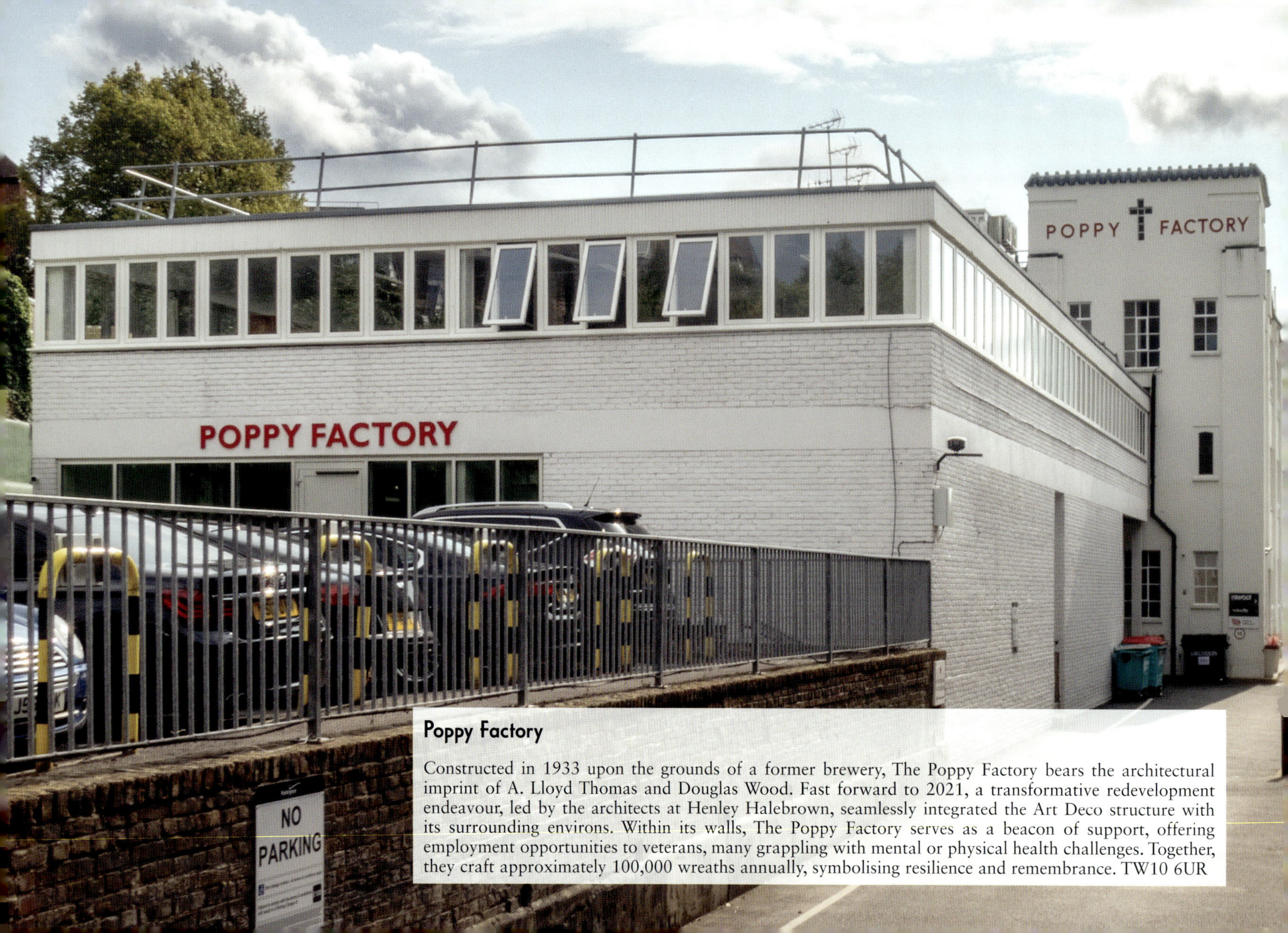

Poppy Factory

Constructed in 1933 upon the grounds of a former brewery, The Poppy Factory bears the architectural imprint of A. Lloyd Thomas and Douglas Wood. Fast forward to 2021, a transformative redevelopment endeavour, led by the architects at Henley Halebrown, seamlessly integrated the Art Deco structure with its surrounding environs. Within its walls, The Poppy Factory serves as a beacon of support, offering employment opportunities to veterans, many grappling with mental or physical health challenges. Together, they craft approximately 100,000 wreaths annually, symbolising resilience and remembrance. TW10 6UR

Canteen Block, Perivale

The Canteen Block in Perivale was added to the Hoover Factory in 1938. Like the Hoover Building it was designed by Wallis, Gilbert and Partners and is Grade II* listed. While it mirrors the main building's white and green colour palette, its architectural style diverges notably. Presently, continuing its culinary legacy, it thrives as a spacious Pakistani restaurant. UB6 8DW

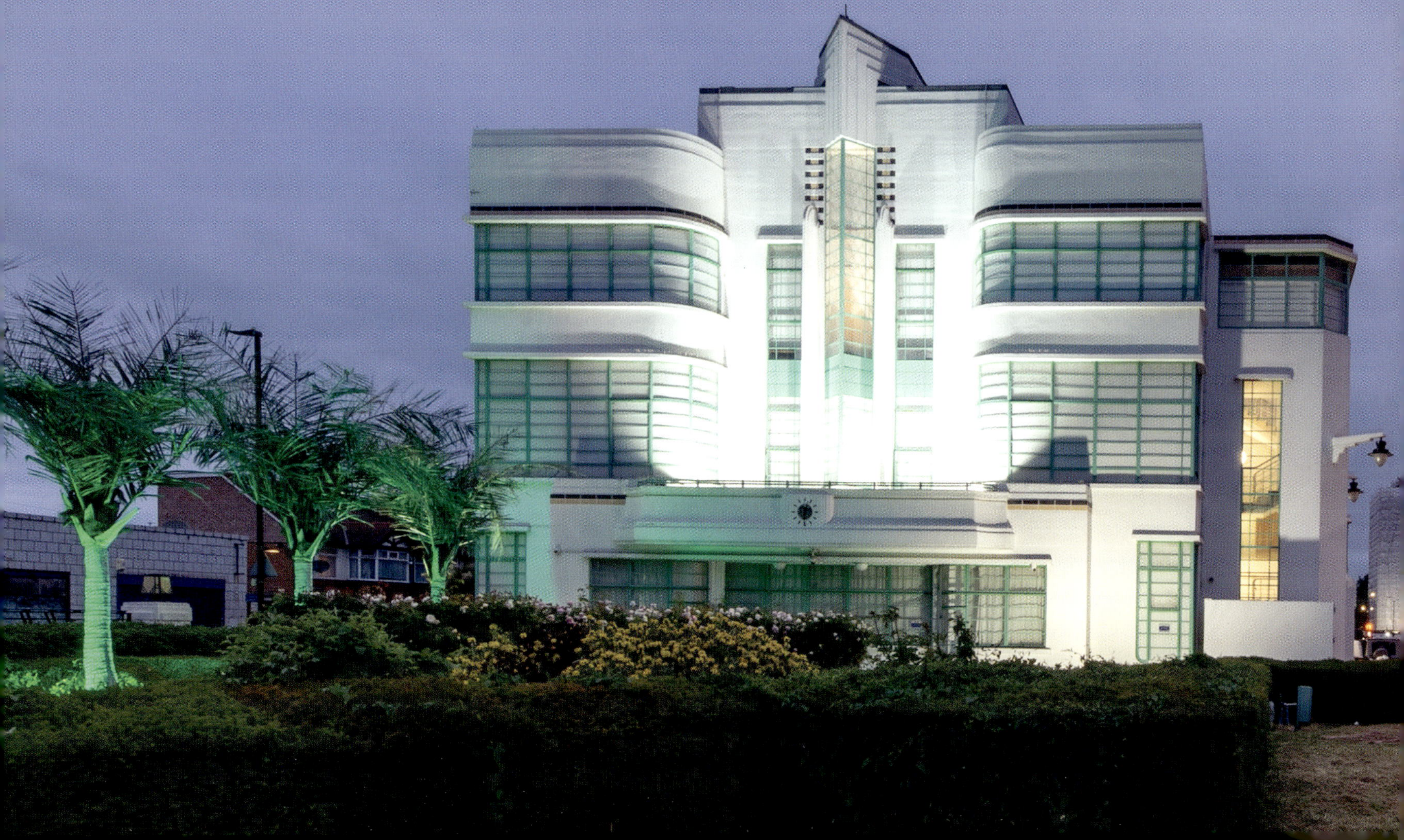

Hoover Building

Designed by Wallis, Gilbert and Partners and listed Grade II* in 1980, this building opened as the headquarters for the Hoover Company in 1933. The listing mentions that this is 'possibly the most significant arterial road factory of its date, and one of the most attractive'. Since 1983 the gates and railings have their own Grade II listing. Not many buildings can claim to have a song written about them, but the Hoover Factory can ('The Hoover Factory' by Elvis Costello). In 2018 the building has been converted by new owners IDM Properties into apartments. UB6 8DW

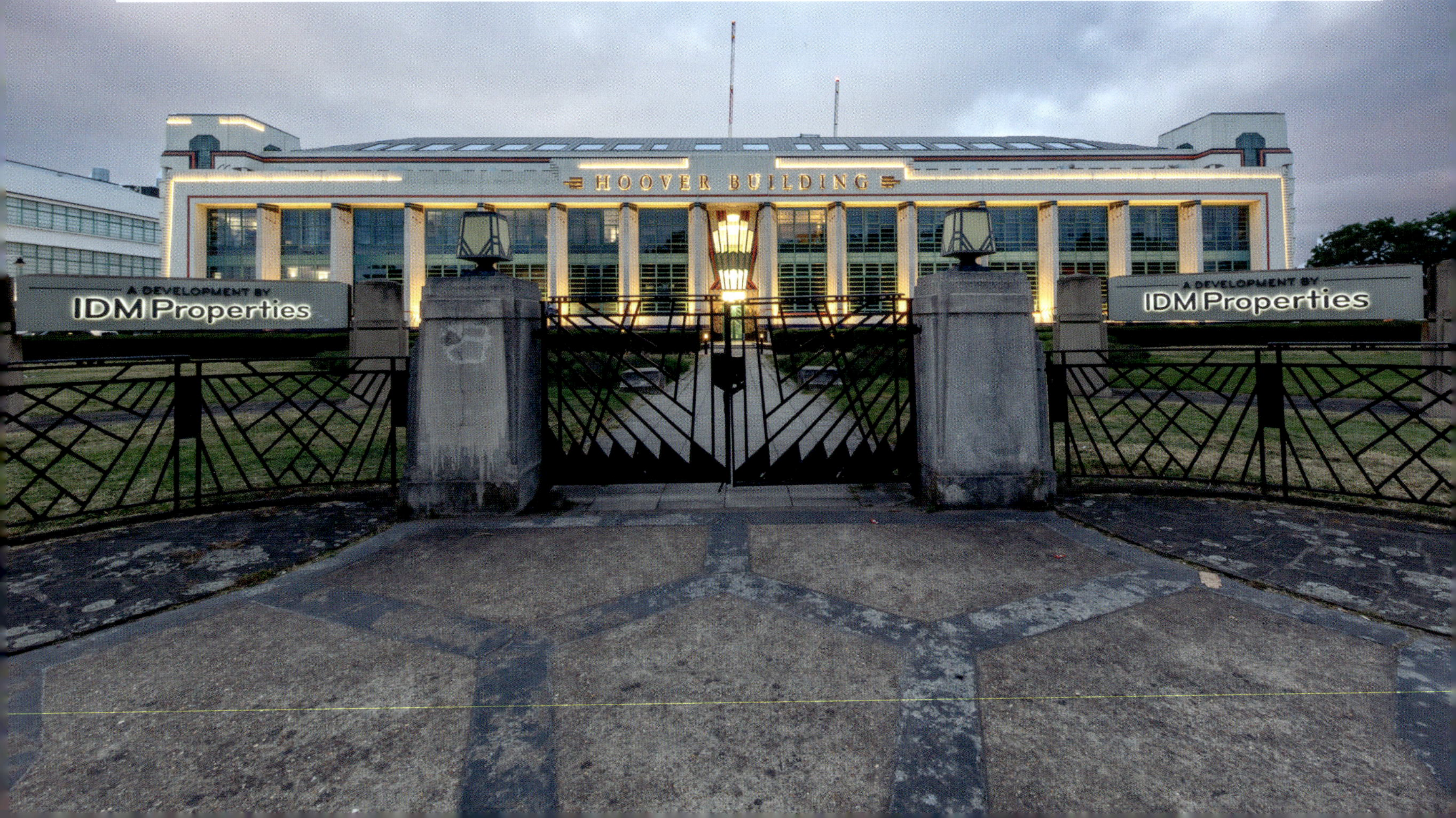

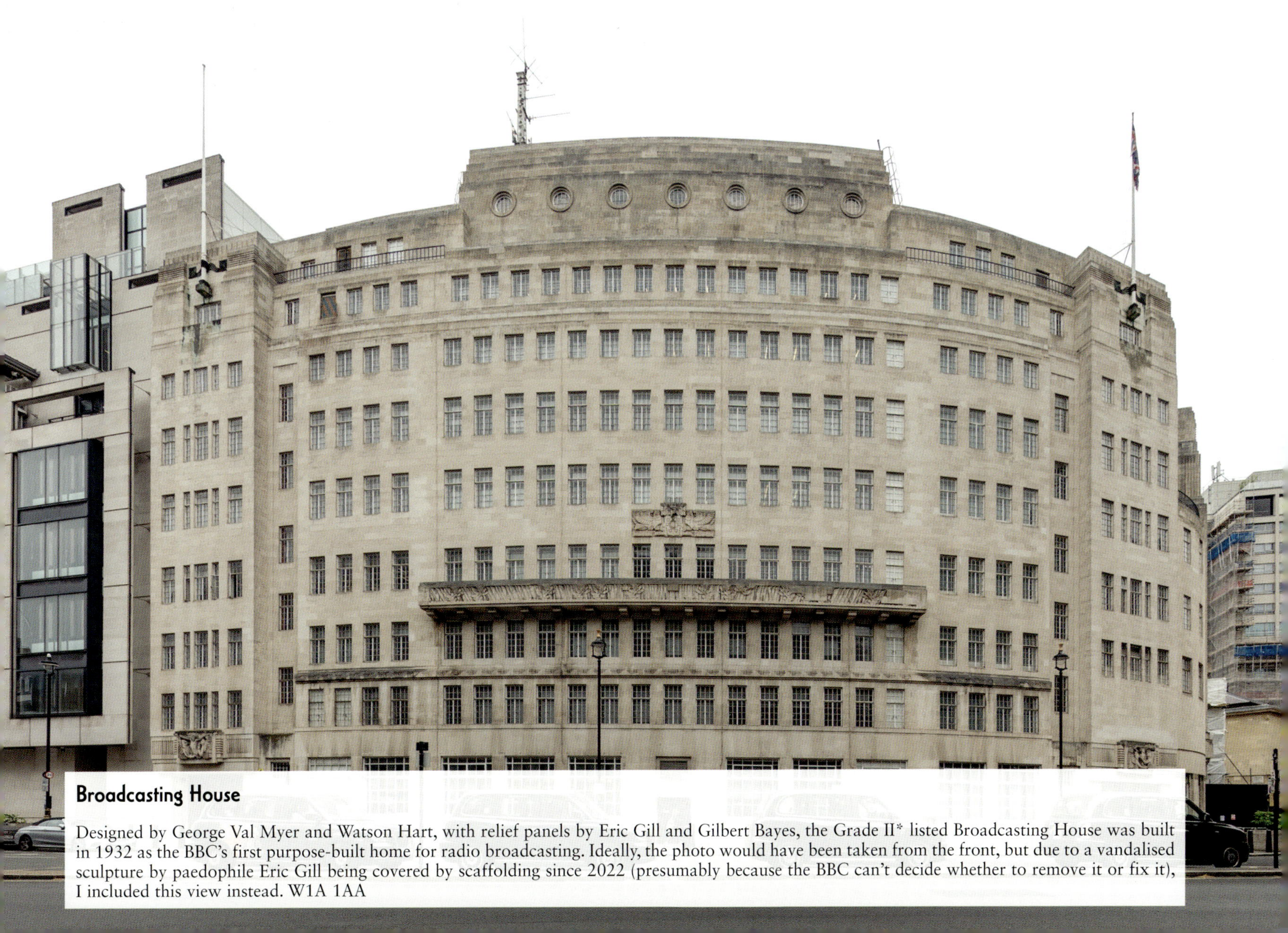

Broadcasting House

Designed by George Val Myer and Watson Hart, with relief panels by Eric Gill and Gilbert Bayes, the Grade II* listed Broadcasting House was built in 1932 as the BBC's first purpose-built home for radio broadcasting. Ideally, the photo would have been taken from the front, but due to a vandalised sculpture by paedophile Eric Gill being covered by scaffolding since 2022 (presumably because the BBC can't decide whether to remove it or fix it), I included this view instead. W1A 1AA

66 Portland Place (RIBA)

The home of the Royal Institute of British Architects better be a significant building. Architect George Grey Wornum won a competition out of 3,600 entries to design the RIBA's new headquarters, which was completed in 1934. The building was opened by King George V and Queen Mary and is now Grade II* listed. W1B 1AD

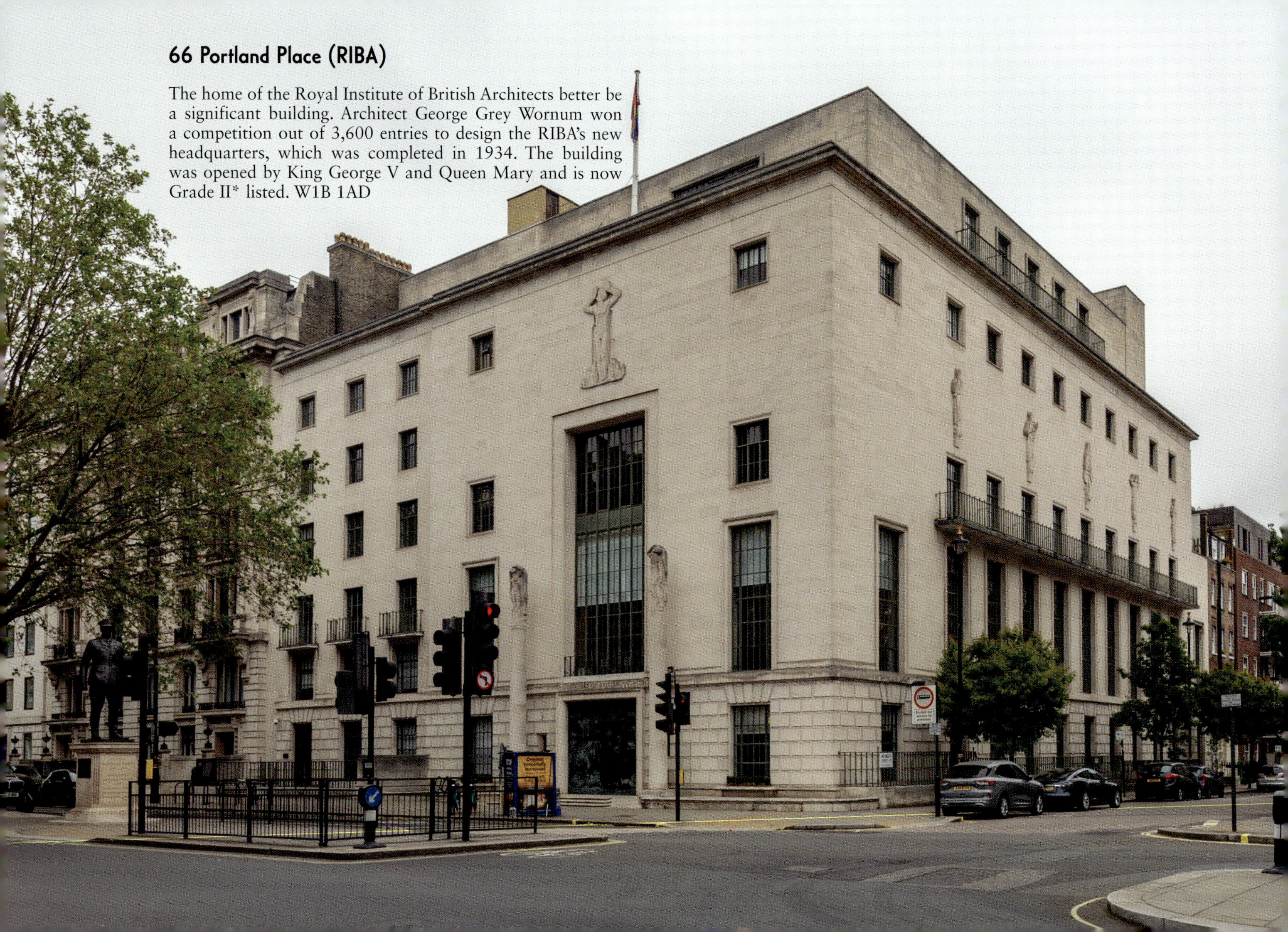

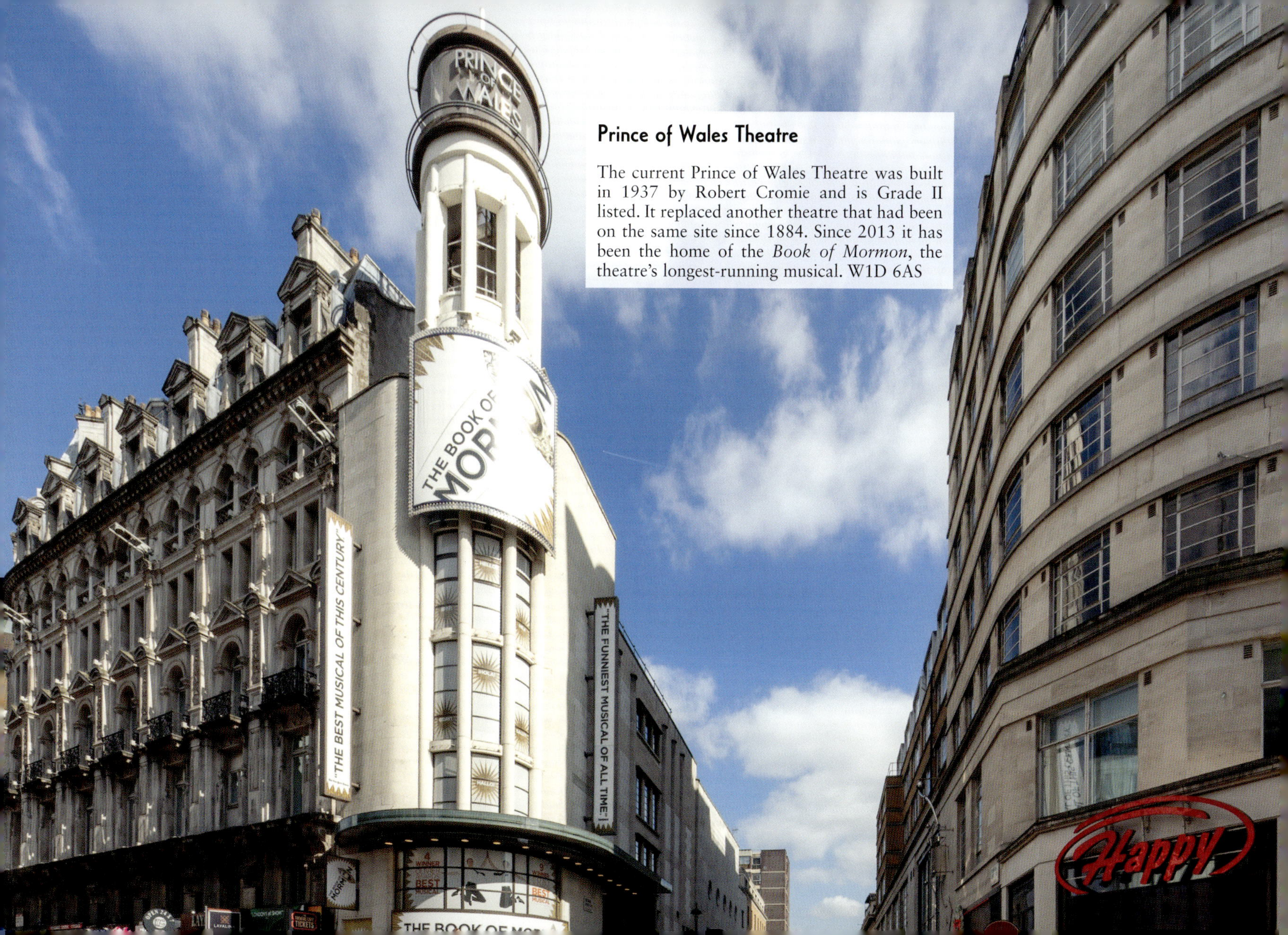

Prince of Wales Theatre

The current Prince of Wales Theatre was built in 1937 by Robert Cromie and is Grade II listed. It replaced another theatre that had been on the same site since 1884. Since 2013 it has been the home of the *Book of Mormon*, the theatre's longest-running musical. W1D 6AS

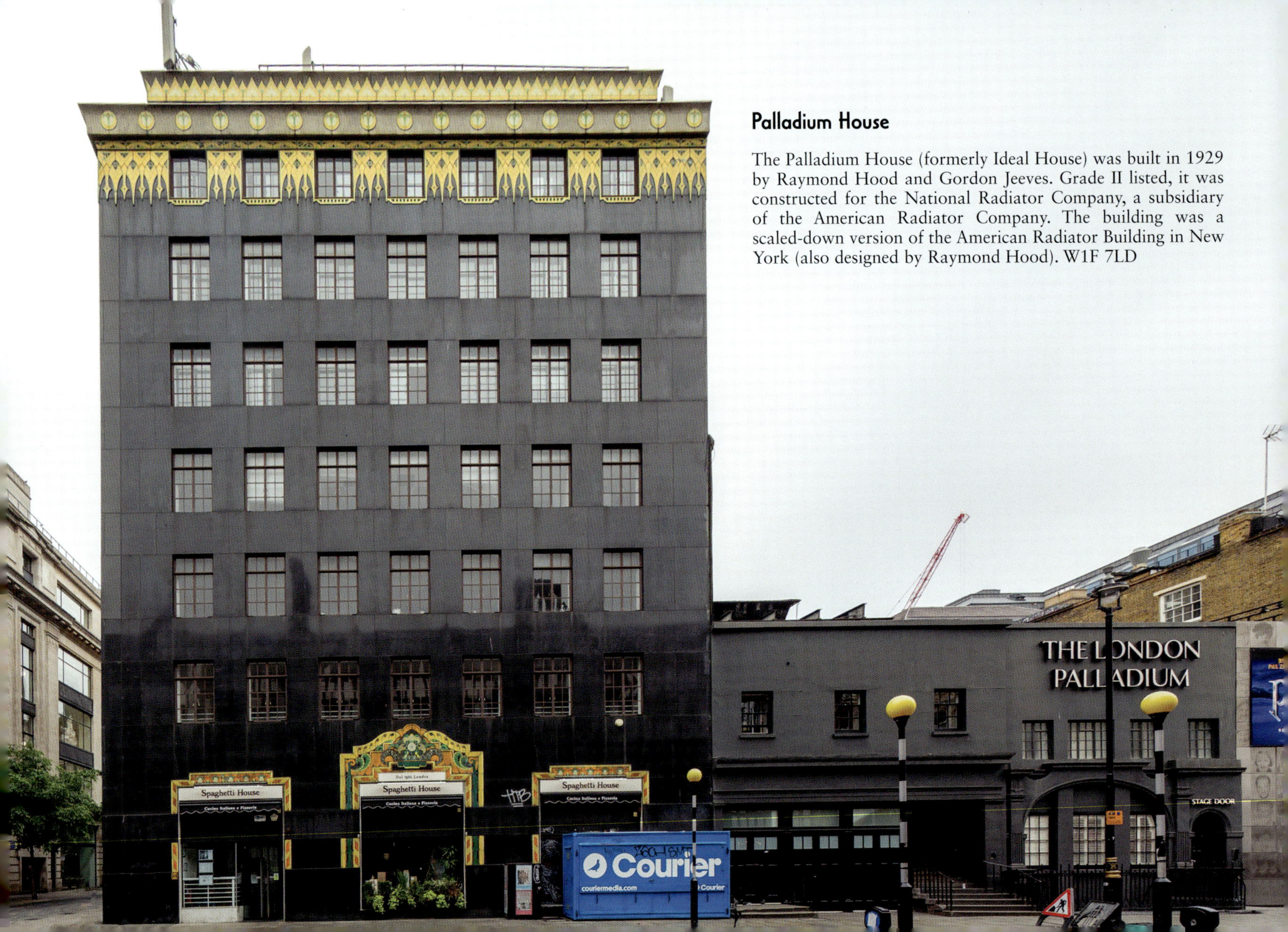

Palladium House

The Palladium House (formerly Ideal House) was built in 1929 by Raymond Hood and Gordon Jeeves. Grade II listed, it was constructed for the National Radiator Company, a subsidiary of the American Radiator Company. The building was a scaled-down version of the American Radiator Building in New York (also designed by Raymond Hood). W1F 7LD

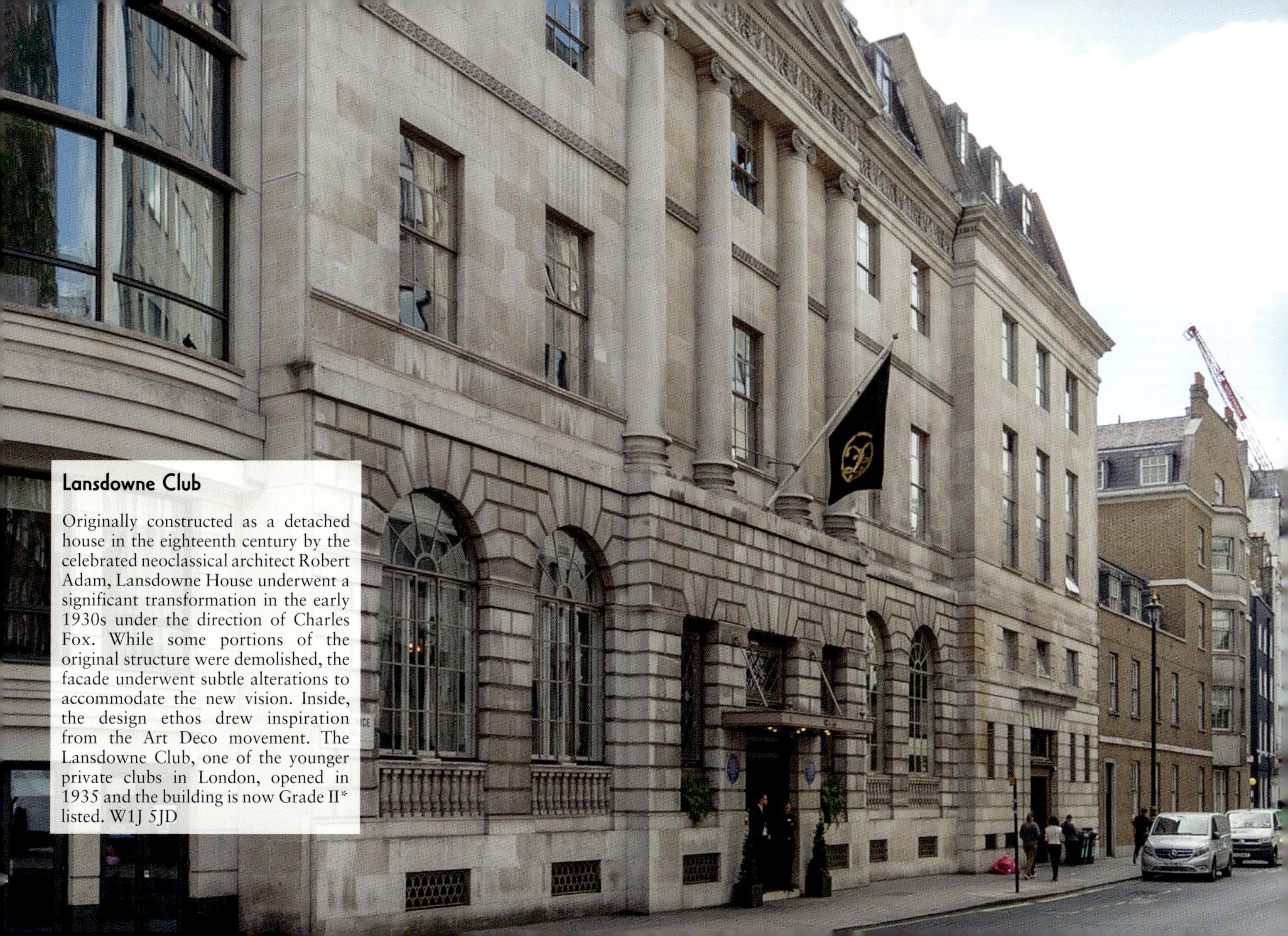

Lansdowne Club

Originally constructed as a detached house in the eighteenth century by the celebrated neoclassical architect Robert Adam, Lansdowne House underwent a significant transformation in the early 1930s under the direction of Charles Fox. While some portions of the original structure were demolished, the facade underwent subtle alterations to accommodate the new vision. Inside, the design ethos drew inspiration from the Art Deco movement. The Lansdowne Club, one of the younger private clubs in London, opened in 1935 and the building is now Grade II* listed. W1J 5JD

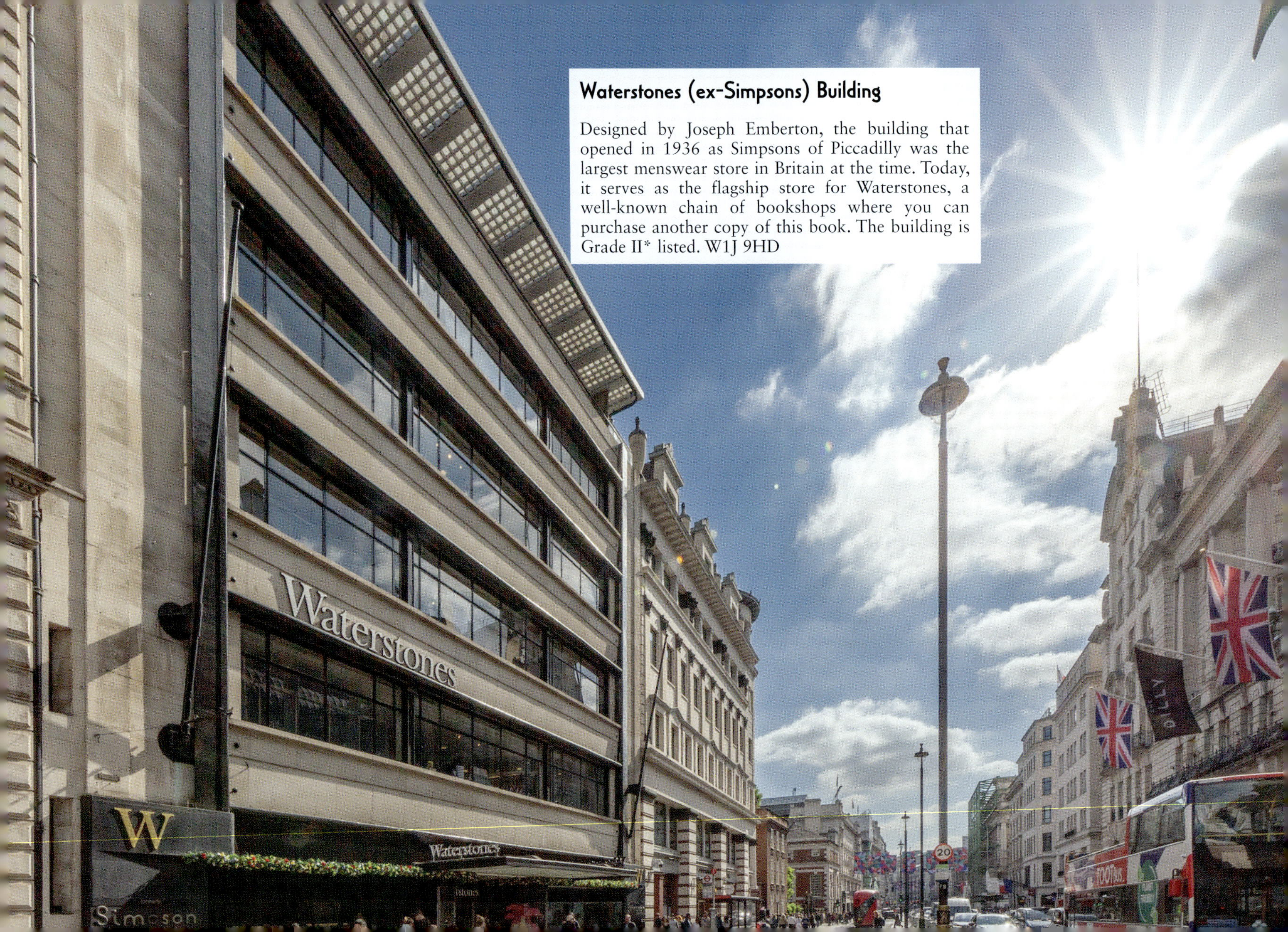

Waterstones (ex-Simpsons) Building

Designed by Joseph Emberton, the building that opened in 1936 as Simpsons of Piccadilly was the largest menswear store in Britain at the time. Today, it serves as the flagship store for Waterstones, a well-known chain of bookshops where you can purchase another copy of this book. The building is Grade II* listed. W1J 9HD

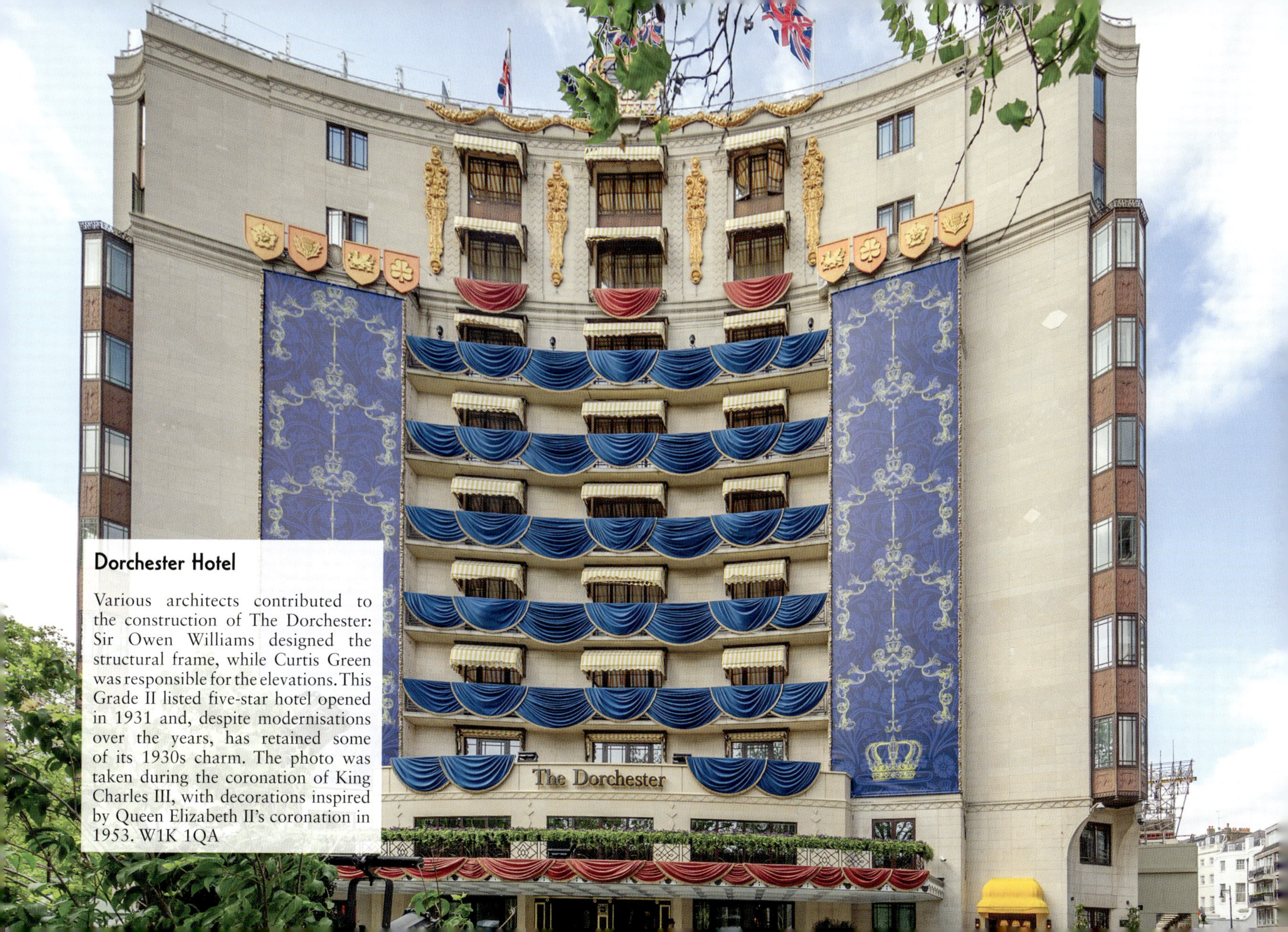

Dorchester Hotel

Various architects contributed to the construction of The Dorchester: Sir Owen Williams designed the structural frame, while Curtis Green was responsible for the elevations. This Grade II listed five-star hotel opened in 1931 and, despite modernisations over the years, has retained some of its 1930s charm. The photo was taken during the coronation of King Charles III, with decorations inspired by Queen Elizabeth II's coronation in 1953. W1K 1QA

Greybrook House

Greybrook House is a Grade II listed building, recognised for being a 'well-detailed, pleasing, and externally little-altered essay in Art Deco in a prominent location'. Designed by John Burnet and Partners in 1929 for the piano manufacturer Bechstein, it now houses a designer store and apartments. W1K 5DH

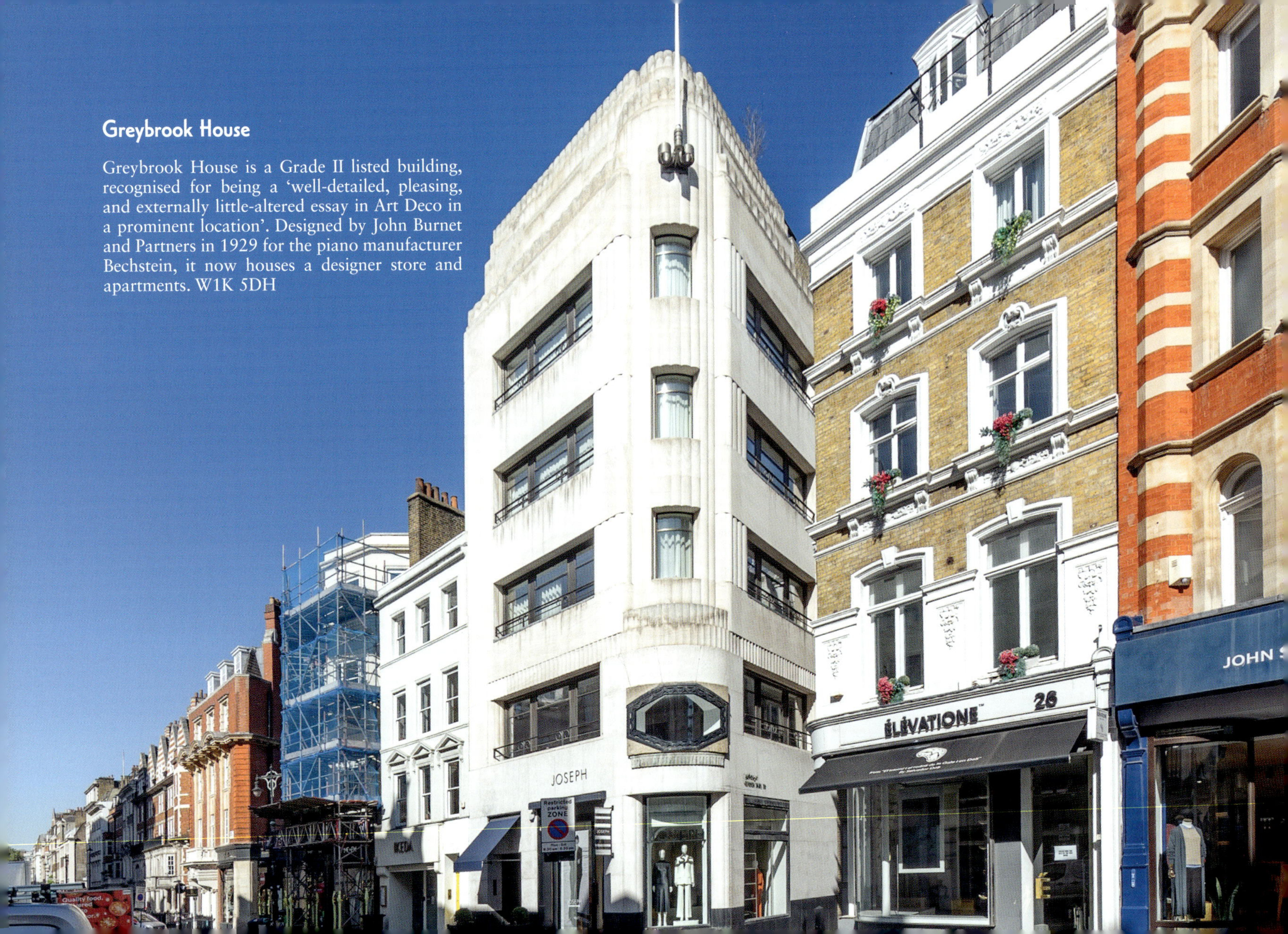

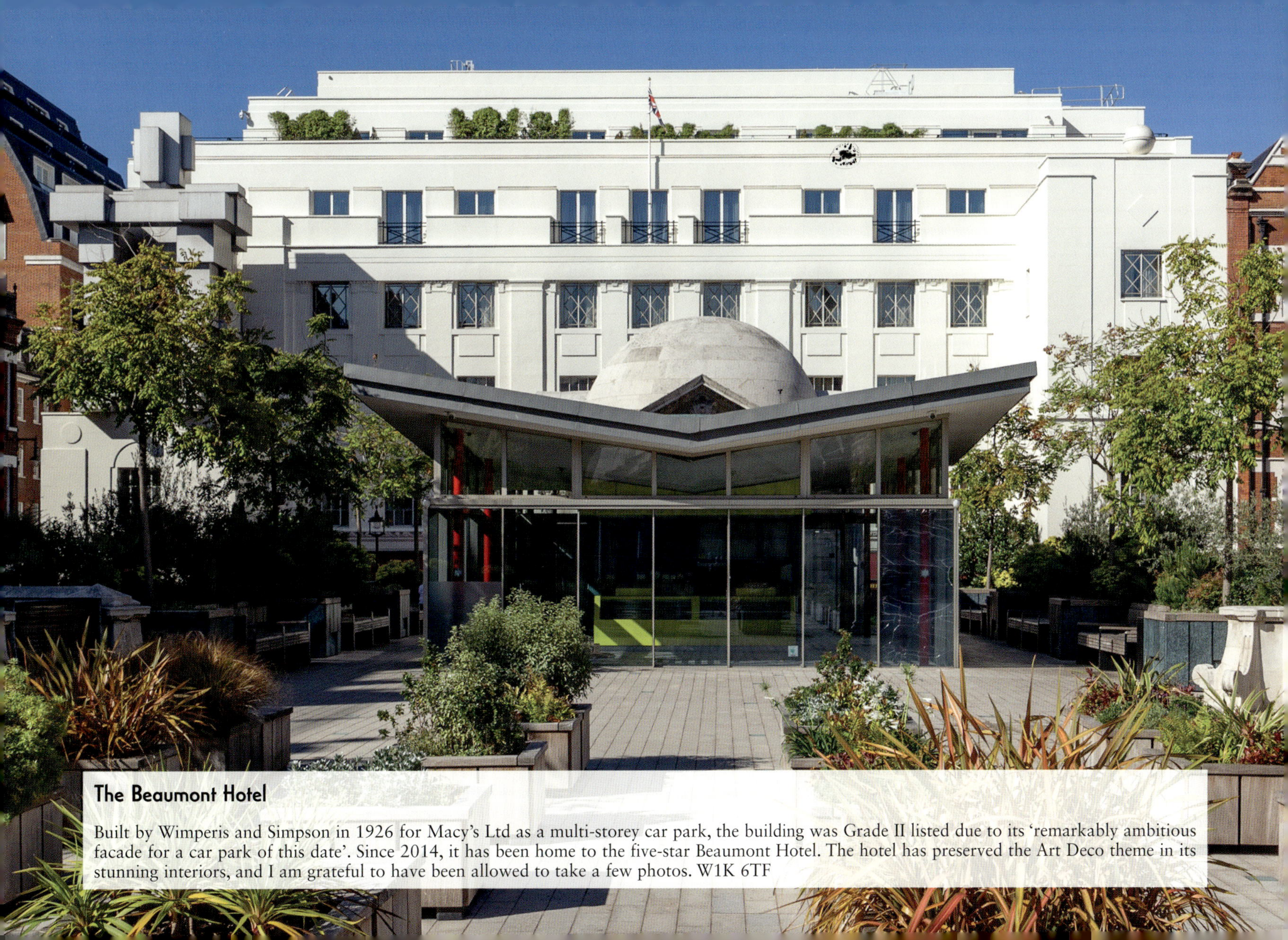

The Beaumont Hotel

Built by Wimperis and Simpson in 1926 for Macy's Ltd as a multi-storey car park, the building was Grade II listed due to its 'remarkably ambitious facade for a car park of this date'. Since 2014, it has been home to the five-star Beaumont Hotel. The hotel has preserved the Art Deco theme in its stunning interiors, and I am grateful to have been allowed to take a few photos. W1K 6TF

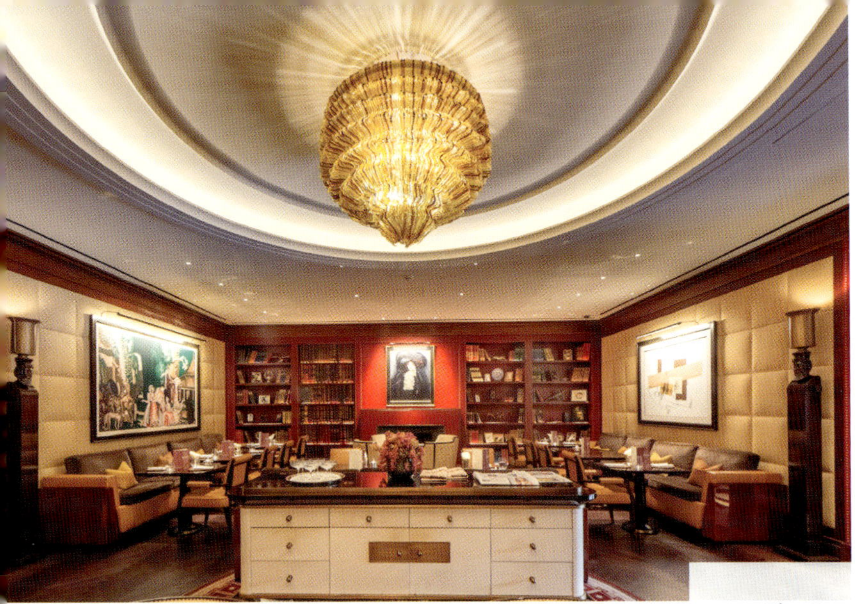

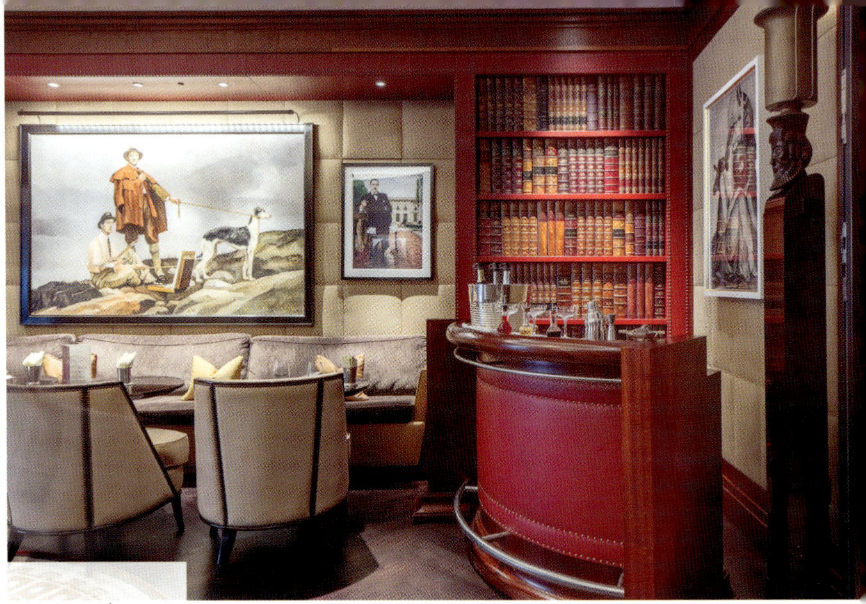

The Beaumont Hotel

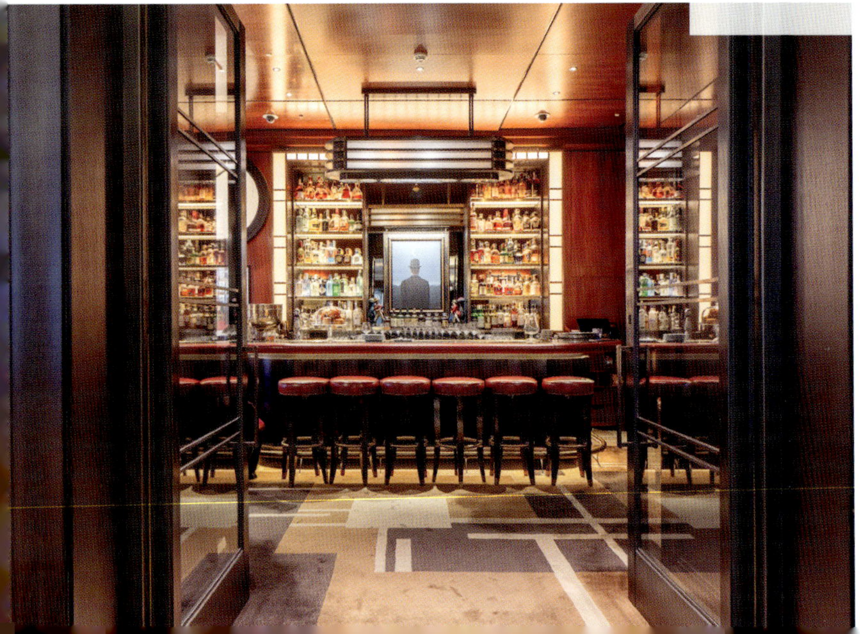

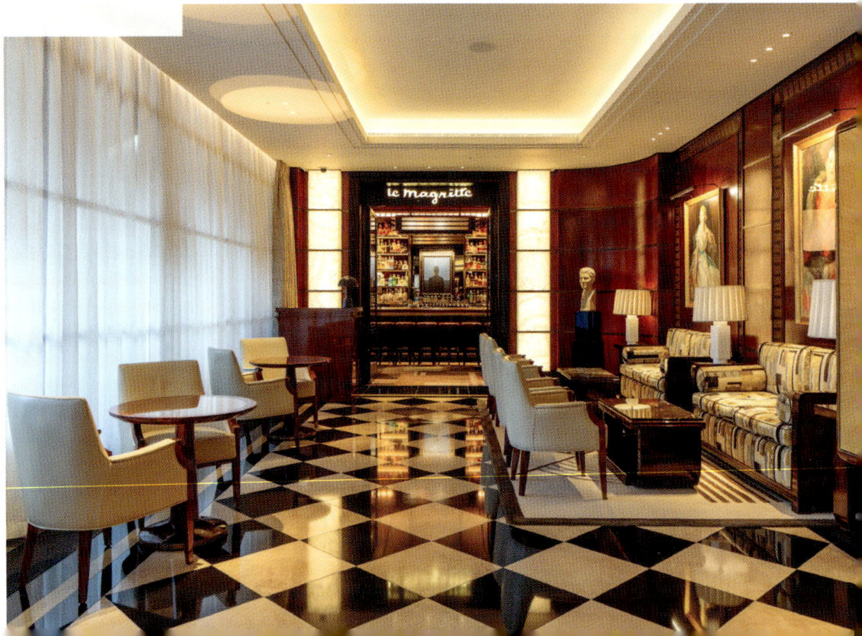

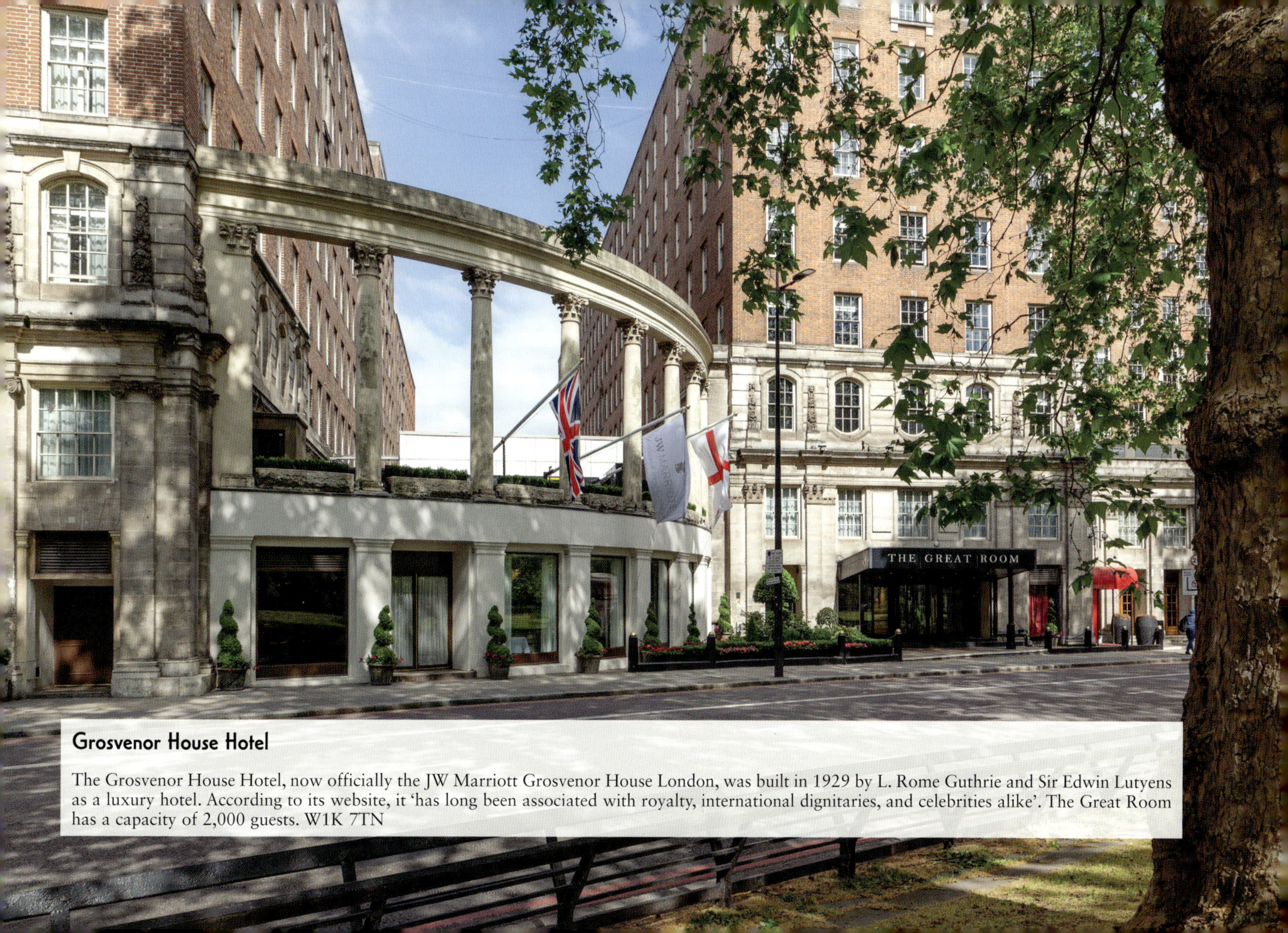

Grosvenor House Hotel

The Grosvenor House Hotel, now officially the JW Marriott Grosvenor House London, was built in 1929 by L. Rome Guthrie and Sir Edwin Lutyens as a luxury hotel. According to its website, it 'has long been associated with royalty, international dignitaries, and celebrities alike'. The Great Room has a capacity of 2,000 guests. W1K 7TN

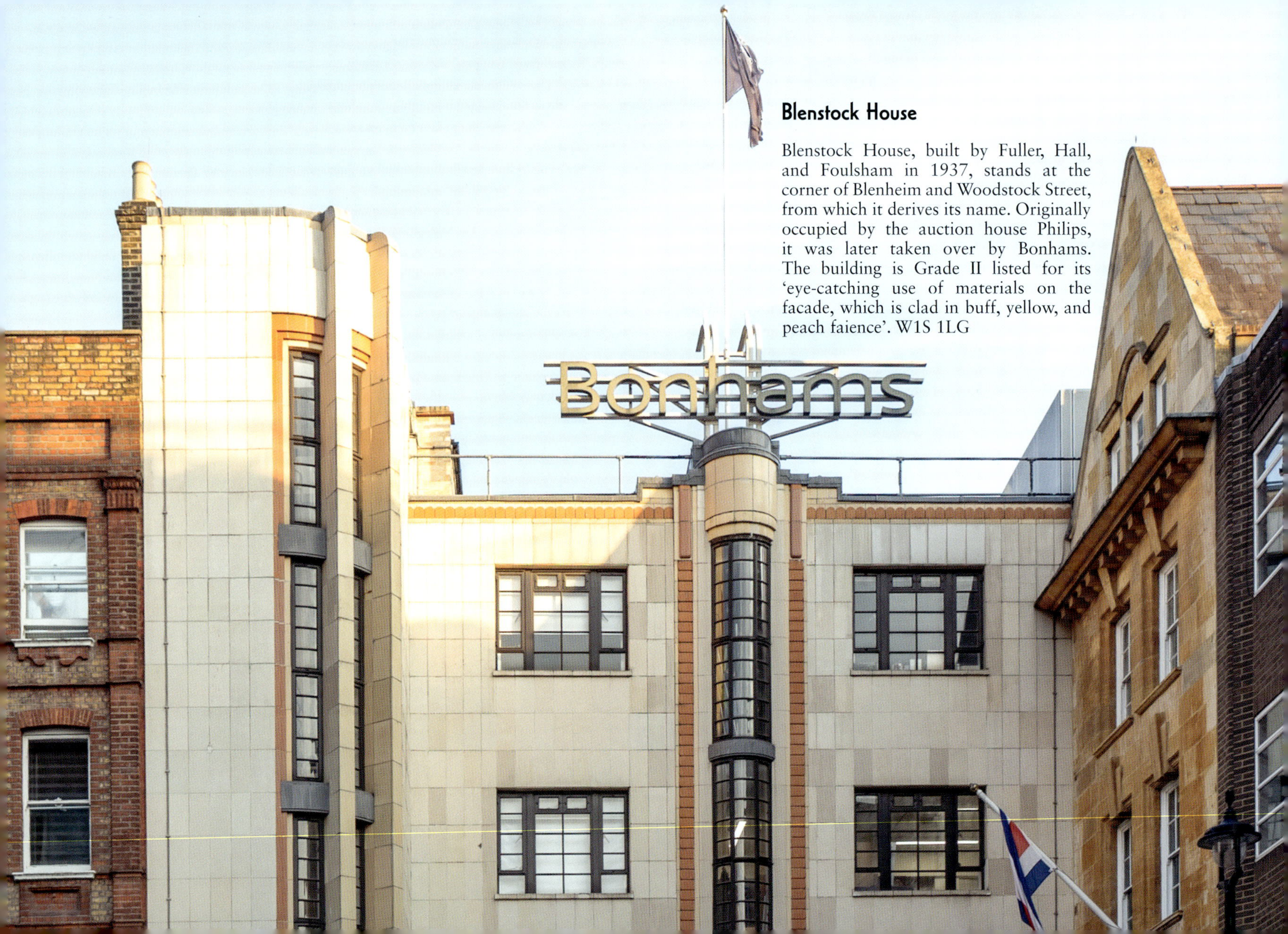

Blenstock House

Blenstock House, built by Fuller, Hall, and Foulsham in 1937, stands at the corner of Blenheim and Woodstock Street, from which it derives its name. Originally occupied by the auction house Philips, it was later taken over by Bonhams. The building is Grade II listed for its 'eye-catching use of materials on the facade, which is clad in buff, yellow, and peach faience'. W1S 1LG

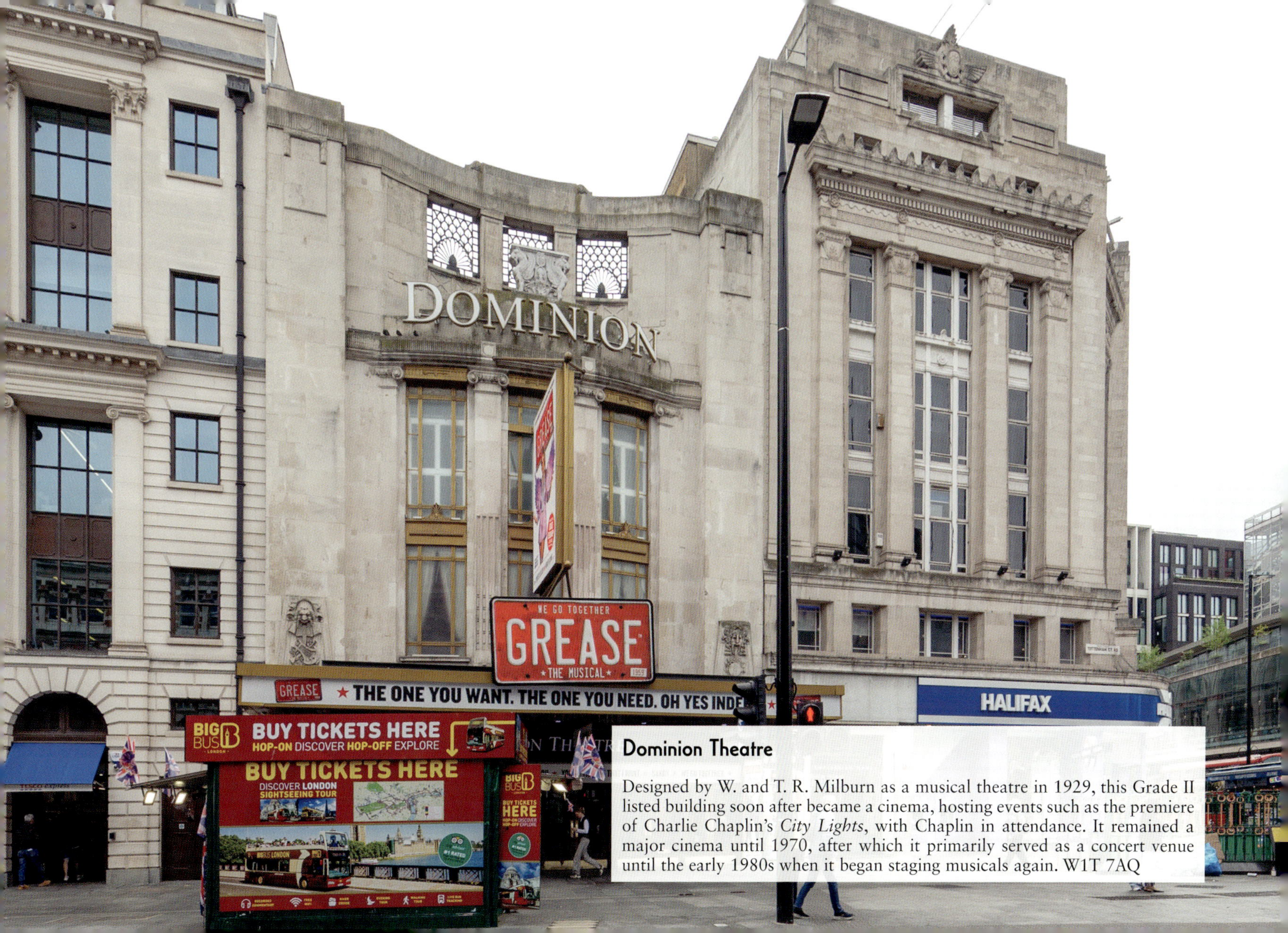

Dominion Theatre

Designed by W. and T. R. Milburn as a musical theatre in 1929, this Grade II listed building soon after became a cinema, hosting events such as the premiere of Charlie Chaplin's *City Lights*, with Chaplin in attendance. It remained a major cinema until 1970, after which it primarily served as a concert venue until the early 1980s when it began staging musicals again. W1T 7AQ

Queens

Originally built as the Queens Cinema, the building was designed by J. Stanley Beard and Clare. It opened in 1932 for W. C. Dawes' Modern Cinemas, a small independent cinema circuit. Over the years, it was managed by various cinema operators. Around the turn of the century, the building was repurposed as a TGI Fridays restaurant. In 2013, it was converted into flats, with the original Art Deco facade tastefully incorporated into the new development. W2 5AA

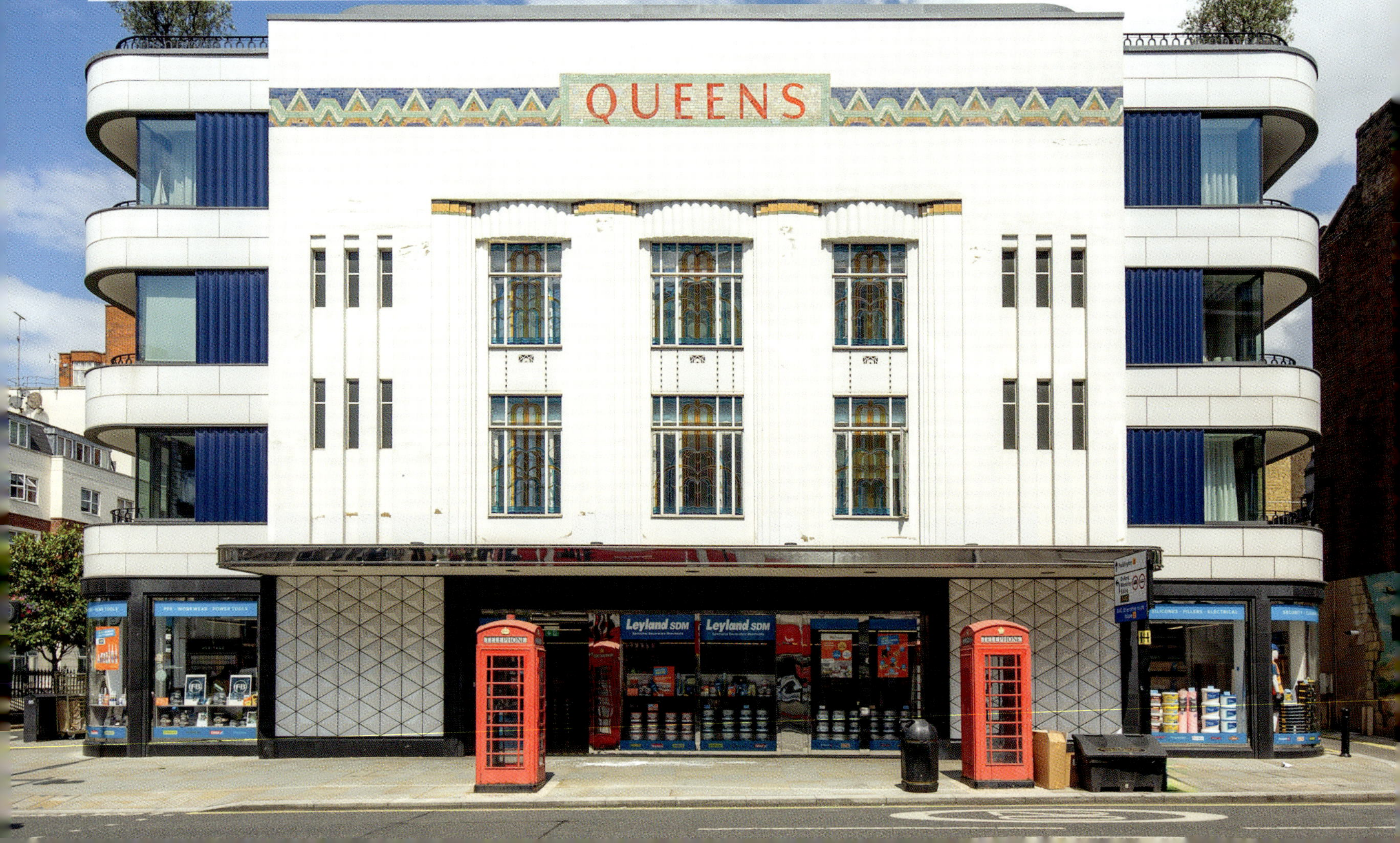

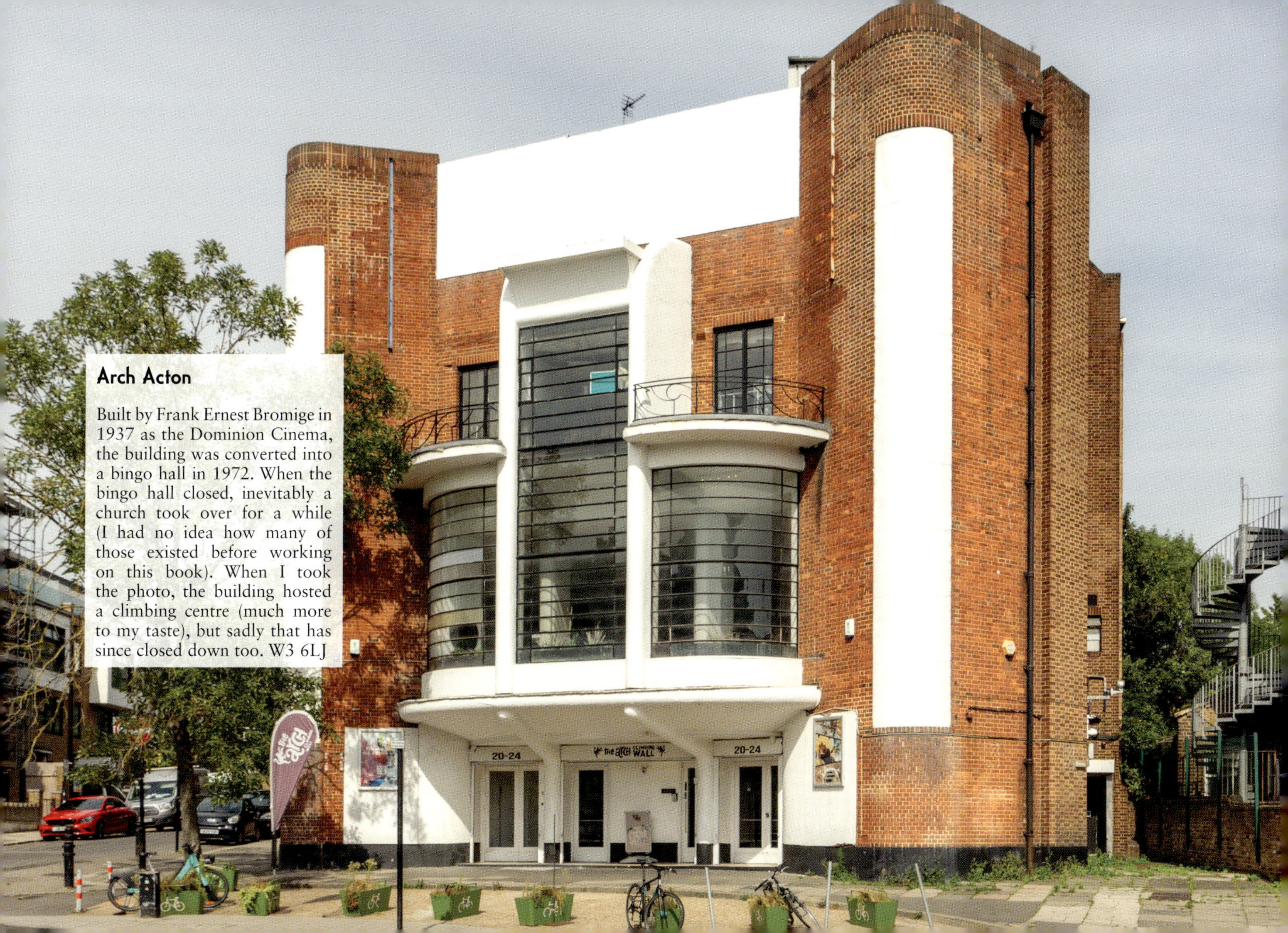

Arch Acton

Built by Frank Ernest Bromige in 1937 as the Dominion Cinema, the building was converted into a bingo hall in 1972. When the bingo hall closed, inevitably a church took over for a while (I had no idea how many of those existed before working on this book). When I took the photo, the building hosted a climbing centre (much more to my taste), but sadly that has since closed down too. W3 6LJ

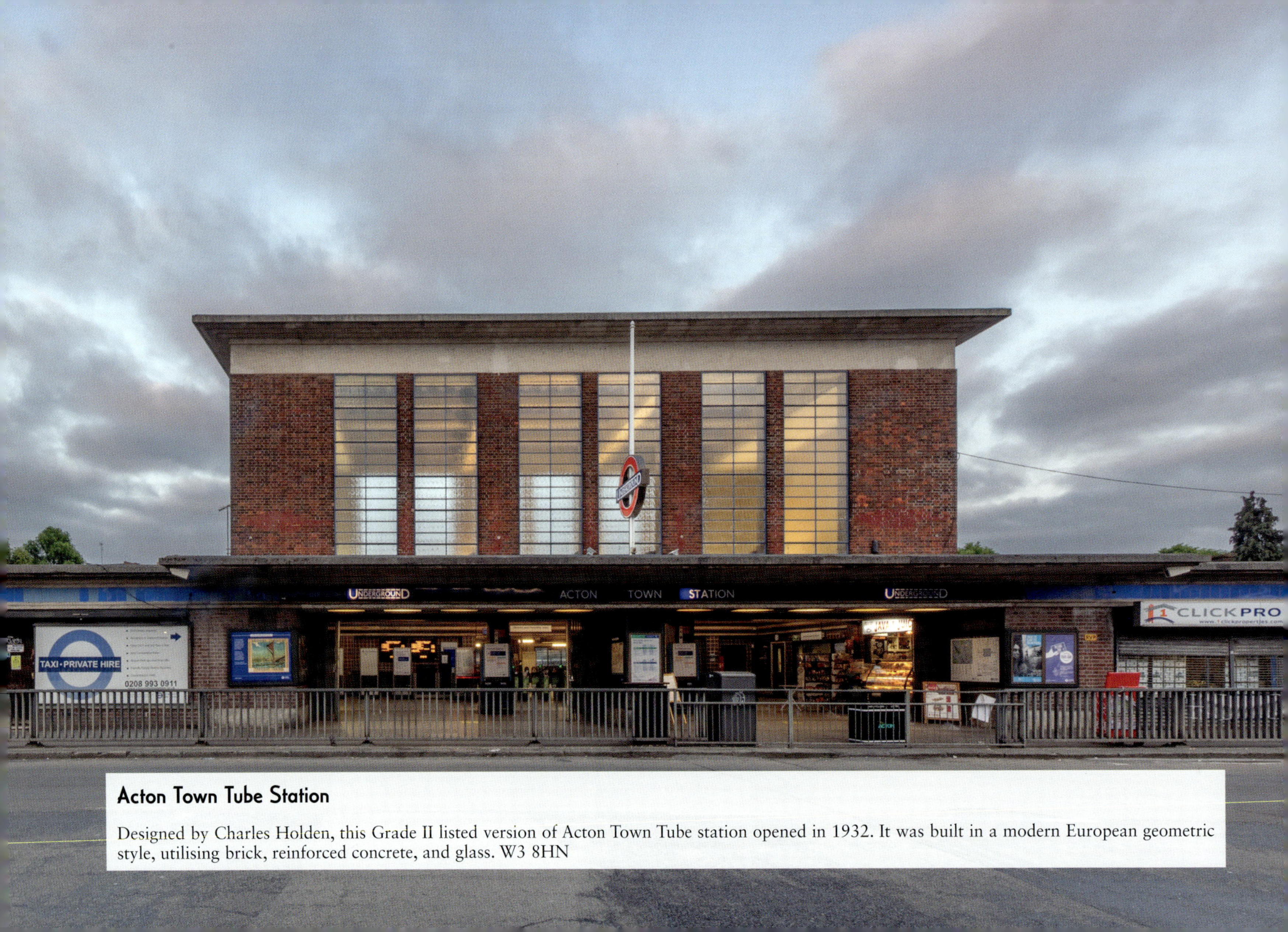

Acton Town Tube Station

Designed by Charles Holden, this Grade II listed version of Acton Town Tube station opened in 1932. It was built in a modern European geometric style, utilising brick, reinforced concrete, and glass. W3 8HN

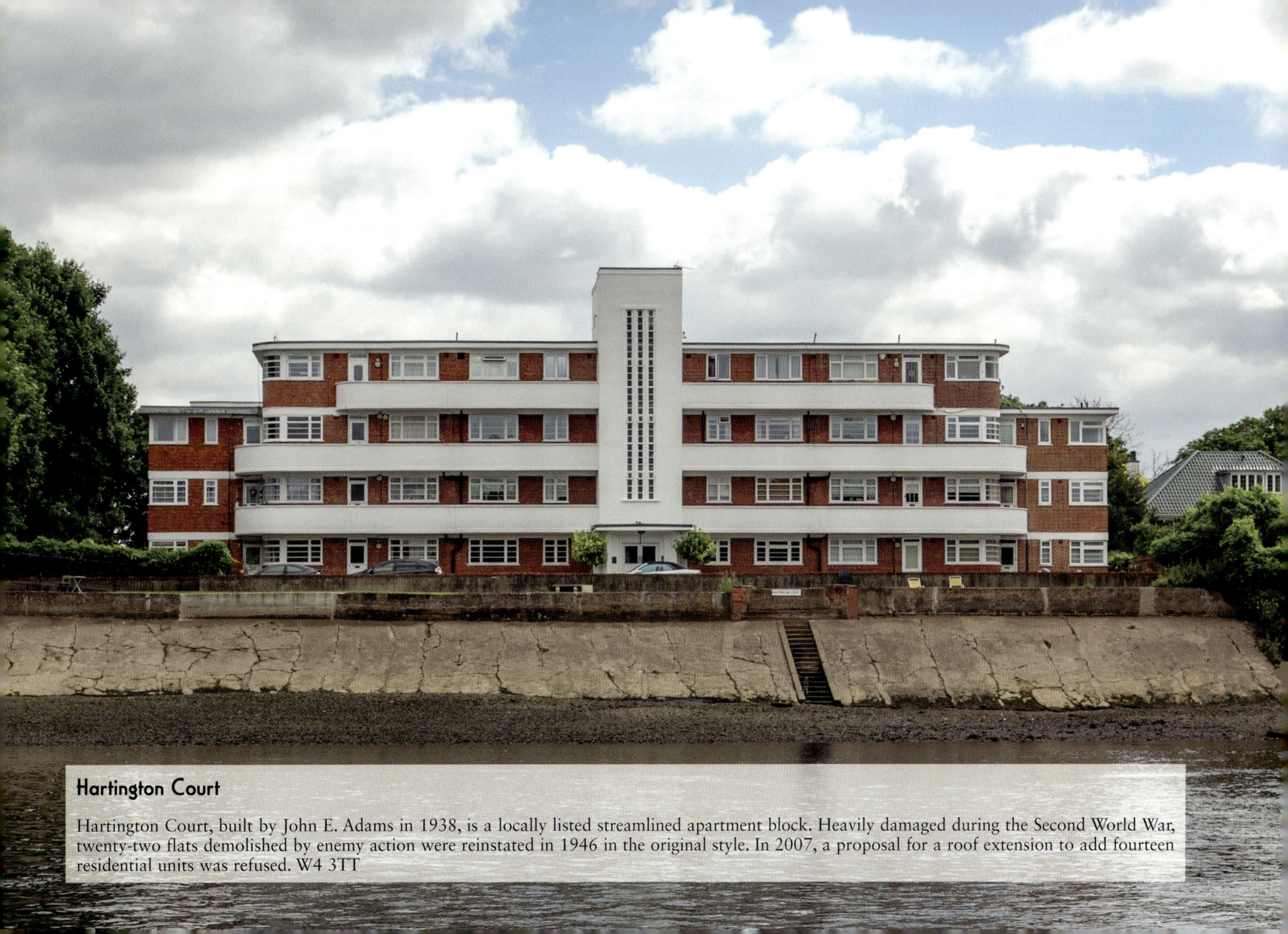

Hartington Court

Hartington Court, built by John E. Adams in 1938, is a locally listed streamlined apartment block. Heavily damaged during the Second World War, twenty-two flats demolished by enemy action were reinstated in 1946 in the original style. In 2007, a proposal for a roof extension to add fourteen residential units was refused. W4 3TT

Chiswick Park Station

It is said that Charles Holden drew inspiration from the Krumme Lanke station in Berlin for the design of the Grade II listed Chiswick Park Station. The station was built in 1933 to accommodate the western expansion of the Piccadilly line, although, ungratefully, the Piccadilly line never stopped there but runs straight through it. W4 5NE

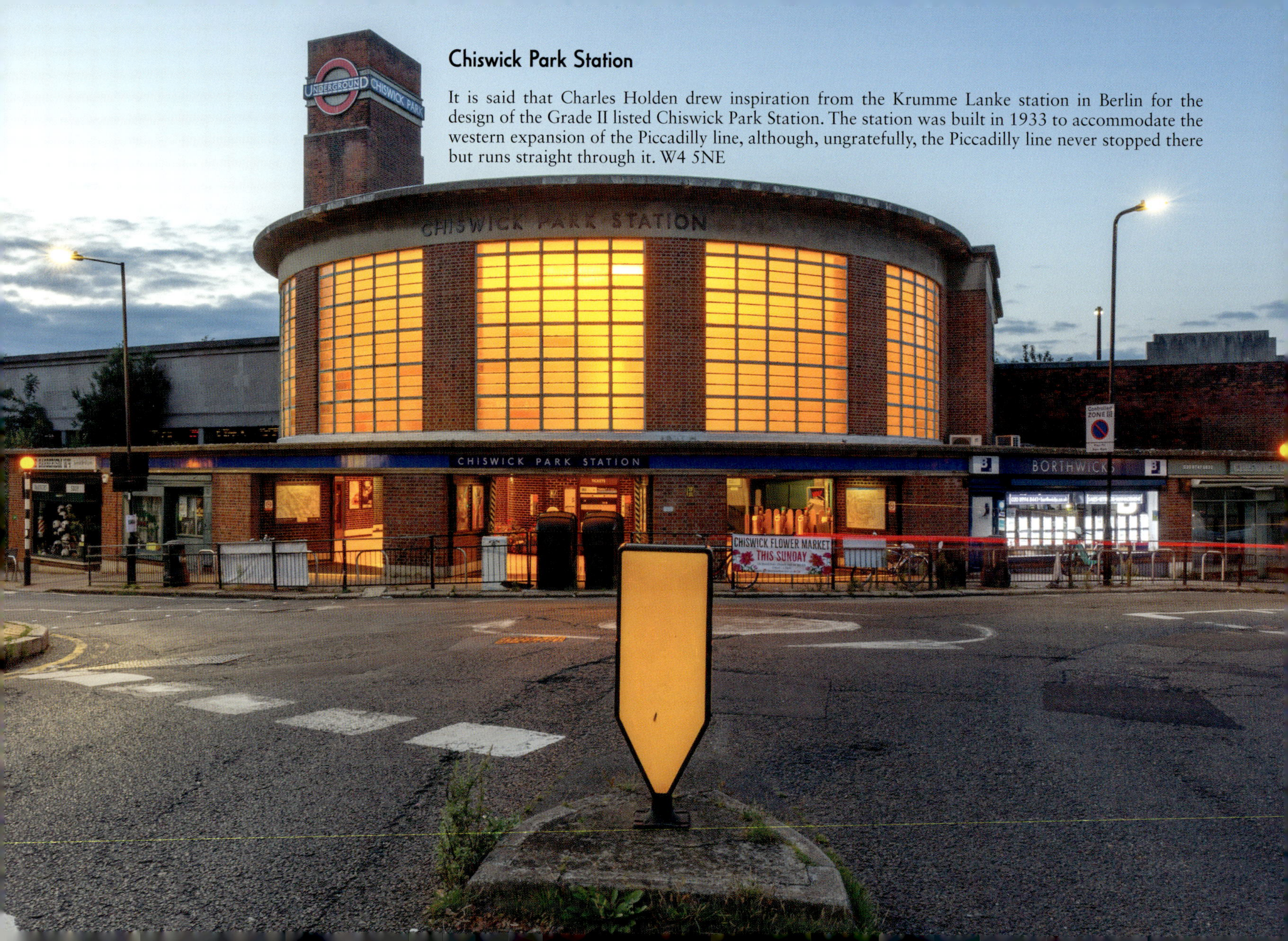

Park Royal Station

Designed by Herbert Welch and Felix Lander, the Grade II listed Park Royal Station opened in 1936 as part of the Piccadilly line's expansion. Felix Lander had previously collaborated with Charles Holden. W5 3EL

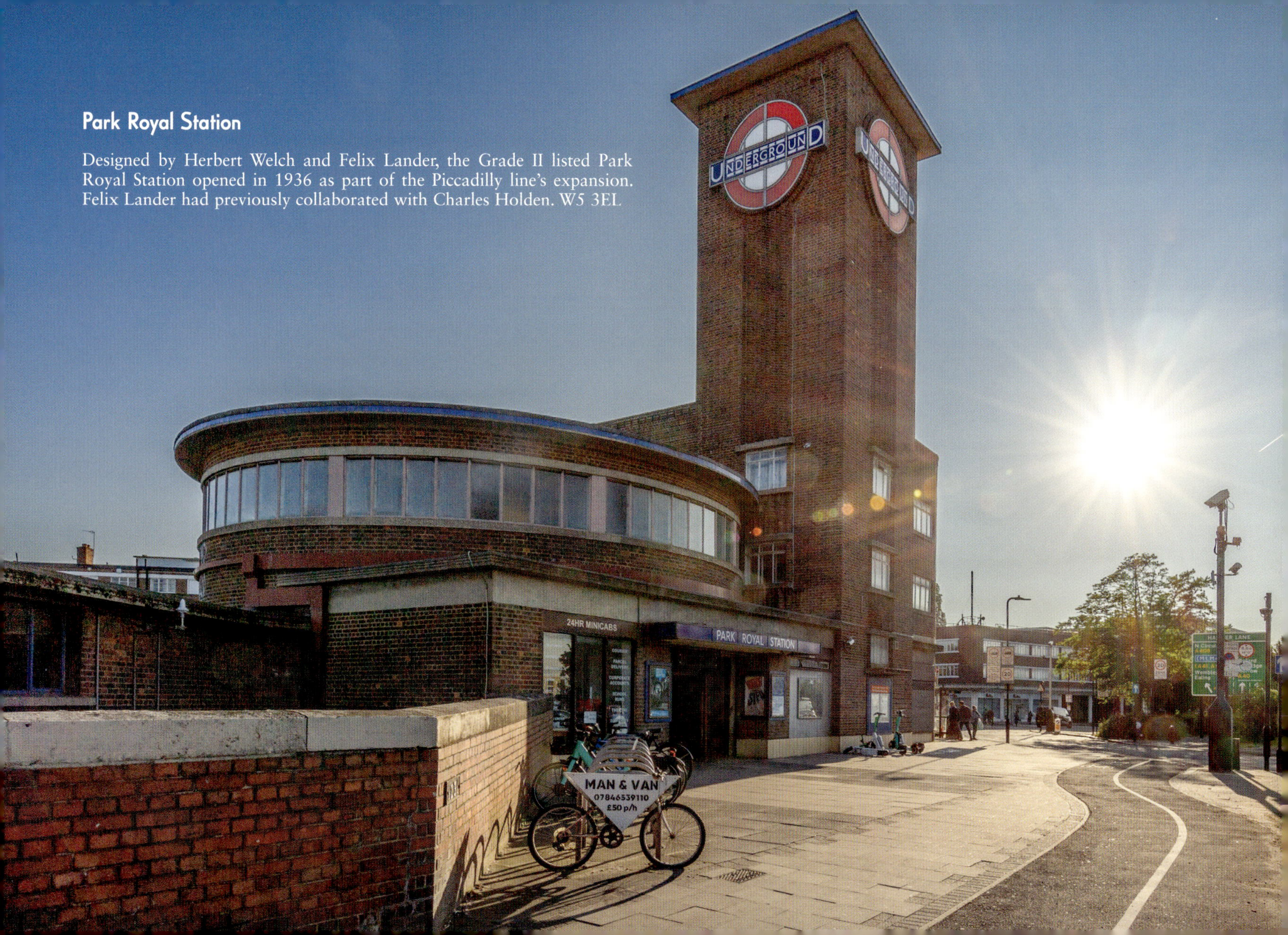

Ealing Common Station

Ealing Common Station, designed by Charles Holden, opened in 1931. This Grade II listed building features a distinctive heptagonal ticket hall. Holden's design philosophy emphasised that a building must be 'fit for purpose', a principle he consistently applied throughout his many projects. W5 3LD

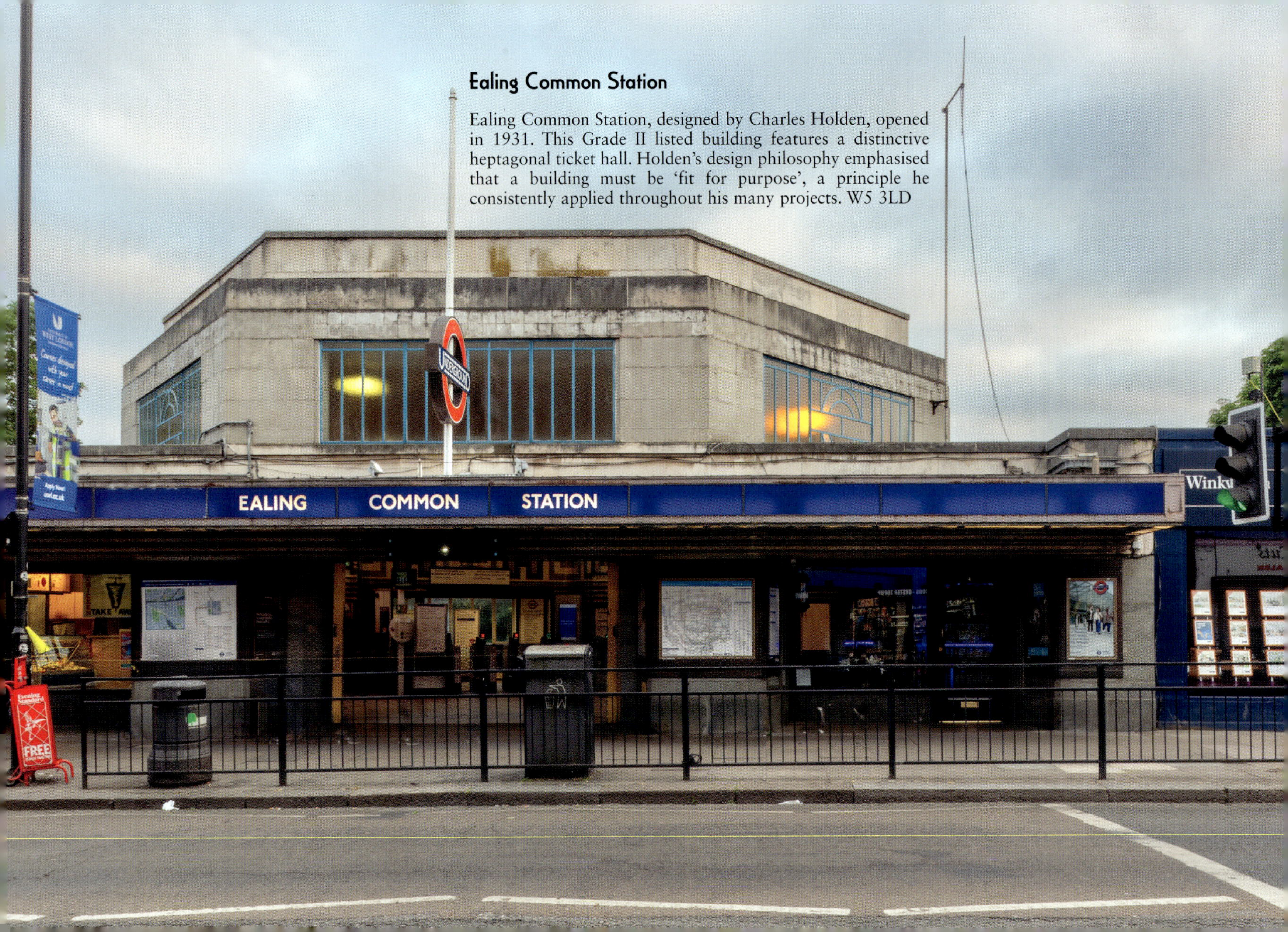

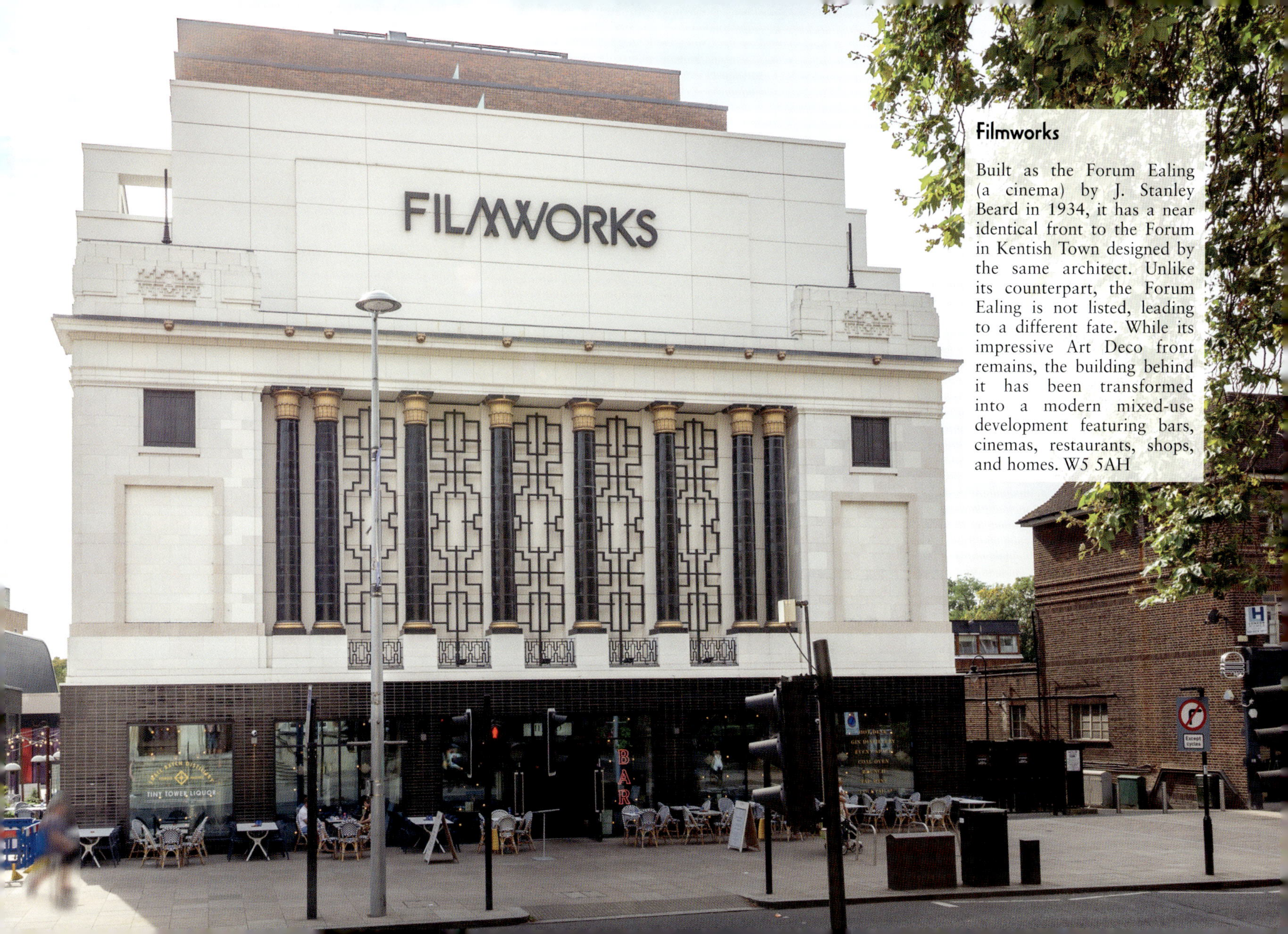

Filmworks

Built as the Forum Ealing (a cinema) by J. Stanley Beard in 1934, it has a near identical front to the Forum in Kentish Town designed by the same architect. Unlike its counterpart, the Forum Ealing is not listed, leading to a different fate. While its impressive Art Deco front remains, the building behind it has been transformed into a modern mixed-use development featuring bars, cinemas, restaurants, shops, and homes. W5 5AH

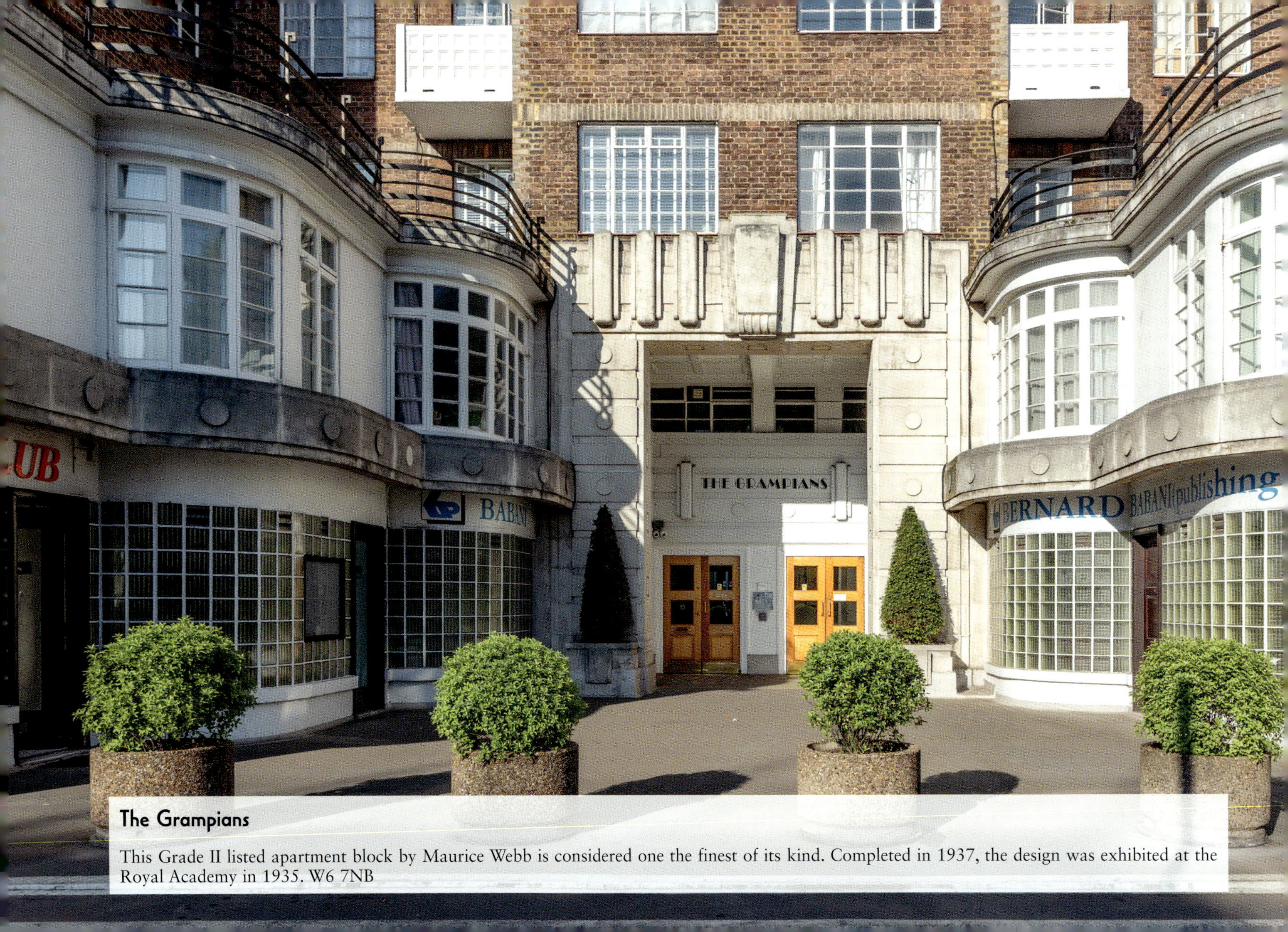

The Grampians

This Grade II listed apartment block by Maurice Webb is considered one the finest of its kind. Completed in 1937, the design was exhibited at the Royal Academy in 1935. W6 7NB

Hammersmith Apollo

Currently known as the Eventim Apollo, this iconic venue was originally built as the Gaumont Palace Cinema in 1932, designed by Robert Cromie. Over the years, it has undergone numerous name changes based on its sponsors. This Grade II* listed building is now one of London's premier live venues for bands and comedians, with many live albums recorded there. It's a shame I didn't have my camera with me when I was among the 5,000 lucky people who got a £10 ticket for AC/DC in 2002. W6 9QH

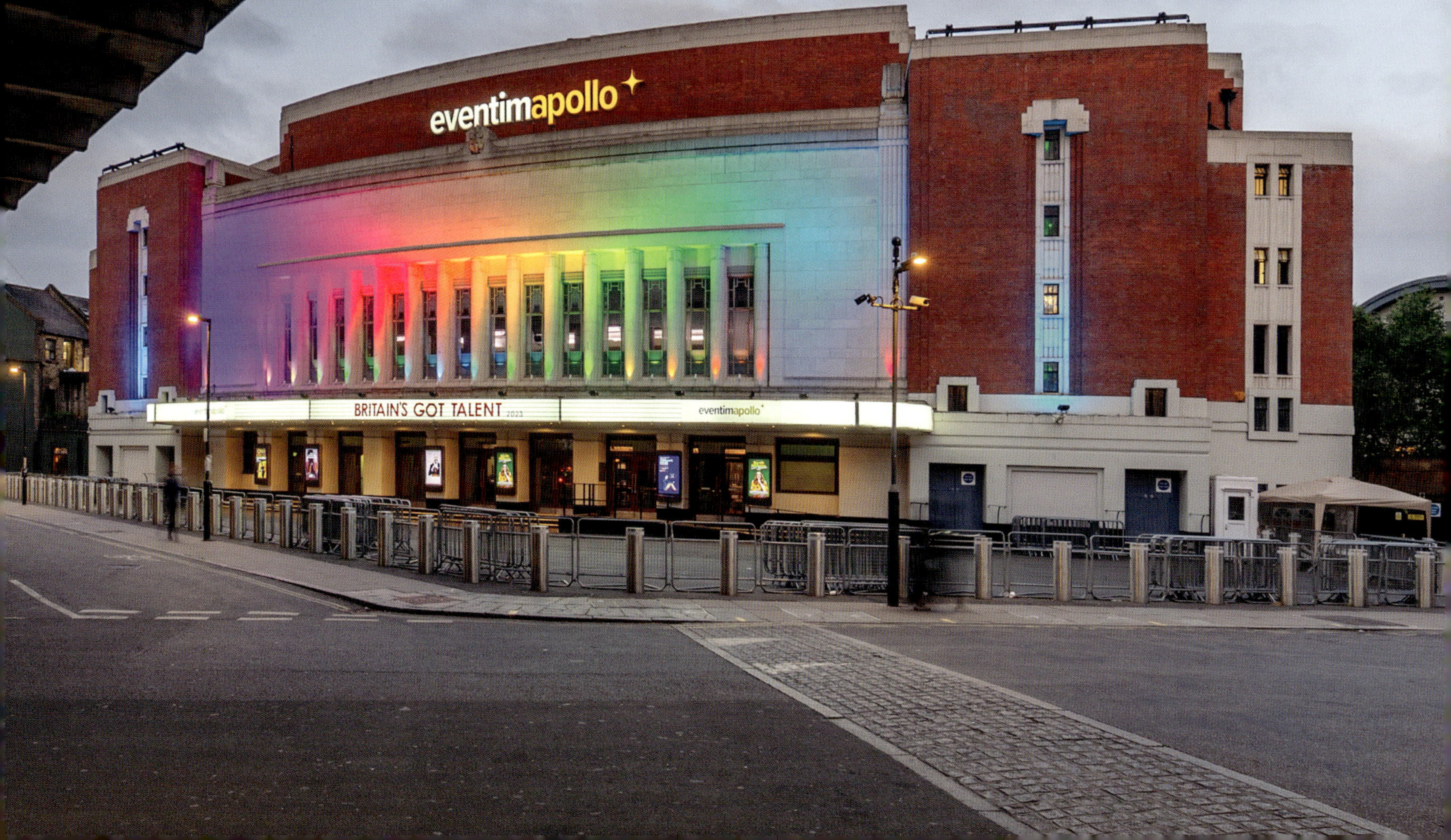

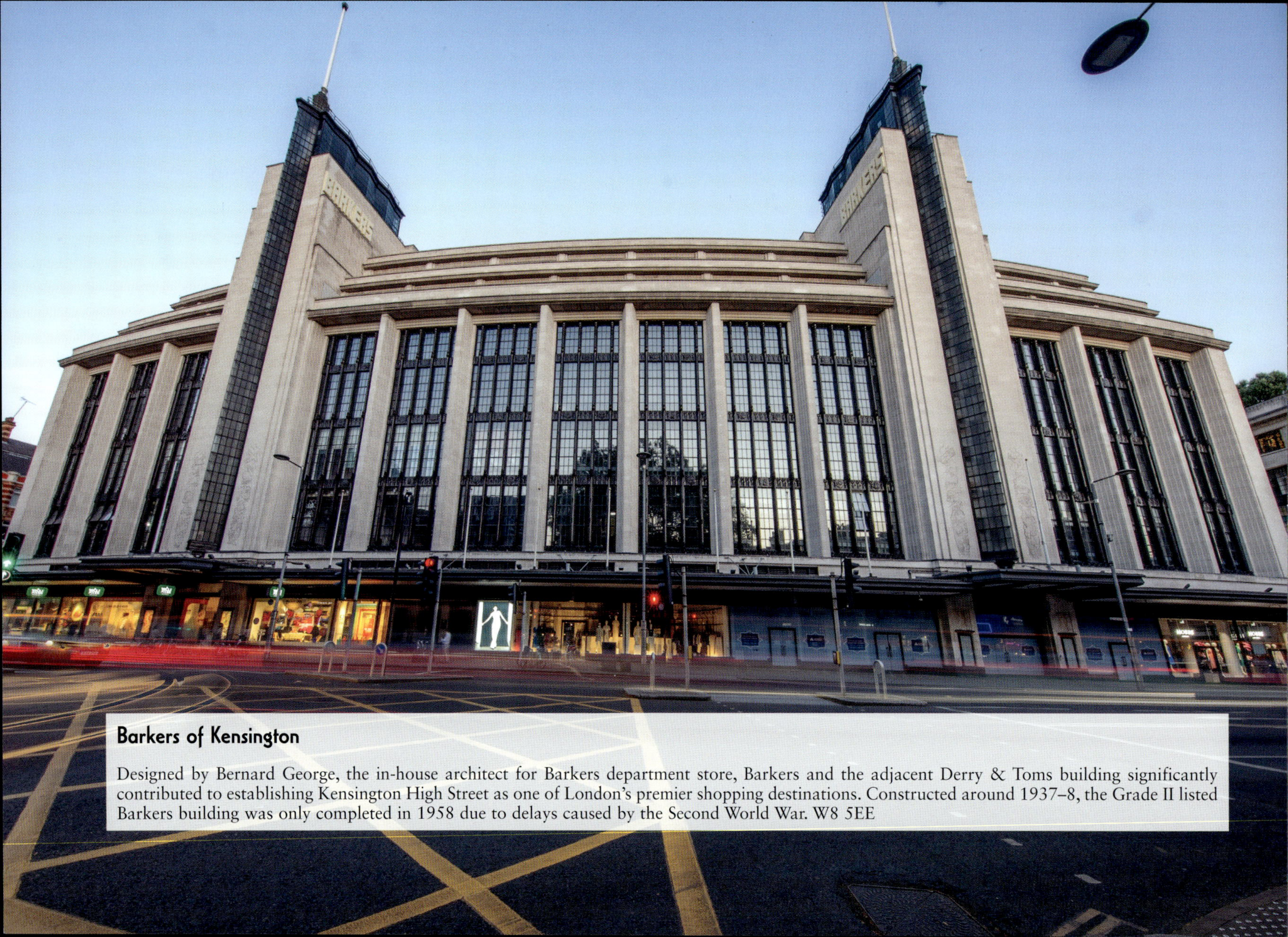

Barkers of Kensington

Designed by Bernard George, the in-house architect for Barkers department store, Barkers and the adjacent Derry & Toms building significantly contributed to establishing Kensington High Street as one of London's premier shopping destinations. Constructed around 1937–8, the Grade II listed Barkers building was only completed in 1958 due to delays caused by the Second World War. W8 5EE

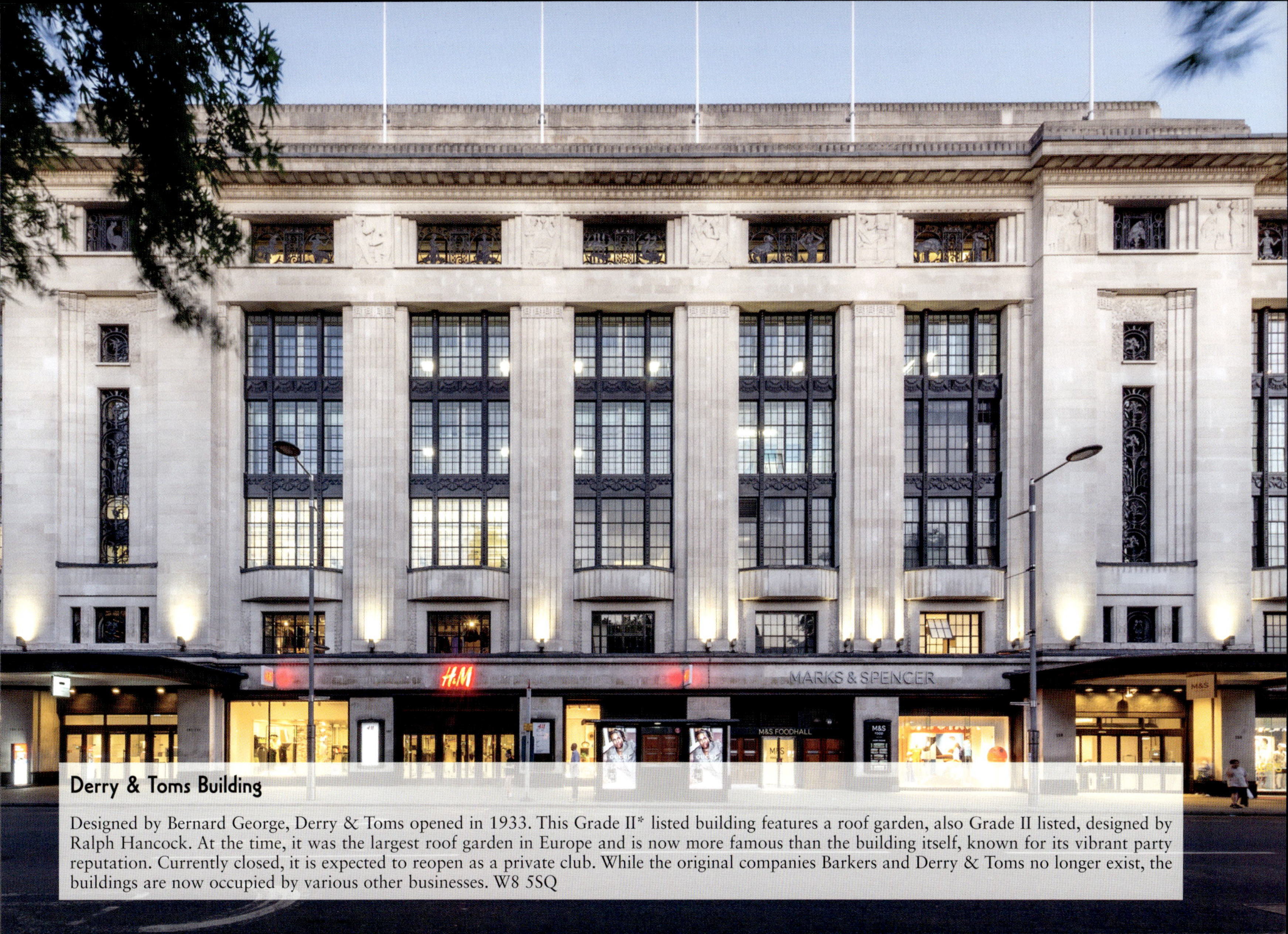

Derry & Toms Building

Designed by Bernard George, Derry & Toms opened in 1933. This Grade II* listed building features a roof garden, also Grade II listed, designed by Ralph Hancock. At the time, it was the largest roof garden in Europe and is now more famous than the building itself, known for its vibrant party reputation. Currently closed, it is expected to reopen as a private club. While the original companies Barkers and Derry & Toms no longer exist, the buildings are now occupied by various other businesses. W8 5SQ

Olympia Central

Olympia Central, originally built as the Empire Hall in 1929 by Joseph Emberton, is a Grade II listed building. It was the first four-storey exhibition building ever constructed in the UK. W14 8UX

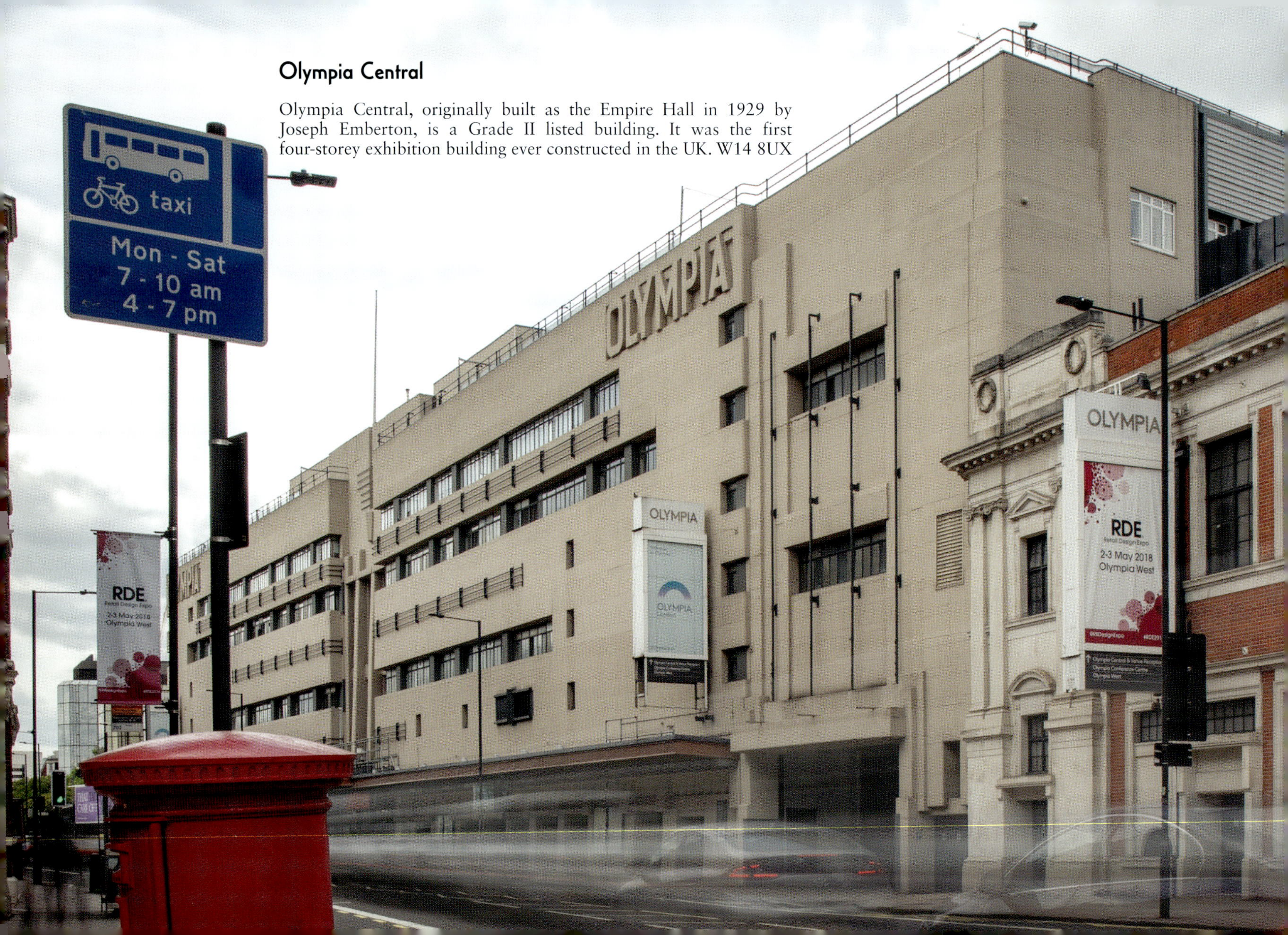

Senate House

The Senate House, home to the University of London, was built to reflect the university's status as the largest in the UK by student numbers. Unlike medieval universities, the brief called for a modern design. Charles Holden designed this Grade II* listed building, originally planned to be even larger. However, due to funding constraints, it was completed in 1937 in its current form. WC1E 7HU

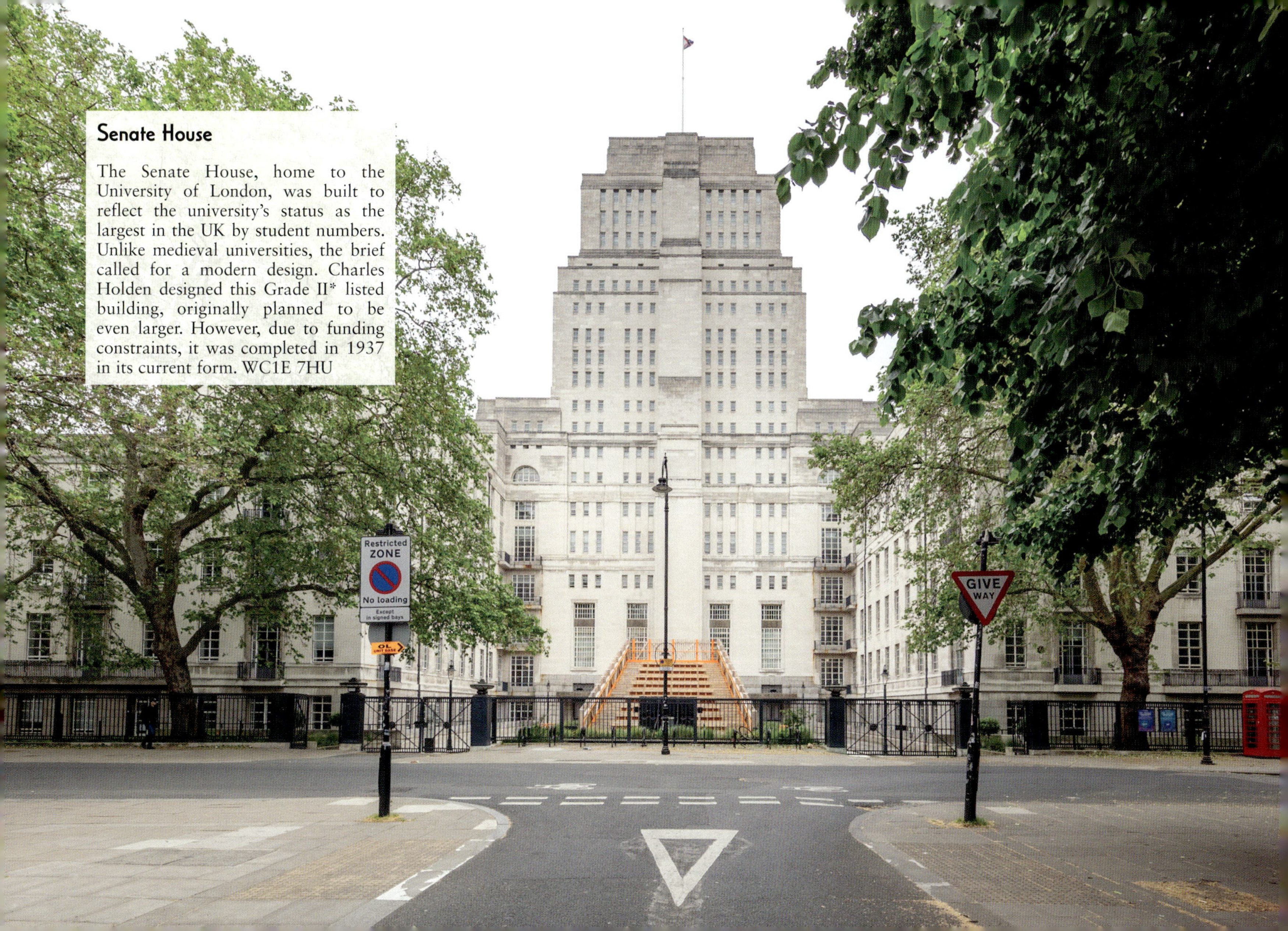

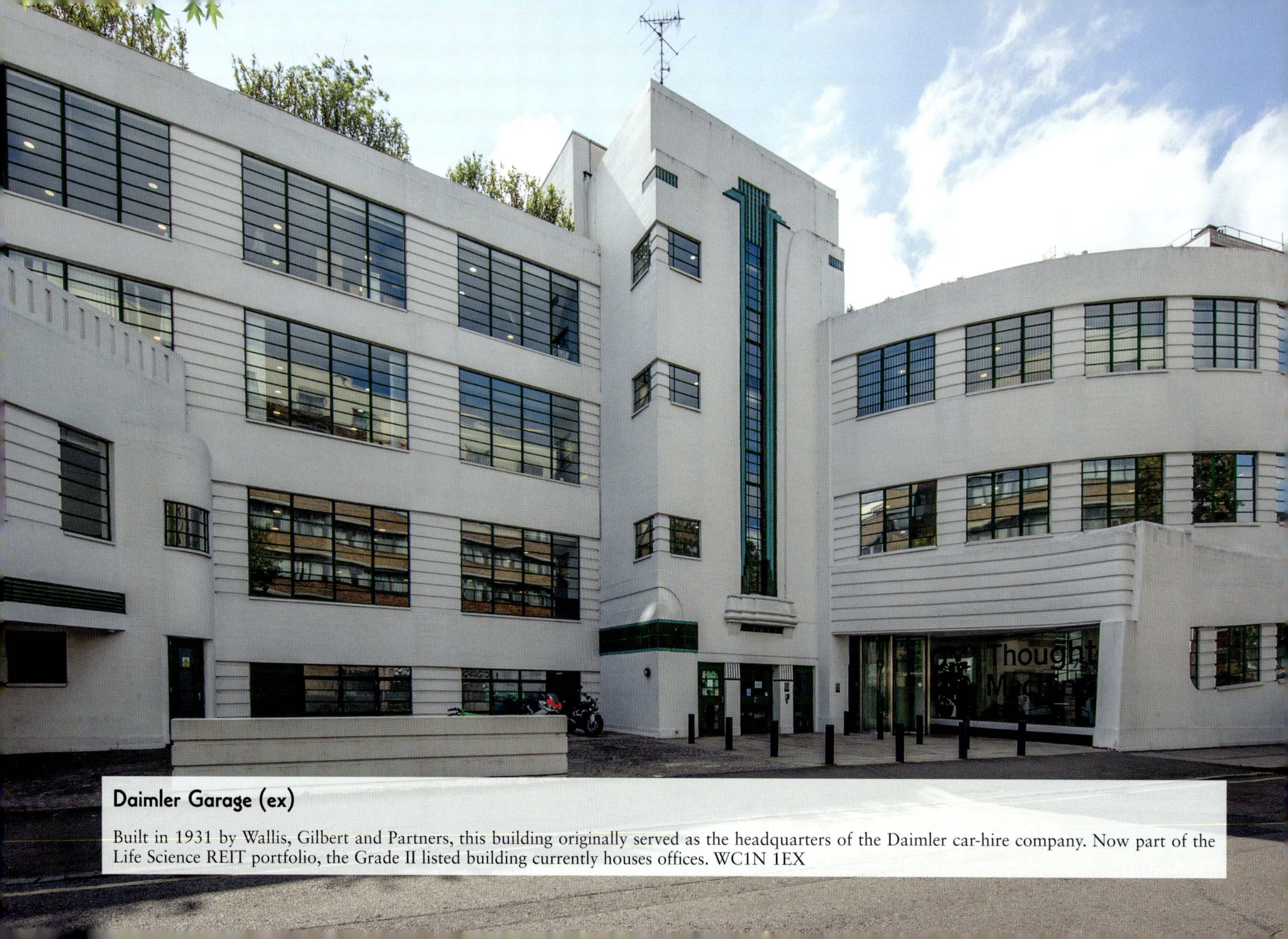

Daimler Garage (ex)

Built in 1931 by Wallis, Gilbert and Partners, this building originally served as the headquarters of the Daimler car-hire company. Now part of the Life Science REIT portfolio, the Grade II listed building currently houses offices. WC1N 1EX

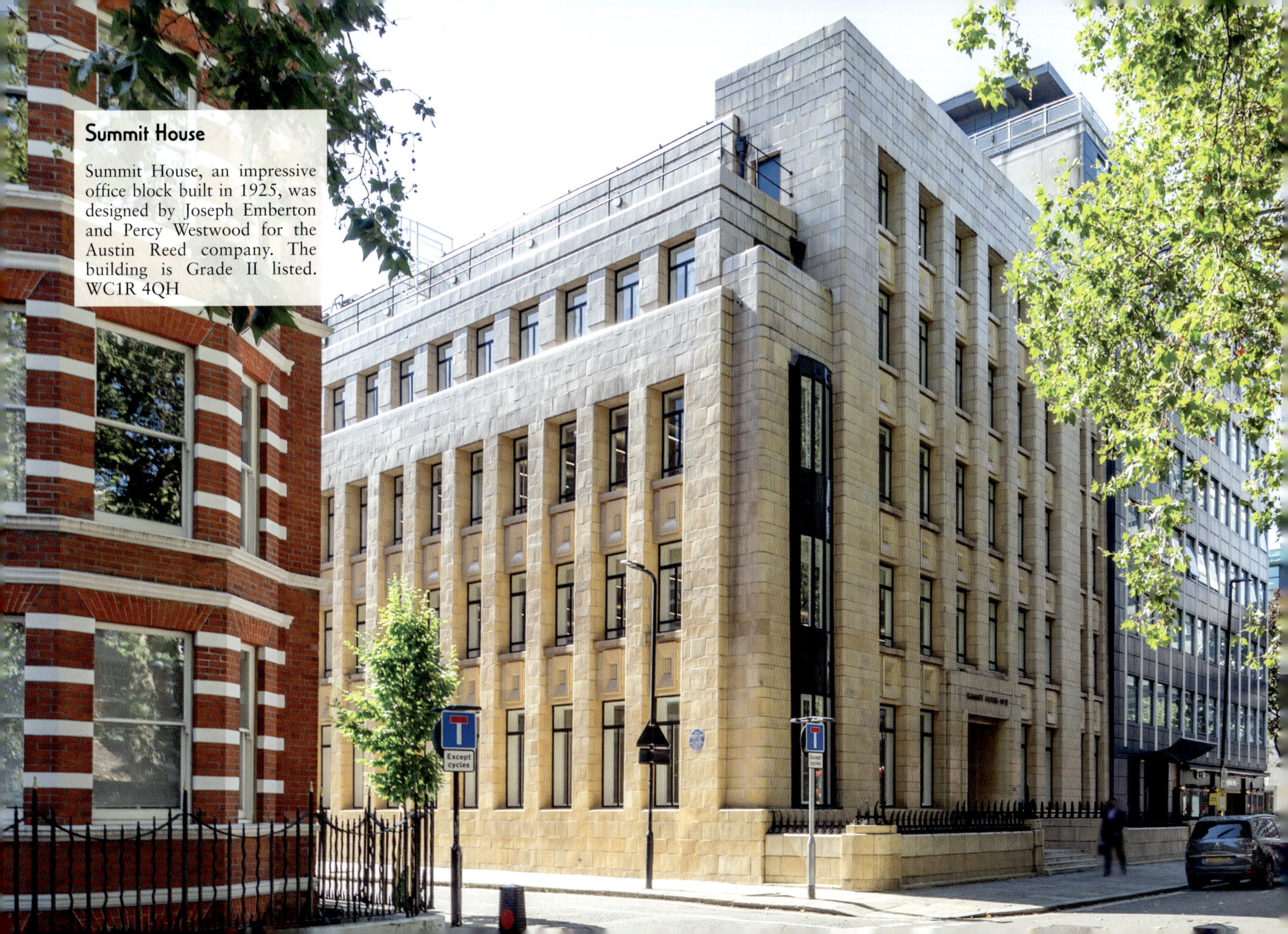

Summit House

Summit House, an impressive office block built in 1925, was designed by Joseph Emberton and Percy Westwood for the Austin Reed company. The building is Grade II listed. WC1R 4QH

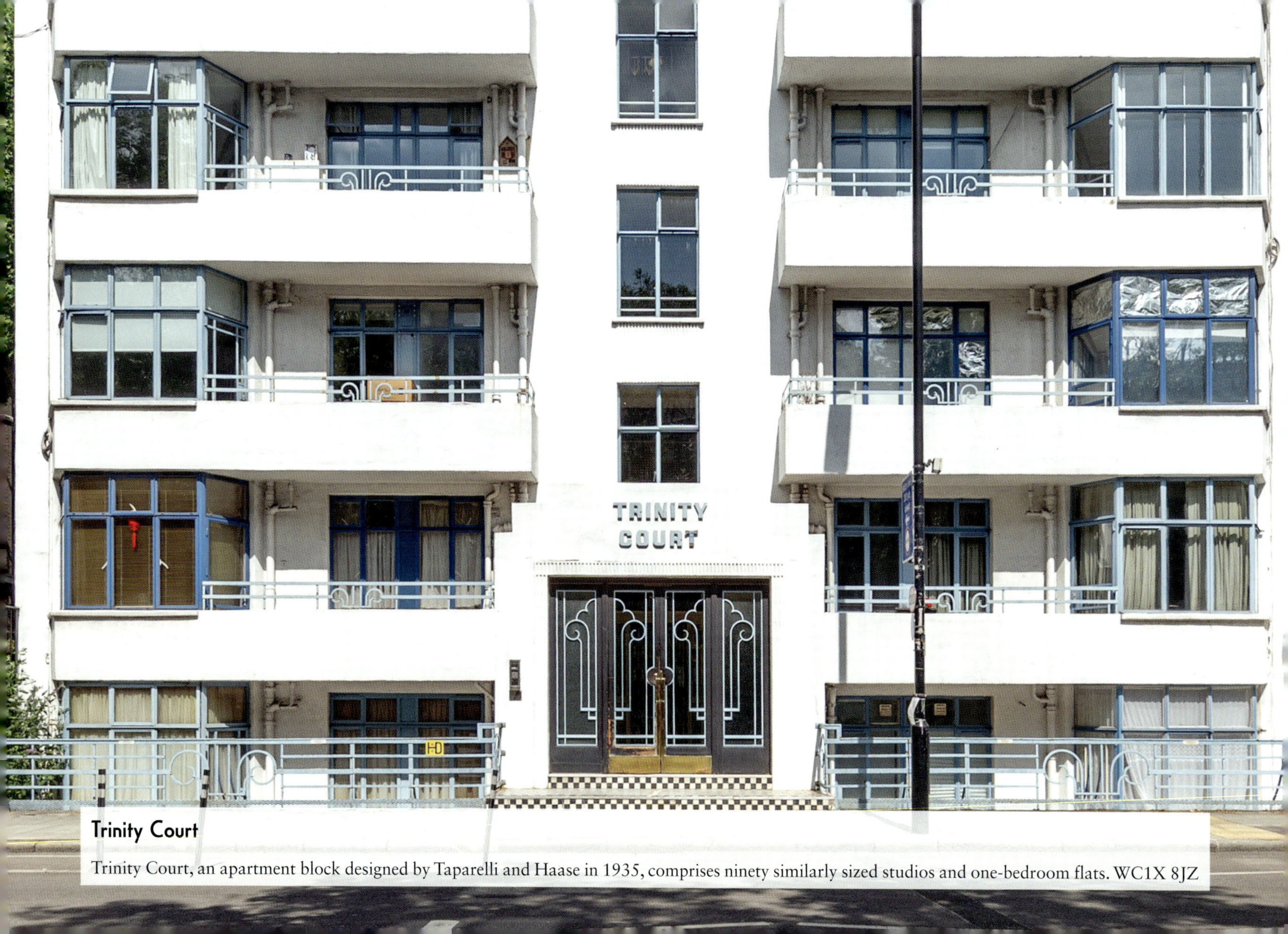

Trinity Court

Trinity Court, an apartment block designed by Taparelli and Haase in 1935, comprises ninety similarly sized studios and one-bedroom flats. WC1X 8JZ

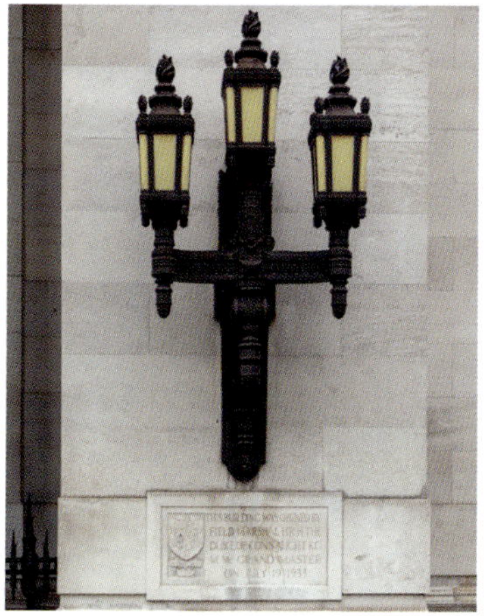

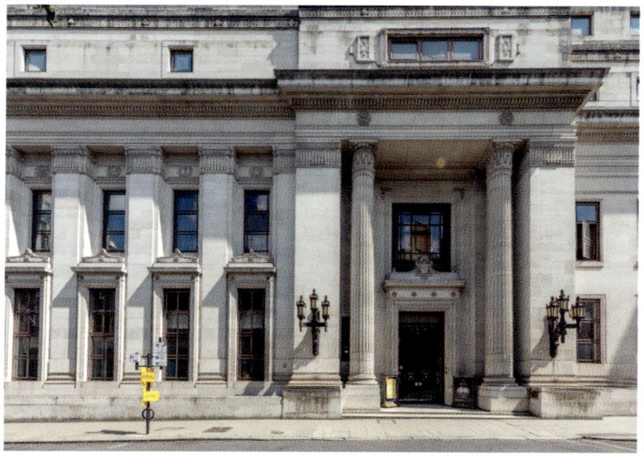

Freemasons' Hall

The Freemasons' Hall, designed by H. V. Ashley and Winton Newman, was built in 1933. This impressive Grade II* listed building covers 2.25 acres and serves as the headquarters of the United Grand Lodge of England, famously known for its secret handshakes. WC2B 5AZ

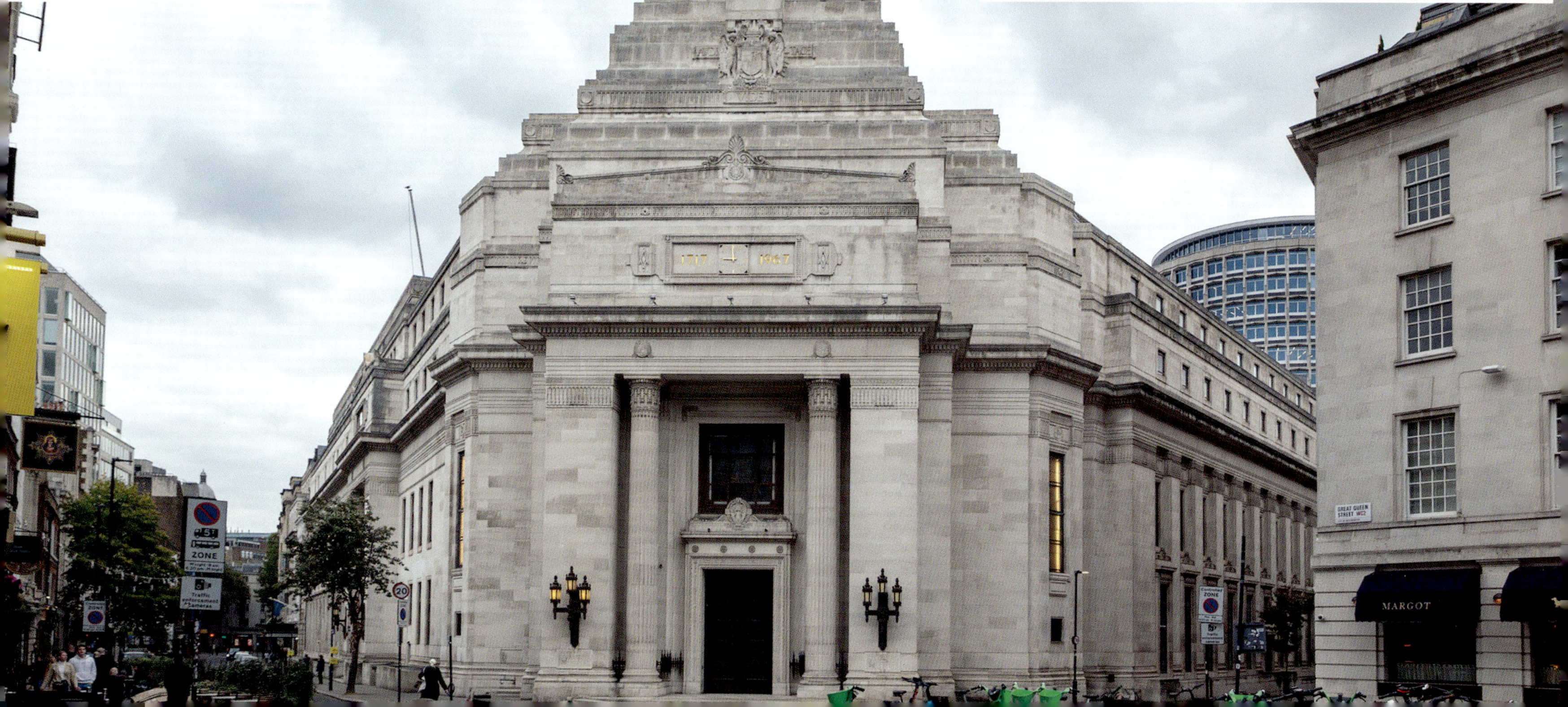

Fortune Theatre

Designed by Ernest Schaufelberg, the Grade II listed Fortune Theatre was built between 1922 and 1924, making it the first theatre erected in Britain after the First World War. With the original Wembley Stadium demolished, it now stands as the oldest public building in Britain designed entirely with a textured and exposed concrete facade. High above the entrance is a figurine of Terpsichore, the goddess of dance and chorus, designed by M. H. Crichton. WC2B 5HH

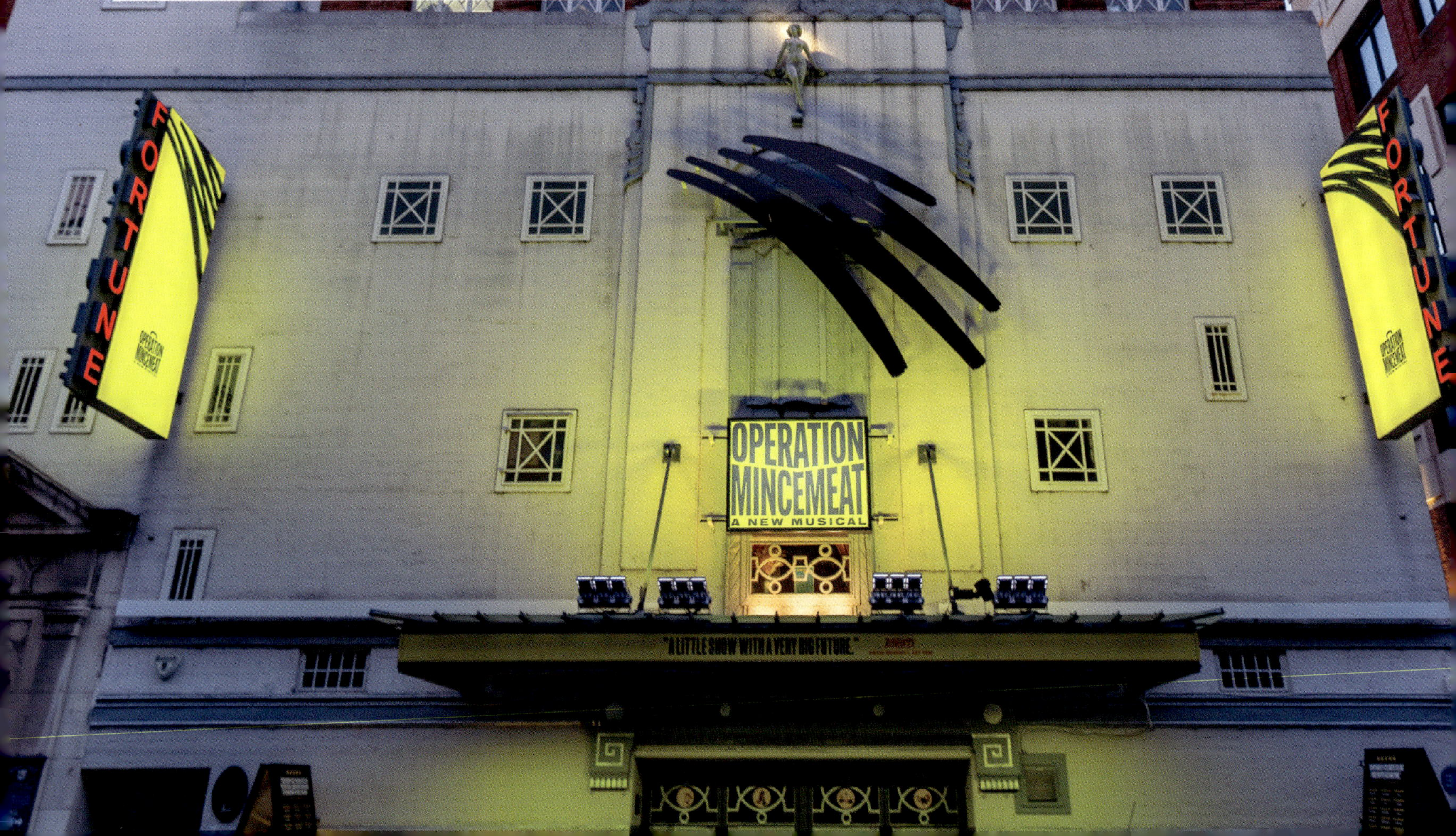

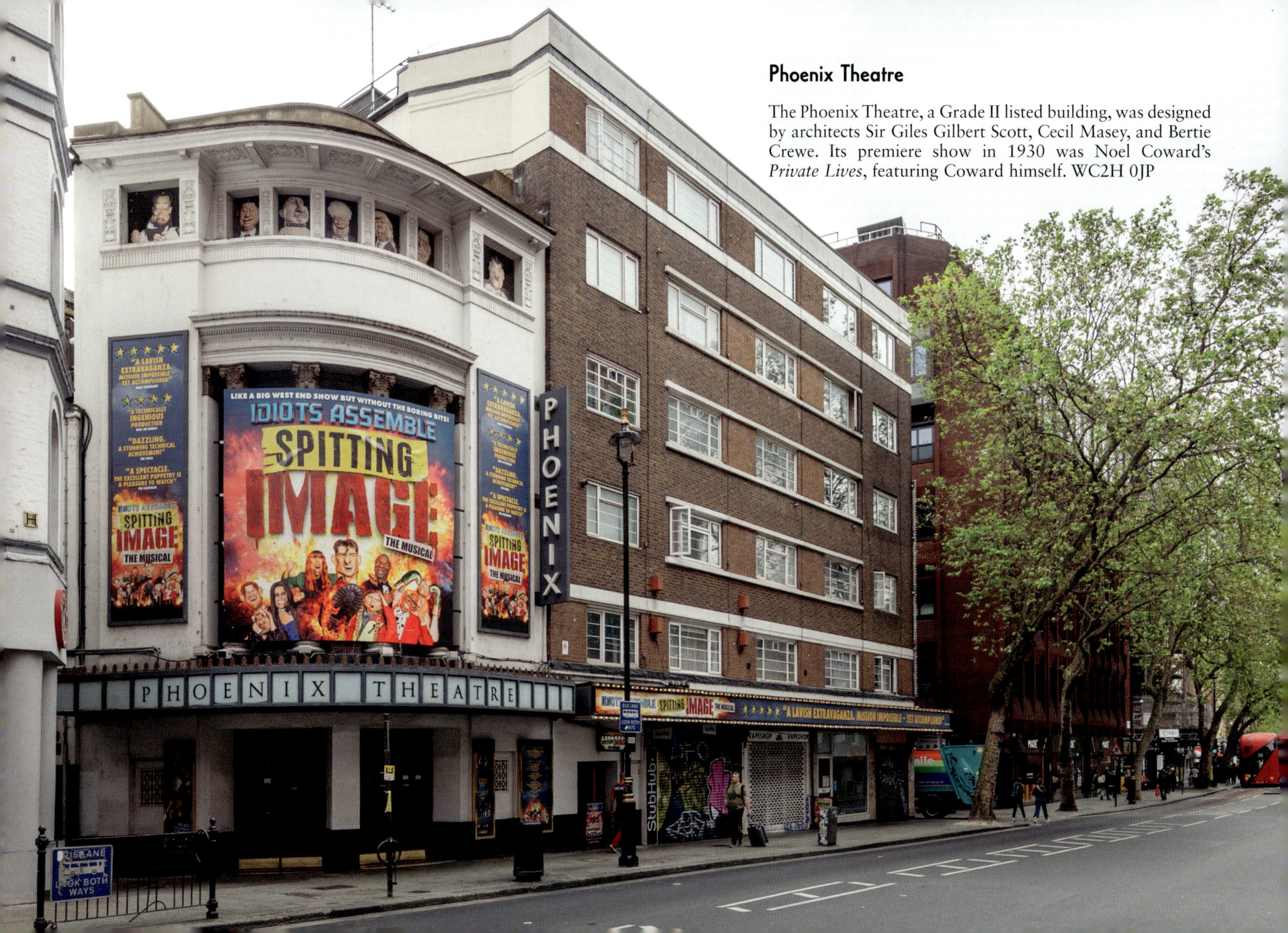

Phoenix Theatre

The Phoenix Theatre, a Grade II listed building, was designed by architects Sir Giles Gilbert Scott, Cecil Masey, and Bertie Crewe. Its premiere show in 1930 was Noel Coward's *Private Lives*, featuring Coward himself. WC2H 0JP

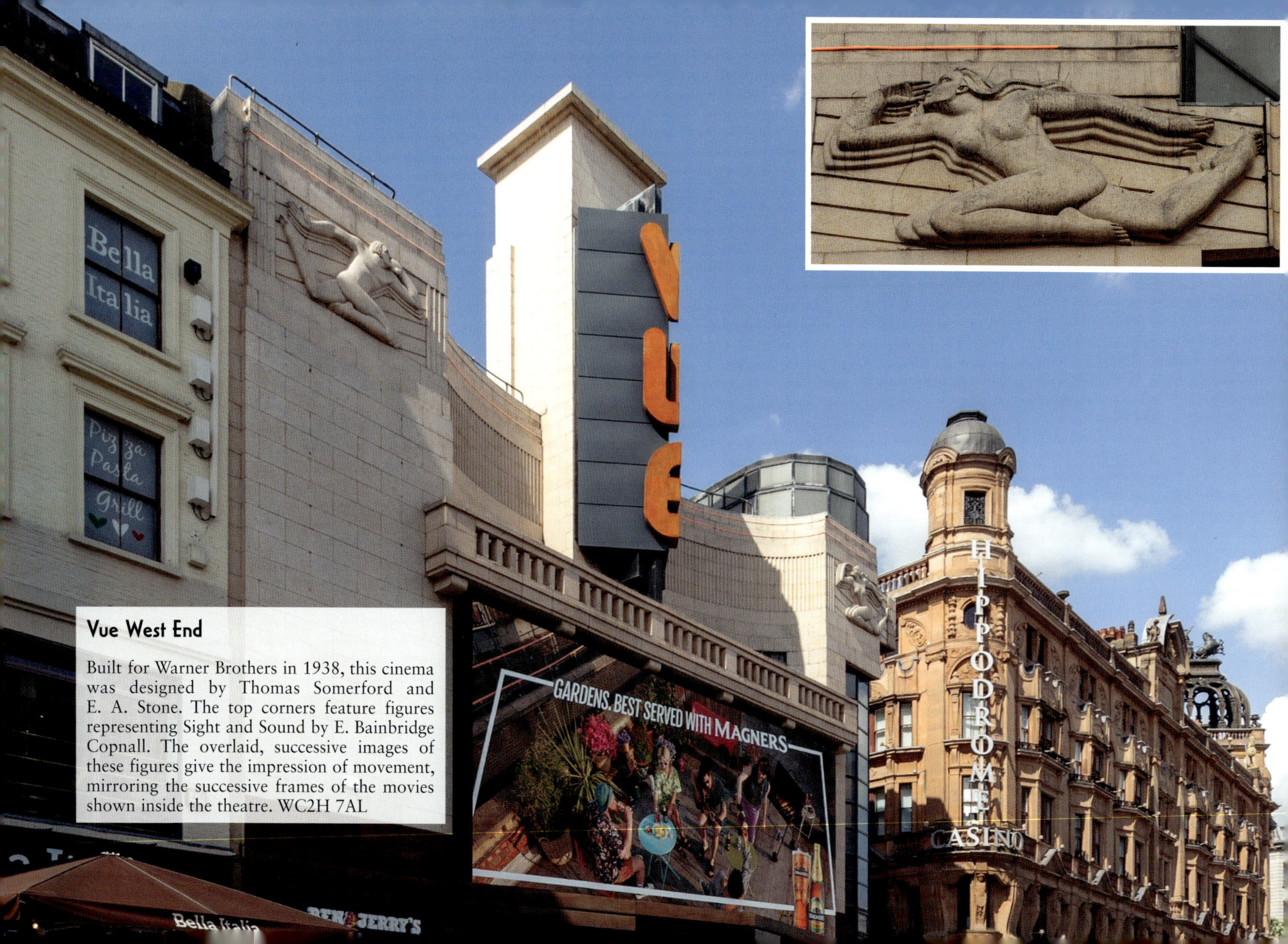

Vue West End

Built for Warner Brothers in 1938, this cinema was designed by Thomas Somerford and E. A. Stone. The top corners feature figures representing Sight and Sound by E. Bainbridge Copnall. The overlaid, successive images of these figures give the impression of movement, mirroring the successive frames of the movies shown inside the theatre. WC2H 7AL

Odeon Luxe Leicester Square

The Odeon Luxe on Leicester Square, built in 1937 for Oscar Deutsch's Odeon cinema chain, was designed by Harry Weedon and Andrew Mather. Intended as the flagship cinema for Odeon, it continues to hold this prestigious position today, hosting numerous European and world premieres. WC2H 7LQ

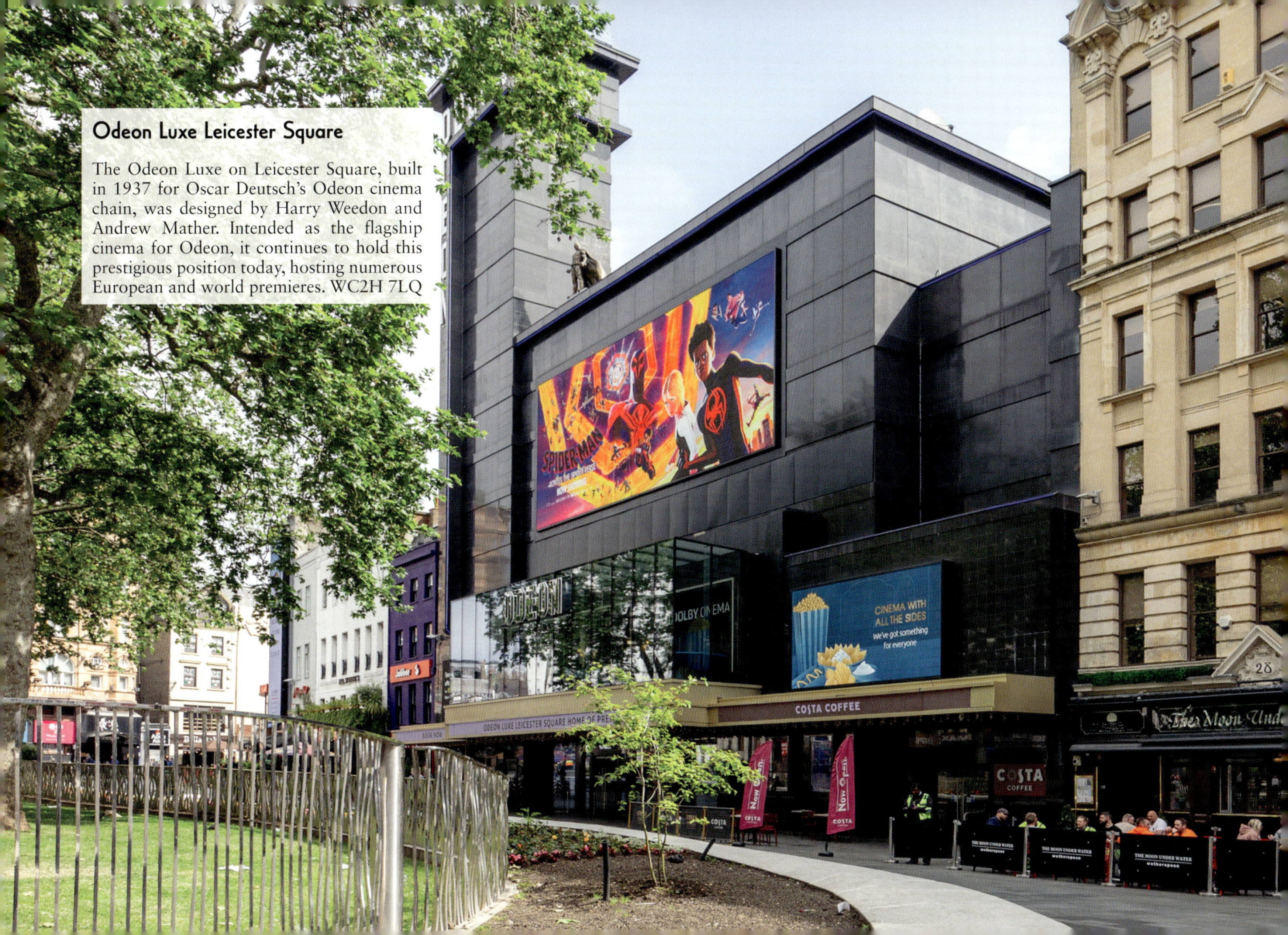

Odeon (ex-Saville Theatre)

The Odeon Covent Garden was originally built as the Saville Theatre for West End shows by T. P. Bennett and Son in 1931. The building features a sculpted frieze by British sculptor Gilbert Bayes, titled *Drama Through the Ages*, which runs across its facade. In the 1960s, Brian Epstein, manager of The Beatles, leased the venue to organise concerts, with legends such as Jimi Hendrix, The Who, and Chuck Berry performing there. The venue was converted into a cinema in the 1970s and remains so today. It is Grade II listed. WC2H 8AH

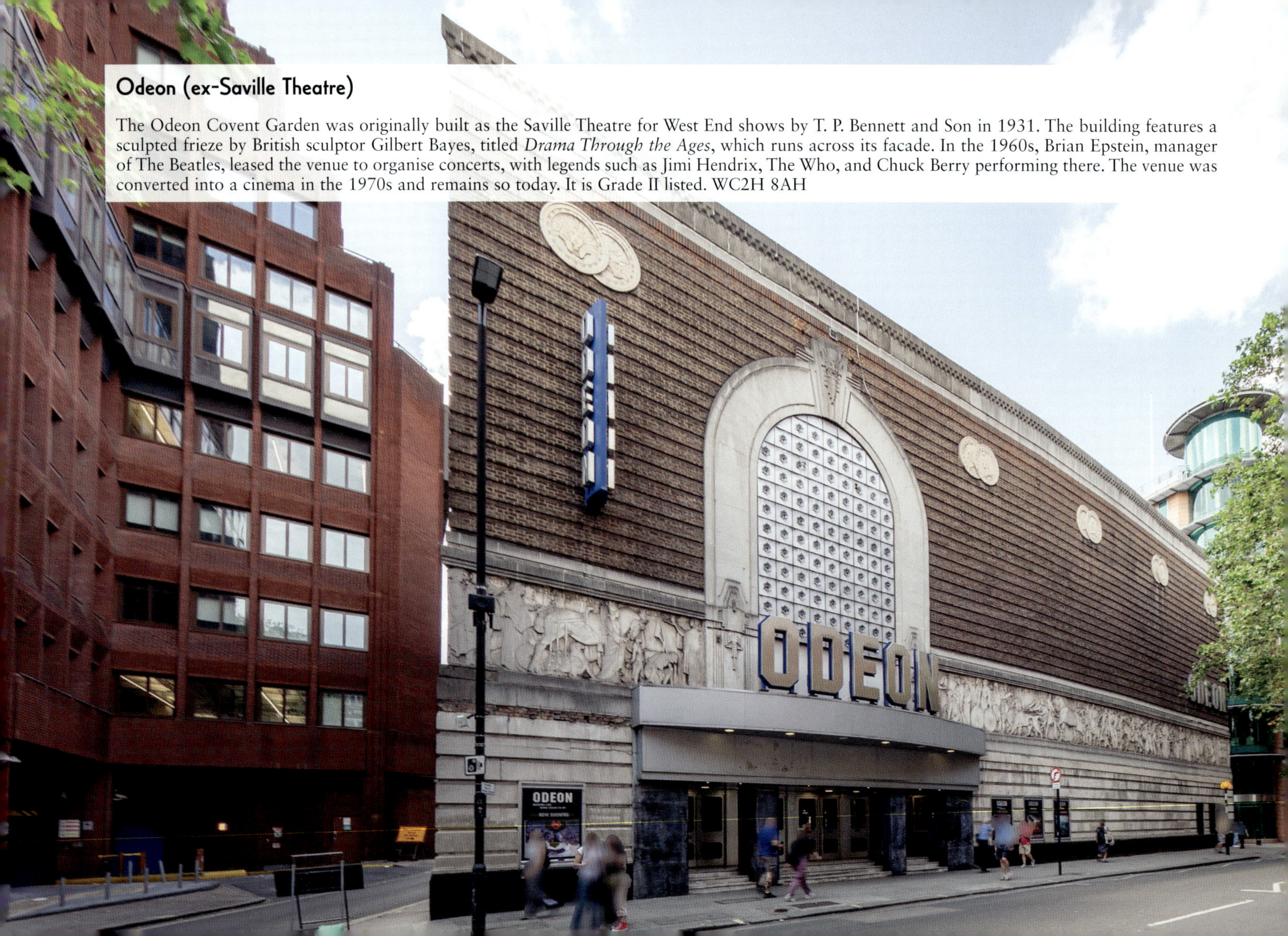

Cambridge Theatre

The Cambridge Theatre, a Grade II listed building, was designed by Wimperis, Simpson, and Guthrie in 1930. It is renowned for its elegant and clean lines, which were unusual for theatres of that era. WC2H 9HU

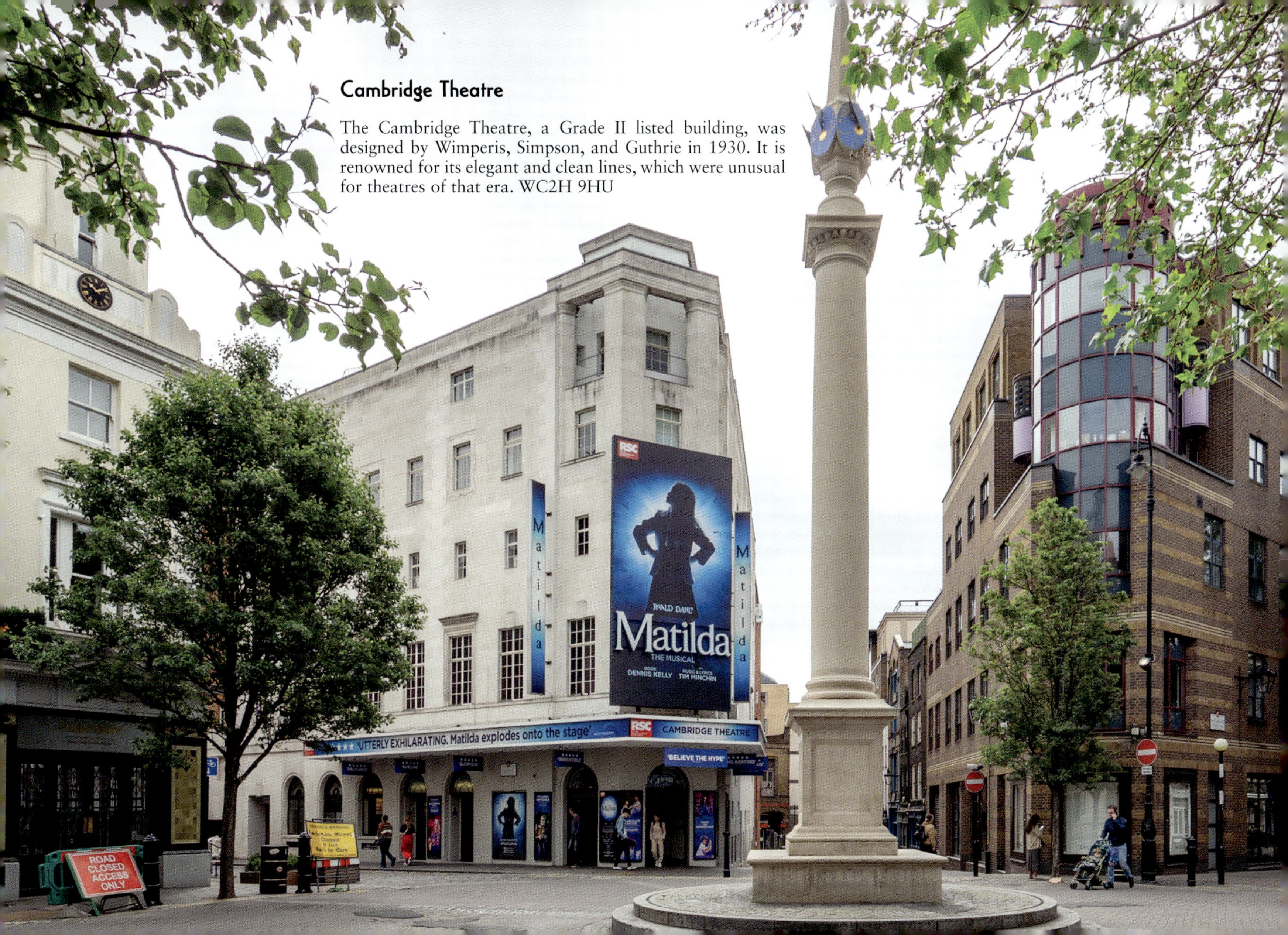

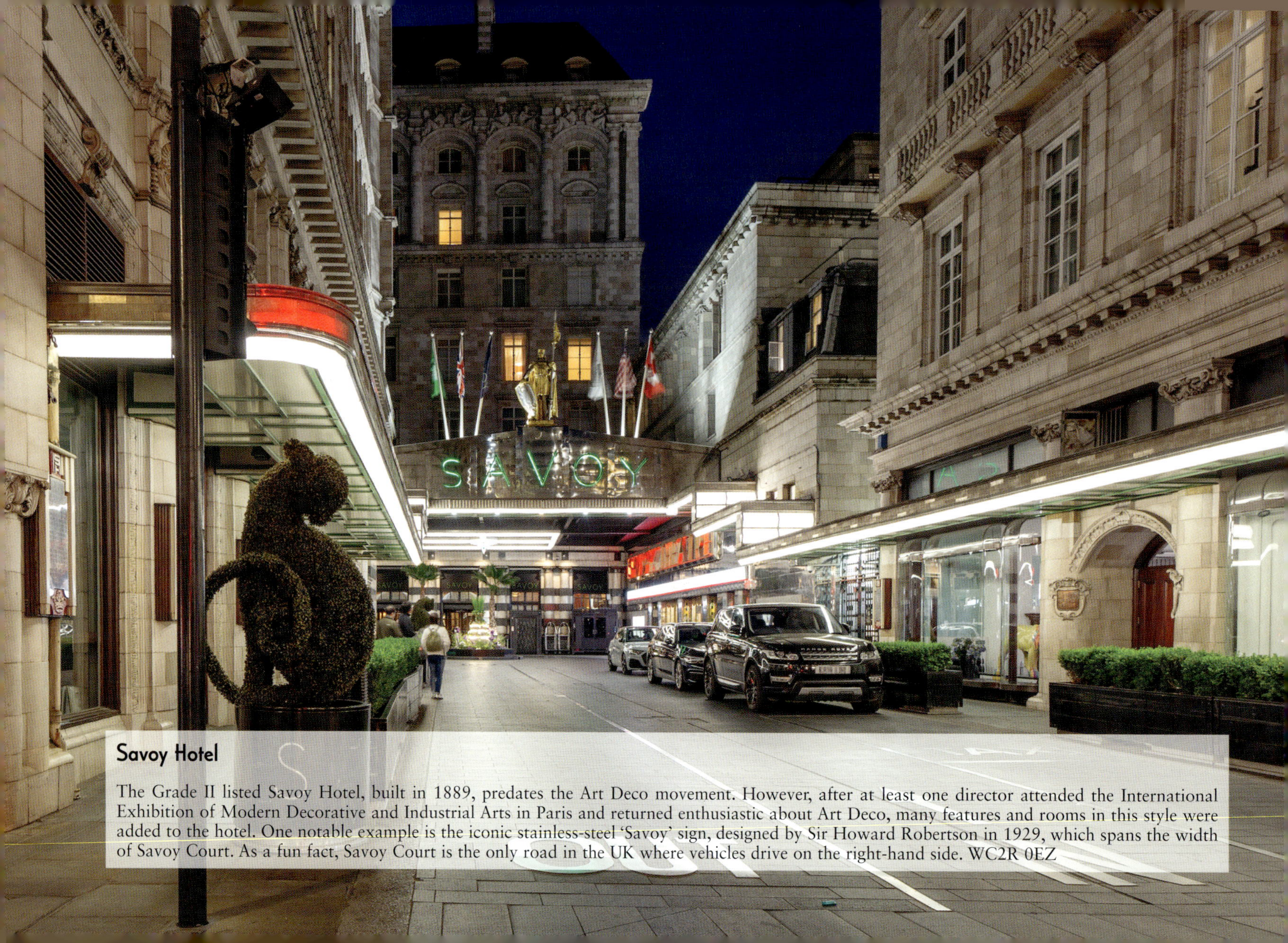

Savoy Hotel

The Grade II listed Savoy Hotel, built in 1889, predates the Art Deco movement. However, after at least one director attended the International Exhibition of Modern Decorative and Industrial Arts in Paris and returned enthusiastic about Art Deco, many features and rooms in this style were added to the hotel. One notable example is the iconic stainless-steel 'Savoy' sign, designed by Sir Howard Robertson in 1929, which spans the width of Savoy Court. As a fun fact, Savoy Court is the only road in the UK where vehicles drive on the right-hand side. WC2R 0EZ

Shell Mex House

Standing next to the Savoy Hotel on the Strand is Shell Mex House, which served for many years as the headquarters of Shell-Mex and BP. Built in 1931 by the architectural firm Messrs Joseph, with F. Milton Cashmore as the principal designer, this Grade II listed building features the UK's largest clock face, measuring 7.62 meters in diameter. Larger than Big Ben, this clock is affectionately nicknamed 'Big Benzene'. WC2R 0DT

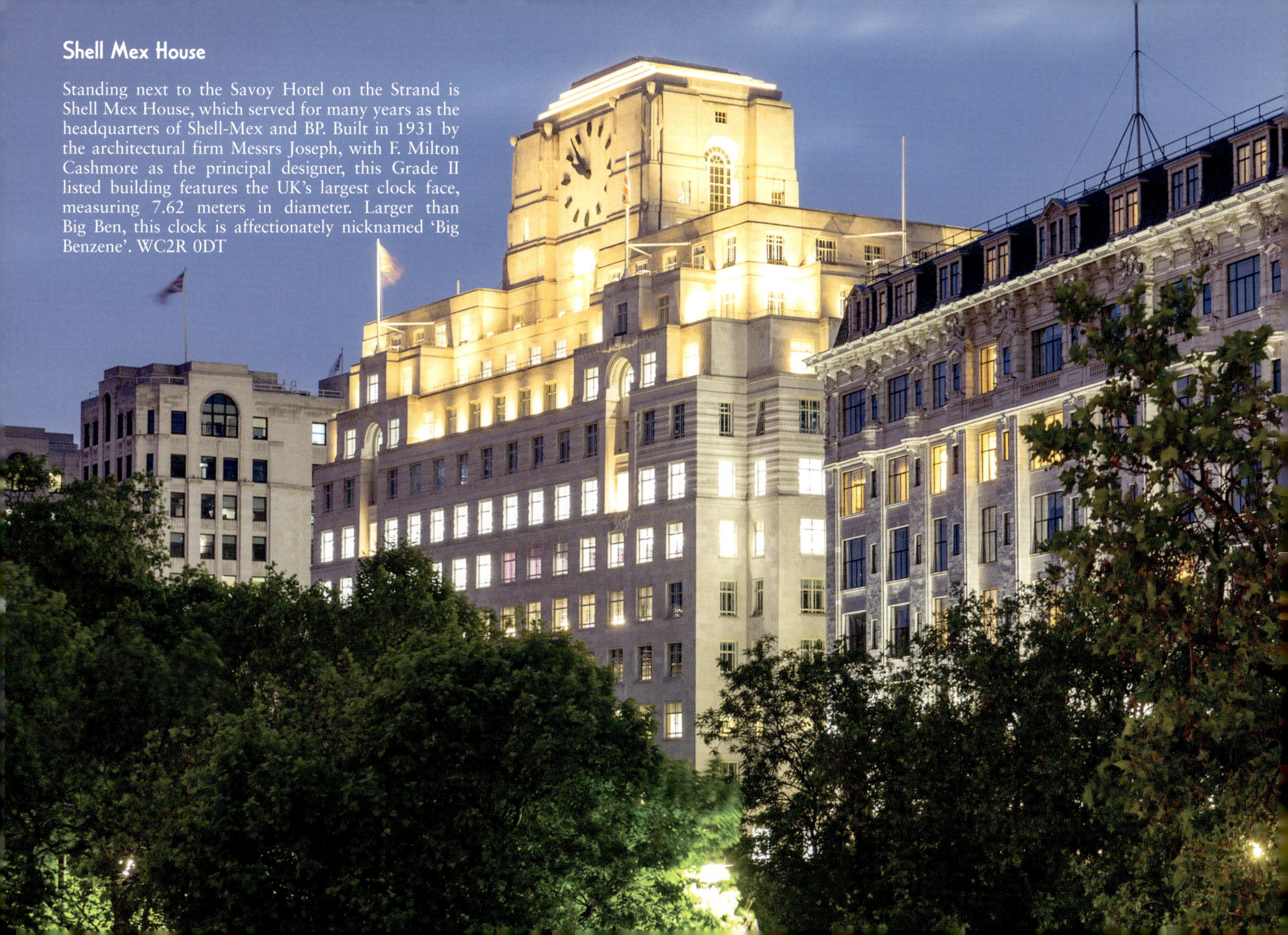

Adelphi Theatre

Founded in 1806 as the 'Sans Pareil', the Adelphi Theatre has undergone many incarnations. The latest transformation occurred in 1930 when Ernest Schaufelberg designed the current Art Deco building, which is now Grade II listed. WC2R 0NS

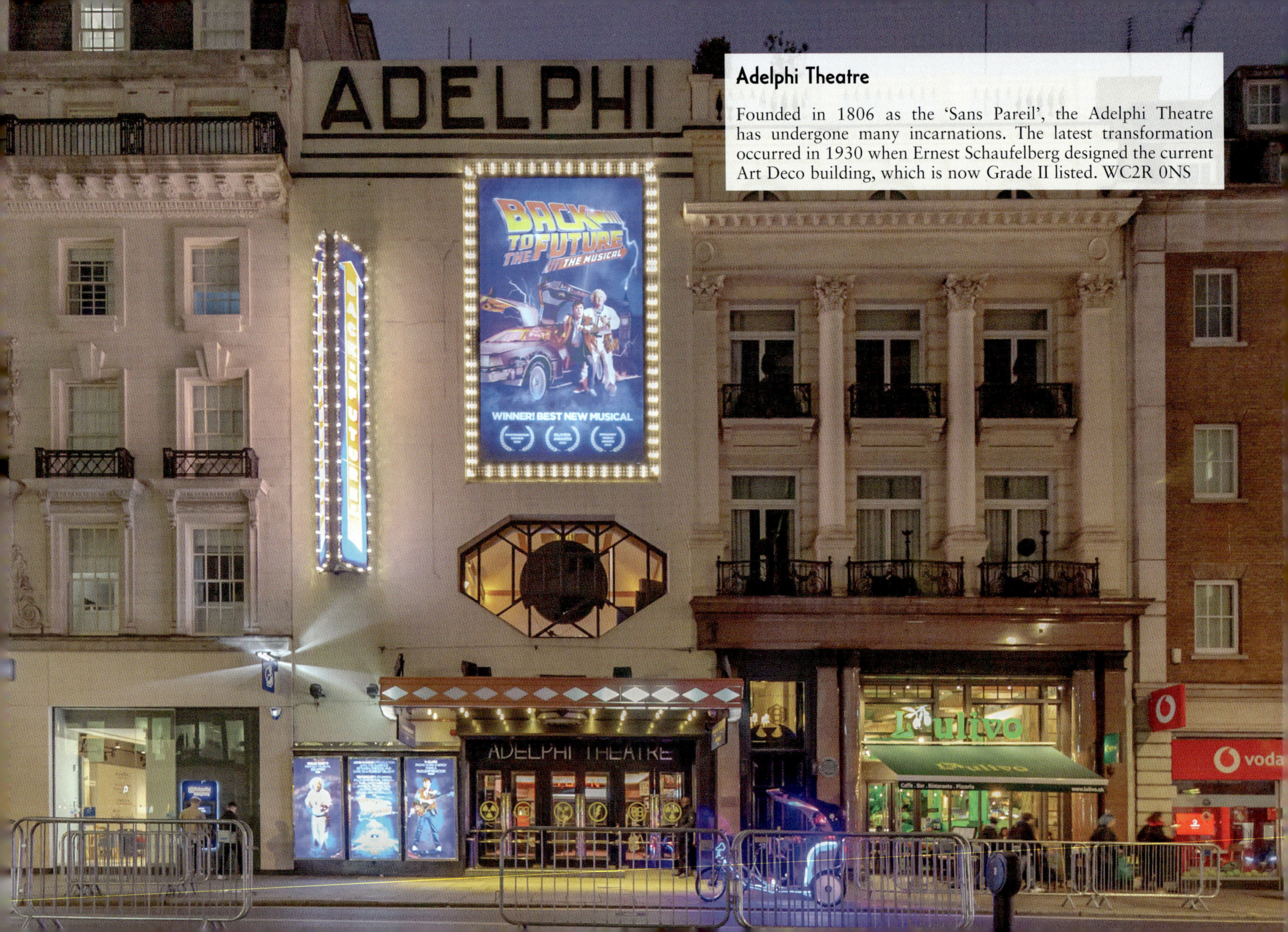

KEY TO MAP

1. Troxy
2. People's Palace
3. Better Gym Walthamstow Stadium
4. Florin Court
5. The Lab Building
6. Ibex House
7. Adelaide House
8. Daily Express Building
9. Daily Telegraph Building
10. Unilever House
11. Sudbury Town Station
12. Zoroastrian Centre
13. Rayners Lane
14. John Keble Church
15. OVO Arena Wembley
16. Sunspan House, New Malden
17. Surbiton Station
18. Gracepoint
19. Islington Assembly Hall
20. Phoenix Cinema London
21. East Finchley Station
22. Rainbow Theatre (ex)
23. Old Arsenal Stadium
24. 92 Frobisher Rd
25. Arnos Grove Station
26. Southgate Station
27. Grange Park Methodist Church
28. Dorset House
29. Carreras Cigarette Factory
30. Isokon Flats
31. Hillfield Court
32. O2 Forum Kentish Town
33. Parliament Hill Fields Lido
34. Ruach City Church – Kilburn
35. St Olaf House
36. Alaska Building
37. Lambeth Fire Station
38. Oxo Tower
39. William Booth College
40. Guthrie Wing
41. Meridian House
42. Charlton Lido and Lifestyle Club
43. Gateway House
44. Brockwell Lido
45. 55 Broadway
46. Marsham Court
47. Apollo Victoria Theatre
48. Peter Jones
49. National Audit Office
50. Victoria Coach Station
51. Sunlight Laundry
52. Nell Gwynne House
53. Sloane Avenue Mansions
54. Bluebird
55. Michelin House
56. Clapham Common Station
57. O2 Academy Brixton
58. Fulham Road Picturehouse
59. Battersea Power Station
60. Hightrees House
61. Thurleigh Court
62. Majestic (ex Odeon Cinema)
63. Du Cane Court
64. Buzz Bingo Hall
65. Wandsworth Town Hall
66. 265 Merton Rd
67. Colliers Wood Station
68. South Wimbledon Station
69. Tooting Bec Station
70. Balham Station
71. Globe Central
72. 46 Ailsa Rd
73. Pavillion & Clubhouse – Isleworth
74. Gillette Factory
75. 941 Great West Rd – Syon Clinic
76. 1100 Great West Rd – Wallis House
77. 991 Great West Rd – JC Decaux
78. 981 Great West Rd – West Link House
79. Gates of ex-Firestone Factory
80. Lichfield Court
81. Odeon Richmond
82. Richmond Station
83. Mortlake Crematorium
84. The Poppy Factory
85. Canteen Block Perivale
86. Hoover Building
87. BBC Broadcasting House
88. 66 Portland Place (RIBA)
89. Prince of Wales Theatre
90. Palladium House
91. The Lansdowne Club
92. Waterstones
93. The Dorchester
94. Greybrook House
95. The Beaumont
96. JW Marriott Grosvenor House London
97. Blenstock House (Bonhams)
98. Dominion Theatre
99. Queens
100. Arch Climbing Wall: Arch Acton
101. Acton Town Station
102. Hartington Court
103. Chiswick Park Station
104. Park Royal Station
105. Ealing Common Station
106. Filmworks
107. The Grampians
108. Hammersmith Apollo
109. Barkers of Kensington
110. Derry & Toms
111. Olympia Central
112. Senate House Library
113. Daimler Garage (ex)
114. Summit House
115. Trinity Court
116. Freemasons Hall
117. Fortune Theatre
118. Phoenix Theatre
119. Vue West End – Leicester Square
120. Odeon Luxe Leicester Square
121. Odeon (ex-Saville Theatre)
122. Cambridge Theatre
123. The Savoy
124. Shell Mex House
125. Adelphi Theatre

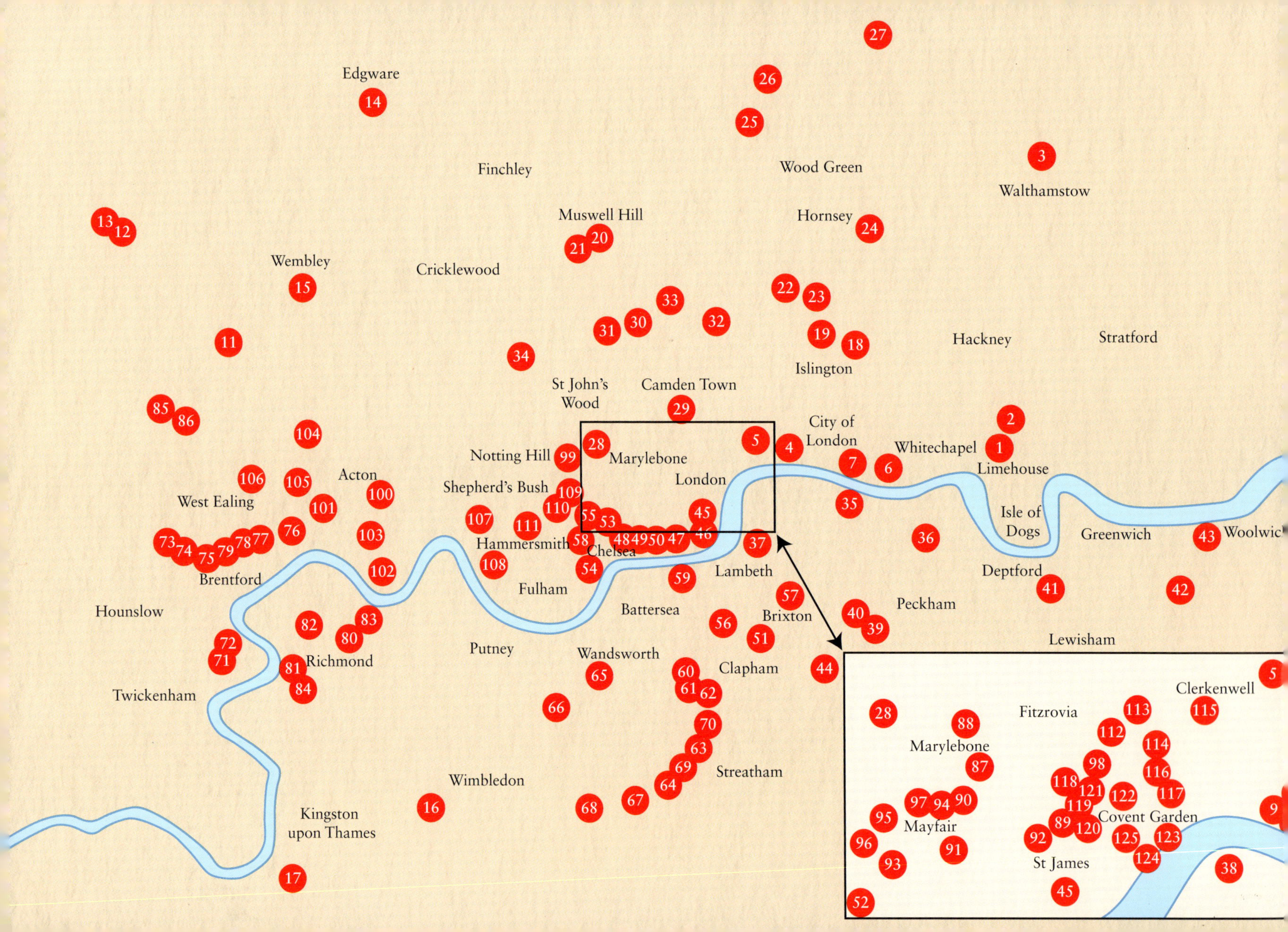
Edgware
Finchley
Wood Green
Walthamstow
Muswell Hill
Hornsey
Wembley
Cricklewood
Hackney
Stratford
Islington
St John's Wood
Camden Town
City of London
Whitechapel
Limehouse
Notting Hill
Marylebone
London
Shepherd's Bush
Acton
West Ealing
Isle of Dogs
Greenwich
Woolwic
Hammersmith
Chelsea
Lambeth
Brentford
Deptford
Fulham
Hounslow
Battersea
Brixton
Peckham
Lewisham
Putney
Wandsworth
Richmond
Clapham
Twickenham
Streatham
Wimbledon
Kingston upon Thames
Clerkenwell
Fitzrovia
Marylebone
Covent Garden
Mayfair
St James